Paton Thomson, John Stockdale, Isaac Weld, James Storer, Samuel Springsguth

Travels through the States of North America, and the Provinces of Upper and Lower Canada during the Years 1795, 1796 and 1797

Vol. 1

Paton Thomson, John Stockdale, Isaac Weld, James Storer, Samuel Springsguth

Travels through the States of North America, and the Provinces of Upper and Lower Canada during the Years 1795, 1796 and 1797
Vol. 1

ISBN/EAN: 9783337346027

Printed in Europe, USA, Canada, Australia, Japan

Cover: Foto ©Andreas Hilbeck / pixelio.de

More available books at **www.hansebooks.com**

TRAVELS

THROUGH THE STATES

OF

NORTH AMERICA,

AND THE

PROVINCES OF

UPPER AND LOWER CANADA,

DURING

THE YEARS 1795, 1796, AND 1797.

BY ISAAC WELD, JUNIOR.

SECOND EDITION.
ILLUSTRATED AND EMBELLISHED WITH SIXTEEN PLATES.

IN TWO VOLUMES.
VOL. I.

LONDON:
PRINTED FOR JOHN STOCKDALE, PICCADILLY.

1799.

PREFACE.

AT a period when war was spreading desolation over the fairest parts of Europe, when anarchy seemed to be extending its frightful progress from nation to nation, and when the storms that were gathering over his native country * in particular, rendered it impossible to say how soon any one of its inhabitants might be forced to seek for refuge in a foreign land; the Author of the following pages was induced to cross the Atlantic, for the purpose of examining with his own eyes into the

* Ireland.

truth of the various accounts which had been given of the flourishing and happy condition of the United States of America, and of ascertaining whether, in case of future emergency, any part of those territories might be looked forward to, as an eligible and agreeable place of abode. Arrived in America, he travelled pretty generally through the states of Pennsylvania, Delaware, Maryland, Virginia, New Jersey, and New York; he afterwards passed into the Canadas, desirous of obtaining equal information as to the state of those provinces, and of determining from his own immediate observations, how far the present condition of the inhabitants of the British dominions in America might be inferior, or otherwise, to that of the people of the States, who had now indeed

indeed thrown off the yoke, but were formerly common members of the same extensive empire.

When abroad, he had not the most distant intention of publishing his travels; but finding on his return home, that much of the matter contained in the following letters was quite new to his friends, and being induced to think that it might prove equally new, and not wholly unacceptable to the Public, he came to the resolution of committing them to print: accordingly the present volume* is now offered to the world, in an humble hope, that if not entertaining to all readers, it will at least be so to some, as well as useful to future travellers.

* The first edition was printed in one quarto volume.

If it shall appear to any one, that he has spoken with too much asperity of American men and American manners, the Author begs that such language may not be ascribed to hasty prejudice, and a blind partiality for every thing that is European. He crossed the Atlantic strongly prepossessed in favour of the people and the country, which he was about to visit; and if he returned with sentiments of a different tendency, they resulted solely from a cool and dispassionate observation of what chance presented to his view when abroad.

An enthusiastic admirer of the beauties of nature, the scenery of the countries through which he passed did not fail to attract a great part of his attention; and interspersed through the

the book will be found views of what he thought would be moſt intereſting to his readers: they are what he himſelf ſketched upon the ſpot, that of Mount Vernon, the Seat of General Waſhington, indeed, excepted, for which he is indebted to an ingenious friend that he met in America, and the View of Bethlehem. He has many more views in his poſſeſſion; but he thought it better to furniſh his Publiſher with a few only, in hopes that the engraving from them would be well executed, rather than with a great many, which, had they been given, muſt either have been in a ſtyle unworthy of the public eye, or elſe have ſwelled the price of the volume beyond the reach of many that may now read it. Of the reſemblance which theſe views bear to

A 4   their

their refpective archetypes, thofe alone can be judges who have been fpectators of the original fcenes. With regard to the Cataract of Niagara, however, it muft be obferved, that in views on fo fmall a fcale no one muft expect to find a lively reprefentation of its wonderful and terrific vaftnefs, even were they executed by artifts of far fuperior merit; the inferting of the three in the prefent work is done merely in the hope that they may help, together with the ground plan of the precipice, if it may be fo called, to give a general idea of the pofition and appearance of that ftupendous Cataract. Thofe who are defirous of becoming more intimately acquainted with it, will foon be gratified, at leaft fo he has been given to underftand by the artift in whofe
hands

hands they at prefent are, with a fet of views from the mafterly pencil of Captain Fifher, of the Royal Britifh Artillery, which are allowed by all thofe who have vifited the Falls of Niagara, to convey a more perfect idea of that wonderful natural curiofity, than any paintings or engravings that are extant.

FINALLY, before the Reader proceeds to the perufal of the enfuing pages, the Author will juft beg leave to apprize him, that they are the production of a very youthful pen, unaccuftomed to write a great deal, far lefs to write for the prefs. It is now for the firft time that one of its productions is ventured to be laid before the public eye. As a firft attempt, therefore, it is humbly hoped that the

prefent

present work may meet with a generous indulgence, and not be too severely criticised on account of its numerous imperfections.

Dublin,
20th December 1798.

ERRATA.

VOL. I.
Page 205 line 10, *for* 60° *read* 6°
— 381 — 7, *dele* there.

VOL. II.
— 18 — 28, *for* take, *read* take on.
— 23 — 14, *for* houses, *read* storehouses.
— 171 — 4 of the note, *dele* not.

CONTENTS

To VOLUME I.

LETTER I.

Arrival on the Coast of America.—Trees the first Object visible.—Description of the Bay and River of Delaware.—Passengers bound for Philadelphia not suffered to land till examined by the Health Officers.—Arrival at Philadelphia.—Poor Appearance of the City from the Water.—Plan of the City.—Wharfs.—Public and private Buildings.—Some Account of the Hospital, and of the Gaol - - - - page 1

LETTER II.

Population of Philadelphia.—Some Account of the Inhabitants, their Character and Manners—Private Amusements.—Americans lose their Teeth prematurely.—Theatrical Amusements only permitted of late.—Quakers.—President's Levee and Drawing Room.—Places of public Worship.—Carriages, what Sort of, used in Philadelphia.—Taverns, how conducted in America.—Difficulty of procuring Servants.—Character of the lower Classes of People in America - - page 20

LETTER III.

Journey to Baltimore.—Description of the Country about Philadelphia.—Floating Bridges over the Schuylkill,

CONTENTS.

Schuylkill, how constructed.—Mills in Brandywine Creek.—Improvement in the Machinery of Flour Mills in America.—Town of Wilmington.—Log Houses.—Bad Roads.— Fine Prospects.—How relished by Americans—Taverns.—Susquehannah River.—Town of Baltimore.—Plan of the Town.—Harbour.—Public and private Buildings.—Inhabitants.—Country between Baltimore and Washington—Execrable Roads - - - - page 31

LETTER IV.

Foundation of the City of Washington.—Not readily agreed to by different States.—Choice of the Ground left to General Washington.—Circumstances to be considered in chusing the Ground.—The Spot fixed upon central to all the States.—Also remarkably advantageously situated for Trade.—Nature of the Back Country Trade.—Summary View of the principal Trading Towns in the United States.—Their Prosperity shewn to depend on the Back Country Trade.—Description of the Patowmac River.—Its Connection with other Rivers pointed out.—Prodigious Extent of the Water Communication from Washington City in all Directions.—Country likely to trade immediately with Washington.—Situation of Washington.—Plan of the City.—Public Buildings.—Some begun, others projected.—Capital President's House.—Hotel.—Stone and other building Materials found in the Neighbourhood.—

CONTENTS.

hood.—*Private Houses and Inhabitants at present in the City.—Different Opinions respecting the future Greatness of the City.—Impediments thrown in the Way of its Improvement.—What has given rise to this* - - page 49

LETTER V.

Some Account of Alexandria.—Mount Vernon, the Seat of General Washington.—Difficulty of finding the Way thither through the Woods.—Description of the Mount, and of the Views from it.—Description of the House and Grounds.—Slaves at Mount Vernon.—Thoughts thereon.—A Person at Mount Vernon to attend to Strangers.—Return to Washington - - page 90

LETTER VI.

Arrival at Philadelphia.—Some Observations on the Climate of the Middle States.—Public Carriages prevented from plying between Baltimore and Philadelphia by the Badness of the Roads.—Left Baltimore during Frost.—Met with American Travellers on the Road.—Their Behaviour preparatory to setting off from an Inn.—Arrival on the Banks of the Susquehannah.—Passage of that River when frozen over.—Dangerous Situation of the Passengers.—American Travellers at the Tavern on the opposite Side of the River.—Their noisy Disputations - - - page 96

LETTER VII.

Philadelphia gayer in the Winter than at any other Season.—Celebration in that City of General Washington's

CONTENTS.

Washington's Birth Day.—Some Account of General Washington's Person and of his Character.—Americans dissatisfied with his Conduct as President.— A Spirit of Dissatisfaction common amongst them   -   -   -   page 104

LETTER VIII.

Singular Mildness of the Winter of 1795-6.—Set out for Lancaster.—Turnpike Road between that Place and Philadelphia.—Summary View of the State of Pennsylvania.—Description of the Farms between Lancaster and Philadelphia. — The Farmers live in a penurious Style.—Greatly inferior to English Farmers.—Bad Taverns on this Road.—Waggons and Waggoners.—Customs of the latter.—Description of Lancaster.—Lately made the Seat of the State Government.—Manufactures carried on there.—Rifle Guns.—Great Dexterity with which the Americans use them.—Anecdote of Two Virginian Soldiers belonging to a Rifle Regiment   -   -   -   page 109

LETTER IX.

Number of Germans in the Neighbourhood of York and Lancaster.— How brought over.— White Slave Trade.—Cruelty frequently practised in the carrying it on.—Character of the German Settlers contrasted with that of the Americans.—Passage of the Susquehannah between York and Lancaster.—Great Beauty of the Prospects along the River.—Description of York.—Courts of Justice there.—Of the Pennsylvanian System of Judicature   -   -   -   page 120

CONTENTS.

LETTER X.

Of the Country near York.—Of the Soil of the Country on each Side of the Blue Mountains.— Frederic-town.—Change in the Inhabitants and in the Country as you proceed towards the Sea.— Numbers of Slaves.—Tobacco chiefly cultivated. —Inquisitiveness of the People at the Taverns.— Observations thereon.—Description of the Great Falls of the Patowmac River.—George Town.— Of the Country between that Place and Hoe's Ferry.— Poisonous Vines.— Port Tobacco.— Wretched Appearance of the Country bordering upon the Ferry.—Slaves neglected.—Passage of the Patowmac very dangerous.—Fresh Water Oysters.—Landed on a deserted Part of the Virginian Shore.—Great Hospitality of the Virginians - - - - - - page 131

LETTER XI.

Of the Northern Neck of Virginia.—First settled by the English.—Houses built by them remaining. —Disparity of Condition amongst the Inhabitants. —Estates worked by Negroes.—Condition of the Slaves.—Worse in the Carolinas.—Lands worn out by Cultivation of Tobacco.—Mode of cultivating and curing Tobacco.—Houses in Virginia. —Those of Wood preferred.—Lower Classes of People in Virginia.—Their unhealthy Appearance - - - - - page 145

CONTENTS.

LETTER XII.

Town of Tappahannock.—Rappahannock River. —Sharks found in it.—Country bordering upon Urbanna.—Fires common in the Woods.—Manner of stopping their dreadful Progress.—Mode of getting Turpentine from Trees.—Gloucester. —York Town.—Remains of the Fortifications erected here during the American War.—Houses shattered by Balls still remaining.—Cave in the Bank of the River.—Williamsburgh.—State House in Ruins.—Statue of Lord Bottetourt.— College of William and Mary.—Condition of the Students - - - - page 158

LETTER XIII.

Hampton.—Ferry to Norfolk.—Danger in crossing the numerous Ferries in Virginia.—Norfolk.— Laws of Virginia injurious to the Trading Interest. —Streets narrow and dirty in Norfolk.—Yellow Fever there.—Observations on this Disorder.— Violent Party Spirit amongst the Inhabitants.— Few Churches in Virginia.—Several in Ruins.— Private Grave Yards - - page 169

LETTER XIV.

Description of Dismal Swamp.—Wild Men found in it.—Bears, Wolves, &c.—Country between Swamp and Richmond.—Mode of making Tar and Pitch.—Poor Soil.—Wretched Taverns.— Corn Bread.—Difficulty of getting Food for Horses.—Petersburgh.—Horse Races there.—
Description

CONTENTS.

Description of Virginian Horses.—Style of Riding in America.— Description of Richmond, Capital of Virginia.—Singular Bridge across James River.—State House.—Falls of James River.—Gambling common in Richmond.—Lower Classes of People very quarrelsome.—Their Mode of Fighting.—Gouging   -   page 178

LETTER XV.

Description of Virginia between Richmond and the Mountains.—Fragrance of Flowers and Shrubs in the Woods.—Melody of the Birds.—Of the Birds of Virginia.—Mocking Bird.—Blue Bird.—Red Bird, &c.—Singular Noises of the Frogs.—Columbia.—Magazine there.— Fire Flies in the Woods.—Green Springs.—Wretchedness of the Accommodation there.—Difficulty of finding the Way through the Woods.—Serpents.—Rattle-Snake.— Copper-Snake.—Black Snake.—South-west, or Green Mountains.—Soil of them.—Mountain Torrents do great Damage.—Salubrity of the Climate.—Great Beauty of the Peasantry.—Many Gentlemen of Property living here.—Monticello, the Seat of Mr. Jefferson.—Vineyards.—Observations on the Culture of the Grape, and the Manufacture of Wine - page 193

LETTER XVI.

Of the Country between the South-west and Blue Mountains.—Copper and Iron Mines.—Lynchburgh.—New London.—Armoury here.—Description of the Road over the Blue Mountains.—

culty of getting forward.—Arrive at Skenesborough.—Dreadfully infested by Musquitoes.—Particular Description of that Insect.—Great Danger ensues sometimes from their Bite.—Best Remedy - - - - page 274

LETTER XXI.

Embark on Lake Champlain.—Difficulty of procuring Provisions at Farms bordering upon it.—Ticonderoga.—Crown Point.—Great Beauty of the Scenery.—General Description of Lake Champlain and the adjacent Country.—Captain Thomas and his Indians arrive at Crown Point.—Character of Thomas.—Reach St. John's.—Description of that Place.—Great Difference observable in the Face of the Country, Inhabitants, &c. in Canada and in the States.—Chambly Castle.—Calashes.—Bons Dieux.—Town of La Prarie.—Great Rapidity of the River Saint Lawrence.—Cross it to Montreal.—Astonishment on seeing large Ships at Montreal.—Great Depth of the River - - - - - page 288

LETTER XXII.

Description of the Town of Montreal.—Of the public Buildings.—Churches.—Funeral Ceremonies —Convents.—Barracks.—Fortifications.—Inhabitants mostly French.—Their Character and Manners.—Charming Prospects in the Neighbourhood of the Town.—Amusements during Summer.—Parties of Pleasure up the Mountain.—

CONTENTS. xxi

tain.—Of the Fur Trade.—The Manner in which it is carried on.—Great Enterprise of the North West Company of Merchants.—Sketch of Mr. M'Kenzie's Expeditions over Land to the Pacific Ocean.—Differences between the North West and Hudson's Bay Companies - page 309

LETTER XXIII.

Voyage to Quebec down the St. Lawrence.—A Bateau preferable to a Keel Boat.—Town of Sorelle.—Ship-building there.—Description of Lake St. Pierre.—Baliscon.—Charming Scenery along the Banks of St. Lawrence.—In what respects it differs from the Scenery along any other River in America.—Canadian Houses.—Sketch of the Character and Manners of the lower Classes of Canadians.—Their Superstition.—Anecdote.—St. Augustin Calvaire.—Arrive at Quebec - - - - - page 331

LETTER XXIV.

Situation of the City of Quebec.—Divided into Upper and Lower Town.—Description of each.—Great Strength of the Upper Town.—Some Observations on the Capture of Quebec by the English Army under General Wolfe.—Observations on Montgomery's and Arnold's Attack during the American War.—Census of Inhabitants of Quebec.—The Chateau.—The Residence of the Governor.—Monastery of the Recollects.—College of the Jesuits.—One Jesuit remaining of great Age.—His great Wealth.—His Character.
—Nun-

—Nunneries.—Engineer's Drawing Room.— State House. — Armoury.—Barracks.—Market-place.—Dogs used in Carts.—Grandeur of the Prospects from Parts of the Upper Town.— Charming Scenery of the Environs.—Description of Montmorenci Water Fall.—Of La Chaudiere Water Fall - - page 341

LETTER XXV.

Of the Constitution, Government, Laws, and Religion of the Provinces of Upper and Lower Canada.—Estimate of the Expences of the Civil List, of the Military Establishment, and the Presents to the Indians.—Salaries of certain Officers of the Crown.—Imports and Exports.— Taxes. - - - - - page 361

LETTER XXVI.

Of the Soil and Productions of Lower Canada— Observations on the Manufacture of Sugar from the Maple-tree.—Of the Climate of Lower Canada. —Amusements of People of all Descriptions during Winter.— Carioles.—Manner of guarding against the Cold.—Great Hardiness of the Horses.—State of the River St. Lawrence on the Dissolution of Winter.— Rapid Progress of Vegetation during Spring. — Agreeableness of the Summer and Autumn Seasons - - - - page 379

LETTER XXVII.

Inhabitants of Lower Canada.—Of the Tenures by which Lands are held.—Not favourable to the Improvement of the Country.—Some Observations thereon.—Advantages of settling in Canada and the United States compared.—Why Emigrations to the latter Country are more general.—Description of a Journey to Stoneham Township near Quebec.—Description of the River St. Charles.—Of Lake St. Charles—Of Stoneham Township - - - page 299

LIST OF PLATES.

Vol. I.

Map of the NORTHERN STATES of America - - - - - Page 1
Plan of the CITY of WASHINGTON - 81
—— MOUNT VERNON, the Seat of General Washington - - - - - - 92
American STAGE WAGGON - - - 27
View of the Natural ROCK BRIDGE in Virginia - - - - - - 221
View on the HUDSON RIVER * - - 263
View of the COHOZ FALL - - - 275
Map of Upper and Lower CANADA - - 305
Plan of the CITY of QUEBEC - - - 342
View of CAPE DIAMOND, from Wolfe's Cove, near Quebec - - - - - - 346
CANADIAN CALASH or Marche-donc - 306

Vol. II.

An Eye Sketch of the FALLS of Niagara 118
View of the HORSE SHOE FALL of Niagara 118
—— Lesser FALLS of NIAGARA - 118
General View of the FALLS of Niagara - 121
View of BETHLEHEM, a Moravian Settlement 355

* In some of the Impressions, by mistake, called "View of the Patowmac River from Mount Vernon."

TRAVELS

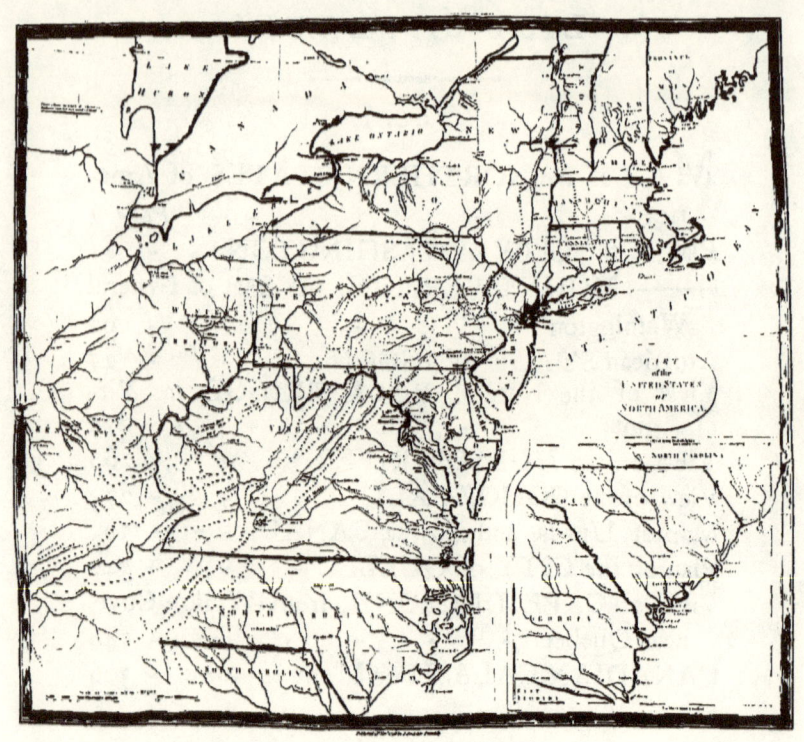

from Philadelphia

TRAVELS

THROUGH THE STATES OF

NORTH AMERICA.

LETTER I.

Arrival on the Coast of America.—Trees the first Object visible.—Description of the Bay and River of Delaware.—Passengers bound for Philadelphia not suffered to land till examined by the Health Officers.—Arrival at Philadelphia.—Poor Appearance of the City from the Water.—Plan of the City.—Wharfs.—Public and private Buildings.—Some Account of the Hospital, and of the Gaol.

MY DEAR SIR,   Philadelphia, November, 1795.

OUR passage across the Atlantic was disagreeable in the extreme. The weather for the most part was bad, and calms and heavy adverse gales so frequently retarded our progress to the westward, that it was not until the fifty-ninth day from that on which we left Ireland, that we discovered the American coast. I shall not attempt to describe the joy which the sight of land, a sight that at once relieved the eye from the uninteresting and wearisome view of sky and water, and that afforded to each individual a speedy prospect of delivery from the narrow confines of a small trading vessel, diffused amongst the passengers. You, who have yourself made a long voyage, can best imagine what it must have been.

The first objects which meet the eye on approaching the American coast, south of NewYork, are the tops of trees, with which the shore is thickly covered to the very edge of the water. These, at a distance, have the appearance of small islands; but as you draw nearer they are seen to unite; and the tall forest rising gradually out of the ocean, at last presents itself in all its majesty to your view. The land which we made was situated very near to the bay of Delaware, and before noon we passed between the capes Henlopen and May, which guard the entrance of the bay. The capes are only eighteen miles apart, but within them the bay expands to the breadth of thirty miles. It afterwards becomes gradually narrower, until it is lost in the river of the same name, at Bombay Hook, seven leagues distant from the Atlantic. The river Delaware, at this place, is about six miles wide; at Reedy Island, twenty miles higher up, it is three miles wide; and at Philadelphia, one hundred and twenty miles from the sea, one mile wide.

The shores of the bay and of the river Delaware, for a very considerable distance upwards, are low; and they are covered, like the coast, with one vast forest, excepting merely in a few places, where extensive marshes intervene. Nothing, however, could be more pleasing than the views with which we were entertained as we sailed up to Philadelphia. The trees had not yet quite lost their foliage, and the rich red and yellow tints which autumn had suffused over the leaves of the oaks and poplars appeared beautifully blended with the sombre green of the lofty pines; whilst the river, winding slowly and smoothly along under the banks, reflected in its glassy surface the varied colours of the objects on shore, as well as the images of multitudes of vessels of various sizes, which, as far as the eye could reach, were seen gliding silently along with the tide. As you approach towards Philadelphia, the banks of the river become more elevated; and on the left hand side, where they are much cleared, they are interspersed with numberless neat farm-houses, with villages and towns; and are in some parts cultivated down to the very edge of the water. The New Jersey shore, on the right hand

hand fide, remains thickly wooded, even as far as the city.

Veffels very commonly afcend to Philadelphia, when the wind is favourable, in twenty-four hours; but unfortunately, as our fhip entered the river, the wind died away, and fhe had to depend folely upon the tide, which flows at the rate of about three miles only in the hour. Finding that the paffage up to the city was likely therefore to become tedious, I would fain have gone on fhore far below it; but this the captain would not permit me to do. By the laws of Pennfylvania, enacted in confequence of the dreadful peftilence which raged in the capital in the year 1793, the mafter of any veffel bound for that port is made fubject to a very heavy fine, if he fuffers any perfon from on board her, whether mariner or paffenger, to go on fhore in any part of the ftate, before his veffel is examined by the health officer: and any perfon that goes on fhore, contrary to the will of the mafter of the veffel, is liable to be imprifoned for a confiderable length of time. In cafe the exiftence of this law fhould not be known on board a veffel bound for a port in Pennfylvania, it is the bufinefs of the pilot to furnifh the mafter and the paffengers on board with copies of it, with which he always comes provided. The
health

health officer, who is a regular bred phyſician, reſides at Mifflin Fort, four miles below the city, where there is a ſmall garriſon kept. A boat is always ſent on ſhore for him from the ſhip. After having been toſſed about on the ocean for nine weeks nearly, nothing could be more tantalizing than to be kept thus cloſe to the ſhore without being permitted to land.

Philadelphia, as you approach by the river, is not ſeen farther off than three miles, a point of land covered with trees concealing it from the view. On weathering this point it ſuddenly opens upon you, and at that diſtance it looks extremely well; but on a nearer approach, the city makes a poor appearance, as nothing is viſible from the water but confuſed heaps of wooden ſtorehouſes, crowded upon each other, the chief of which are built upon platforms of artificial ground, and wharfs which project a conſiderable way into the river. The wharfs are of a rectangular form, and built of wood; they jut out in every direction, and are well adapted for the accommodation of ſhipping, the largeſt merchant veſſels being able to lie cloſe alongſide them. Behind theſe wharfs, and parallel to the river, runs Waterſtreet. This is the firſt ſtreet which you uſually enter after landing, and it does not ſerve to give a ſtranger a very favourable opinion either of the neatneſs or commodiouſneſs of the public ways of Philadelphia. It is no more than thirty feet wide; and immediately behind the houses, which stand on the side fartheſt from the water, a high bank, ſuppoſed to be the old bank of the river, riſes, which renders the air very confined. Added to this, ſuch ſtenches at times prevail in it, owing in part to the quantity of filth and dirt that is ſuffered to remain on the pavement, and in part to what is depoſited in waſte houſes, of which there are ſeveral in the ſtreet, that it is really dreadful to paſs through it. It was here that the malignant yellow fever broke out in the year 1793, which made ſuch terrible ravages; and in the ſummer ſeaſon, in general, the ſtreet is found extremely unhealthy. That the inhabitants, after ſuffering ſo much from the ſickneſs that originated in it, ſhould remain thus inattentive to the cleanlineſs of Water-ſtreet is truly ſurpriſing; more eſpecially ſo, when it is conſidered, that the ſtreets in the other parts of the town are as much diſtinguiſhed for the neatneſs that prevails throughout them, as this one is for its dirty condition.

On the level plot of ground on the top of the bank which riſes behind Water-ſtreet, the city of Philadelphia was originally laid out, and it was intended by the founder that no houſes ſhould have been erected at the bottom

of

of it; however, as there was no positive law to this effect, the convenience of the situation soon tempted numbers to build there, and they are now encroaching, annually, on the river, by throwing wharfs farther out into the stream. In another respect also the original plan of the city was not adhered to. The ground allotted for it was in the form of an oblong square, two miles in length, reaching from the river Schuylkill to the Delaware, and one mile in breadth. Pursuant to this scheme, the houses were begun on the Delaware side; but instead of having been carried on towards the Schuylkill, the current of building has kept entirely on one side. The houses extend for two miles nearly along the Delaware, but, on an average, not more than half a mile towards the Schuylkill: this is to be attributed to the great superiority of the one river over the other. All the houses built beyond the boundary line of the oblong square are said to be in the "Liberties," as the jurisdiction of the corporation does not extend to that part of the town. Here the streets are very irregularly built, but in the city they all intersect each other at right angles, according to the original plan. The principal street is one hundred feet wide; the others vary from eighty to fifty. They are all tolerably well paved with pebble stones in the middle; and on each side, for the convenience of passengers, there is a footway paved with red brick.

The houses within the limits of the city are for the most part built of brick; a few, and a few only, are of wood.

In the old parts of the town they are in general small, heavy, and inconvenient; but amongst those which have been lately erected, many are to be found that are light, airy, and commodious. In the whole city, however, there are only two or three houses that particularly attract the attention, on account of their size and architecture, and but little beauty is observable in the designs of any of these. The most spacious and the most remarkable one amongst them stands in Chesnut-street, but it is not yet quite finished. At present it appears a huge mass of red brick and pale blue marble, which bids defiance to simplicity and elegance. This superb mansion, according to report, has already cost upwards of fifty thousand guineas, and stands as a monument of the increasing luxury of the city of Philadelphia.

As for the public buildings, they are all heavy tasteless piles of red brick, ornamented with the same sort of blue marble as that already mentioned, and which but ill accord together, unless indeed we except the new Bank of the United States, and the presbyterian

terian church in High-street. The latter building is ornamented with a handsome portico in front, supported by six pillars in the Corinthian order; but it is seen to great disadvantage on account of the market house, which occupies the center of the street before it. The buildings next to these, that are most deserving of notice, are the State House, the President's House, the Hospital, the Bettering House, and the Gaol.

The State House is situated in Chesnut-street; and, considering that no more than fifty-three years elapsed from the time the first cabin was built on the spot marked out for the city, until it was erected, the architecture calls forth both our surprise and admiration. The State House is appropriated to the use of the legislative bodies of the state. Attached to this edifice are the congress and the city-halls. In the former, the congress of the United States meets to transact business. The room allotted to the representatives of the lower house is about sixty feet in length, and fitted up in the plainest manner. At one end of it is a gallery, open to every person that chuses to enter it; the stair-case leading to which runs directly from the public street. The senate chamber is in the story above this, and it is furnished and fitted up in a much superior style to that of the lower

lower houfe. In the city hall the courts of juftice are held, the fupreme court of the United States, as well as that of the ftate of Pennfylvania, and thofe of the city.

The prefident's houfe, as it is called, was erected for the refidence of the prefident, before the removal of the feat of the federal government from Philadelphia was agitated. The original plan of this building was drawn by a private gentleman, refident in the neighbourhood of Philadelphia, and was poffeffed, it is faid, of no fmall fhare of merit; but the committee of citizens, that was appointed to take the plan into confideration, and to direct the building, conceiving that it could be improved upon, reverfed the pofitions of the upper and lower ftories, placing the latter at top, fo that the pilafters, with which it is ornamented, appear fufpended in the air. The committee alfo contrived, that the windows of the principal apartments, inftead of opening into a fpacious area in front of the houfe, as was defigned at firft, fhould face towards the confined back yards of the adjoining houfes. This building is not yet finifhed, and as the removal of the feat of government to the federal city of Wafhington is fo fhortly to take place, it is moft probable that it will never be occupied by the prefident. To what purpofe it will be now applied is yet undetermined.

mined. Some imagine, that it will be converted into a city hotel; others, that it will be deftined for the refidence of the governor of the ftate. For the latter purpofe, it would be unfit in the extreme, the falary of the governor being fo inconfiderable, that it would not enable him to keep up an eftablifhment fuitable to a dwelling of one-fourth part the fize of it.

The hofpital, for its airinefs, for its convenient accommodation for the fick and infirm, and for the neatnefs exhibited throughout every part of it, cannot be furpaffed by any inftitution of the kind in the world. The plan of the building is in the form of the letter H. At prefent but one wing and a part of the center are finifhed; but the reft of the building is in a ftate of forwardnefs. It is two ftories high, and underneath the whole are cells for lunatics. Perfons labouring under any diforder of body or mind are received into this hofpital, excepting fuch as have difeafes that are contagious, and of a malignant nature; fuch patients, however, have the advice of the attending phyficians gratis, and are fupplied with medicine from the hofpital difpenfary.

The productive ftock of this hofpital, in the year 1793, was eftimated £.17,065 currency; befides which there are eftates belonging to it that

that as yet produce nothing. The same year, the legiſlature granted £.10,000 for enlarging the building, and adding thereto a Lying-in and Foundling hoſpital. The annual private donations are very conſiderable. Thoſe that contribute a certain ſum have the power of electing the directors, who are twelve in number, and choſen yearly. The directors appoint ſix of the moſt ſkilful ſurgeons and phyſicians in the city to attend; there is alſo a ſurgeon and apothecary reſident in the houſe. From the year 1756, when it was built, to the year 1793 incluſive, nearly 9,000 patients were admitted into this hoſpital, upwards of 6,000 of whom were relieved or cured. The hoſpital ſtands within the limits of the city, but it is more than a quarter of a mile removed from any of the other buildings. There are ſpacious walks within the incloſure for ſuch of the patients as are in a ſtate of convaleſcence.

The Bettering Houſe, which is under the care of the overſeers of the poor, ſtands in the ſame neighbourhood, ſomewhat farther removed from the houſes of the city. It is a ſpacious building of brick, with extenſive walks and gardens. The poor of the city and neighbourhood are here furniſhed with employment, and comfortably lodged and dieted. During the ſeverity of the winter ſeaſon, many aged

aged and reduced perfons feek refuge in this place, and leave it again on the return of spring. Whilst they stay there, they are under very little restraint, and go in and out when they please; they must, however, behave orderly. This institution is supported by a tax on the town.

The gaol is a spacious building of common stone, one hundred feet in front. It is fitted up with solitary cells, on the new plan, and the apartments are all arched, to prevent the communication of fire. Behind the building are extensive yards, which are secured by lofty walls. This gaol is better regulated, perhaps, than any other on the face of the globe. By the new penal laws of Pennsylvania, lately enacted, no crime is punishable with death, excepting murder of the first degree, by which is meant, murder that is perpetrated by wilful premeditated intention, or in attempts to commit rape, robbery, or the like. Every other offence, according to its enormity, is punished by solitary imprisonment of a determined duration. Objections may be made to this mode of punishment, as not being sufficiently severe on the individual to atone for an atrocious crime; nor capable, because not inflicted in public, of deterring evil-minded persons in the community from the commission of offences which incur the rigour of the law; but on a
close

cloſe examination, it will be found to be very
ſevere; and as far as an opinion can be formed
from the trial that has been hitherto made by
the ſtate of Pennſylvania, it ſeems better calculated to reſtrain the exceſſes of the people
than any other. If any public puniſhment
could ſtrike terror into the lawleſs part of the
multitude, it is as likely that the infliction of
death would do it as any whatſoever: but
death is diveſted of many of his terrors, after
being often preſented to our view; ſo that
we find in countries, for inſtance in England,
where it occurs often as puniſhment, the ſa-
lutary effects that might be expected from it
are in a great meaſure loſt. The unfortunate
wretch, who is doomed to forfeit his life in
expiation of the crimes he has committed, in
numberleſs inſtances, looks forward with apparent unconcern to the moment in which he
is to be launched into eternity; his compa-
nions around him only condole with him, becauſe his career of iniquity has ſo ſuddenly
been impeded by the courſe of juſtice: or, if
he is not too much hardened in the paths of
vice, but falls a prey to remorſe, and ſees all
the horrors of his impending fate, they endeavour to rally his broken ſpirits by the con-
ſoling remembrance, that the pangs he has to
endure are but the pangs of a moment, which
they illuſtrate by the ſpeedy exit of one whoſe
death

death he was perhaps himself witness to but a few weeks before. A month does not pass over in England without repeated executions; and there is scarcely a vagabond to be met with in the country, who has seen a fellow creature suspended from the gallows. We all know what little good effect such spectacles produce. But immured in darkness and solitude, the prisoner suffers pangs worse than death a hundred times in the day: he is left to his own bitter reflections; there is no one thing to divert his attention, and he endeavours in vain to escape from the horrors which continually haunt his imagination. In such a situation the most hardened offender is soon reduced to a state of repentance.

But punishment by imprisonment, according to the laws of Pennsylvania, is imposed, not only as an expiation of past offences, and an example to the guilty part of society, but for another purpose, regarded by few penal codes in the world, the reform of the criminal. The regulations of the gaol, are calculated to promote this effect as soon as possible, so that the building, indeed, deserves the name of a penitentiary house more than that of a gaol. As soon as a criminal is committed to the prison he is made to wash; his hair is shorn, and if not decently clothed, he is furnished with clean apparel; then he is thrown into a solitary

litary cell,-about nine feet long and four wide, where he remains debarred from the fight of every living being excepting his gaoler, whofe duty it is to attend to the bare neceffities of his nature, but who is forbidden, on any account, to fpeak to him without there is abfolute occafion. If a prifoner is at all refractory, or if the offence for which he is imprifoned is of a very atrocious nature, he is then confined in a cell fecluded even from the light of heaven. This is the worft that can be inflicted upon him.

The gaol is infpected twice every week by twelve perfons appointed for that purpofe, who are chofen annually from amongft the citizens of Philadelphia. Nor is it a difficult matter to procure thefe men, who readily and voluntarily take it upon them to go through the troublefome functions of the office without any fee or emolument whatever. They divide themfelves into committees; each of thefe takes it in turn, for a ftated period, to vifit every part of the prifon; and a report is made to the infpectors at large, who meet together at times regularly appointed. From the report of the committee an opinion is formed by the infpectors, who, with the confent of the judges, regulate the treatment of each individual prifoner during his confinement. This is varied according to his crime,

and

and according to his subsequent repentance. Solitary confinement in a dark cell is looked upon as the severest usage; next, solitary confinement in a cell with the admission of light; next, confinement in a cell where the prisoner is allowed to do some sort of work; lastly, labour in company with others. The prisoners are obliged to bathe twice every week, proper conveniencies for that purpose being provided within the walls of the prison, and also to change their linen, with which they are regularly provided. Those in solitary confinement are kept upon bread and water; but those who labour are allowed broth, porridge, puddings, and the like: meat is dispensed only in small quantities, twice in the week. Their drink is water; on no pretence is any other beverage suffered to be brought into the prison. This diet is found, by experience, to afford the prisoners strength sufficient to perform the labour that is imposed upon them; whereas a more generous one would only serve to render their minds less humble and submissive. Those who labour, are employed in the particular trade to which they have been accustomed, provided it can be carried on in the prison; if not acquainted with any, something is soon found that they can do. One room is set apart for shoemakers, another for taylors, a third for carpenters,

penters, and so on; and in the yards are stonecutters, smiths, nailers, &c. &c.

Excepting the cells, which are at a remote part of the building, the prison has the appearance of a large manufactory. Good order and decency prevail throughout, and the eye of a spectator is never assailed by the sight of such ghastly and squalid figures as are continually to be met with in our prisons; so far, also, is a visitor from being insulted, that he is scarcely noticed as he passes through the different wards. The prisoners are forbidden to speak to each other without there is necessity; they are also forbidden to laugh, or to sing, or to make the smallest disturbance. An overseer attends continually to see that every one performs his work diligently; and in case of the smallest resistance to any of the regulations, the offender is immediately cast into a solitary cell, to subsist on bread and water till he returns to a proper sense of his behaviour; but the dread all those have of this treatment, who have once experienced it, is such, that it is seldom found necessary to repeat it. The women are kept totally apart from the men, and are employed in a manner suitable to their sex. The labourers all eat together in one large apartment; and regularly, every Sunday, there is divine service, at which all attend. It is the duty of the chaplain to converse at times

with

with the prisoners, and endeavour to reform their minds and principles. The inspectors, when they visit the prison, also do the same; so that when a prisoner is liberated, he goes out, as it were, a new man; he has been habituated to employment, and has received good instructions. The greatest care is also taken to find him employment the moment he quits the place of his confinement. According to the regulations, no person is allowed to visit the prison without permission of the inspectors. The greatest care is also taken to preserve the health of the prisoners, and for those who are sick there are proper apartments and good advice provided. The longest period of confinement is for a rape, which is not to be less than ten years, but not to exceed twenty-one. For high treason, the length of confinement is not to be less than six nor more than twelve years. There are prisons in every county throughout Pennsylvania, but none as yet are established on the same plan as that which has been described. Criminals are frequently sent from other parts of the state to receive punishment in the prison of Philadelphia.

So well is this gaol conducted, that instead of being an expense, it now annually produces a considerable revenue to the state.

LETTER II.

Population of Philadelphia.—Some Account of the Inhabitants, their Character and Manners—Private Amusements.—Americans lose their Teeth prematurely.—Theatrical Amusements only permitted of late.—Quakers.—President's Levee and Drawing Room.—Places of public Worship.—Carriages, what sort of, used in Philadelphia.—Taverns, how conducted in America.—Difficulty of procuring Servants.—Character of the lower Classes of People in America.

MY DEAR SIR,   Philadelphia, November.

PHILADELPHIA, according to the census taken in the Year 1790, contained 42,000 people. From the natural increase, however, of population, and the influx of strangers, the number is supposed now to be near 50,000, notwithstanding the ravages of the yellow fever in 1793, which swept off 4,000 people. The inhabitants consist of English, Irish, Scotch, Germans, French, and of American born citizens, descended from people of these different nations, who are of course by far the most numerous class. The inhabitants are for the most part engaged in some sort of business; a few, and a few only, live with-

out

out any oftenfible profeffions, on the fortunes which they themfelves have raifed; but thefe men are not idle or inattentive to the increafe of their property, being ever on the watch to profit by the fale of lands, which they have purchafed, and to buy more on advantageous terms. It would be a difficult matter to find a man of any property in the country, who is not concerned in the buying or felling of land, which may be confidered in America as an article of trade.

In a large city, like Philadelphia, where people are affembled together from fo many different quarters, there cannot fail to be a great diverfity in the manners of the inhabitants. It is a remark, however, very generally made, not only by foreigners, but alfo by perfons from other parts of the United States, that the Philadelphians are extremely deficient in hofpitality and politenefs towards ftrangers. Amongft the uppermoft circles in Philadelphia, pride, haughtinefs, and oftentation are confpicuous; and it feems as if nothing could make them happier than that an order of nobility fhould be eftablifhed, by which they might be exalted above their fellow citizens, as much as they are in their own conceit. In the manners of the people in general there is a coldnefs and referve, as if they were fufpicious of fome defigns againft them, which chills

chills to the very heart those who come to visit them. In their private societies a *tristesse* is apparent, near which mirth and gaiety can never approach. It is no unusual thing, in the genteelest houses, to see a large party of from twenty to thirty persons assembled, and seated round a room, without partaking of any other amusement than what arises from the conversation, most frequently in whispers, that passes between the two persons who are seated next to each other. The party meets between six and seven in the evening; tea is served with much form; and at ten, by which time most of the company are wearied with having remained so long stationary, they return to their own homes. Still, however, they are not strangers to music, cards, or dancing; their knowledge of music, indeed, is at a very low ebb; but in dancing, which appears to be their most favourite amusement, they certainly excel.

The women, in general, whilst young, are very pretty, but by the time they become mothers of a little family they lose all their beauty, their complexions fade away, their teeth begin to decay, and they hardly appear like the same creatures. In a few instances only it would be possible to find a fine woman of the age of forty, who has had a large family. The sudden decay of the teeth is a circumstance which

has

has engaged the attention of the faculty; both men and women, American born, losing them very generally at an early age. Some ascribe it to the great and sudden changes in the weather, from heat to cold; but negroes, who are exposed to the same transition of climate, are distinguished for the whiteness and beauty of their teeth; and the Indians also, who are more exposed than either, preserve their teeth in good order. Others attribute it to the immoderate use of confectionary. Of confectionary, the Americans in the towns certainly make an inordinate use; but in the country, where the people have not an opportunity of getting such things, the men, but more generally the women, also lose their teeth very prematurely. Most probably it is owing to the very general use they make of salted provisions. In the country parts of America in particular, the people live upon salted pork and salted fish nearly the whole year round.

It is only within a few years past, since 1779, that any public amusements have been suffered in this city; the old corporation, which consisted mostly of the Quakers, and not of the most liberal minded people in the city, having always opposed the establishment of any place for the purpose. Now, however, there are two theatres and an amphitheatre. Little or no use is made of the old theatre, which is of wood, and a very indifferent building. The new one is built of brick, and neatly fitted up within; but it is hardly large enough for the town. A shocking custom obtains here, of smoking tobacco in the house, which at times is carried to such an excess, that those to whom it is disagreeable are under the necessity of going away. To the people in the pit, wine and porter is brought between the acts, precisely as if they were in a tavern. The actors are procured, with a very few exceptions, from Great Britain and Ireland; none of them are very eminent performers, but they are equal to what are usually met with in the country towns of England. The amphitheatre is built of wood; equestrian and other exercises are performed there, similar to those at Astley's. Dancing assemblies are held regularly every fortnight through the winter, and occasionally there are public concerts.

During summer, the people that can make it convenient retire to country houses in the neighbourhood of the town, and all public and private amusements cease; winter is the season for them, the Congress being then assembled, and trade not being so closely attended to, as the navigation of the river is then commonly impeded by ice.

The president finds it necessary, in general,
to

to come to Philadelphia preparatory to the meeting of congress, and resides there during the whole of the session. Once in the week, during his stay in the city, he has levees, between the hours of three and four in the afternoon. At these he always appears himself in a court dress, and it is expected that the foreign ministers should always attend in the same style; this they constantly do, excepting the French minister, who makes a point of going in dishabille, not to say worse of it. Other persons are at liberty to go as they think proper. Mrs. Washington, also, has a drawing room once every week. On this occasion the ladies are seated in great form round the apartment, and tea, coffee, &c. served *.

Philadelphia is the grand residence of the Quakers in America, but their number does not bear the same proportion now to that of the other citizens which it did formerly. At present they form about one fourth only of the inhabitants. This does not arise from any diminution of the number of Quakers, on the contrary they have considerably increased, but

---

* Whether the levee is kept up by the present president, or not, I have not heard. Many objections were made to it by the democratic party during the administration of General Washington, as being inconsistent with the spirit of a republican government, and destructive of that equality which ought to reign amongst the citizens of every class.

from

from the great influx into the city of persons of a different persuasion. Belonging to the Quakers there are five places for public worship; to the Presbyterians and Seceders six; to the English Episcopalians three; to German Lutherans two; to the Roman Catholics four; and one respectively to the Swedish Lutherans, Moravians, Baptists, Universal Baptists, Methodists, and Jews. On a Sunday every citizen appears well dressed; the lower classes of the people in particular are remarkably well clothed. This is a great day also for little excursions into the country.

The carriages made use of in Philadelphia consist of coaches, chariots, chaises, coachees, and light waggons, the greater part of which are built in Philadelphia. The equipages of a few individuals are extremely ostentatious; nor does there appear in any that neatness and elegance which might be expected amongst a set of people that are desirous of imitating the fashions of England, and that are continually getting models over from that country. The coachee is a carriage peculiar, I believe, to America; the body of it is rather longer than that of a coach, but of the same shape. In the front it is left quite open down to the bottom, and the driver sits on a bench under the roof of the carriage. There are two

two seats in it for the paffengers, who fit with their faces towards the horfes. The roof is fupported by fmall props, which are placed at the corners. On each fide of the doors, above the pannels, it is quite open, and to guard againft bad weather there are curtains, which are made to let down from the roof, and faften to buttons placed for the purpofe on the outfide. There is alfo a leathern curtain to hang occafionally between the driver and paffengers.

The light waggons are on the fame conftruction, and are calculated to accommodate from four to twelve people. The only difference between a fmall waggon and a coachee is, that the latter is better finifhed, has varnifhed pannels, and doors at the fide. The former has no doors, but the paffengers fcramble in the beft way they can, over the feat of the driver. The waggons are ufed univerfally for ftage carriages.

The accommodations at the taverns, by which name they call all inns, &c. are very indifferent in Philadelphia; as indeed they are, with a very few exceptions, throughout the country. The mode of conducting them is nearly the fame every where. The traveller is fhewn, on arrival, into a room which is common to every perfon in the houfe, and which is generally the one fet apart for breakfaft, breakfaſt, dinner, and ſupper. All the ſtrangers that happen to be in the houſe ſit down to theſe meals promiſcuouſly, and, excepting in the large towns, the family of the houſe alſo forms a part of the company. It is ſeldom that a private parlour or drawing room can be procured at any of the taverns, even in the towns; and it is always with reluctance that breakfaſt or dinner is ſerved up ſeparately to any individual. If a ſingle bed room can be procured, more ought not to be looked for; but it is not always that even this is to be had, and thoſe who travel through the country muſt often ſubmit to be crammed into rooms where there is ſcarcely ſufficient ſpace to walk between the beds.* Strangers who remain for any length of time in the large towns moſt uſually go to private boarding houſes, of which great numbers are to be met with. It is always a difficult matter to procure furniſhed lodgings without paying for board.

---

* Having ſtopped one night at Elkton, on my journey to Baltimore in the public carriage, my firſt enquiries from the landlord, on alighting, as there were many paſſengers in the ſtage, were to know what accommodation his houſe afforded. He ſeemed much ſurprized that any enquiries ſhould be made on ſuch a ſubject, and with much conſequence told me, I need not give myſelf any trouble about the extent of his accommodations, as he had no leſs than *eleven* beds in *one* of his rooms.

At

At all the taverns, both in town and country, but particularly in the latter, the attendance is very bad; indeed, excepting in the southern states, where there are such great numbers of negroes, it is a matter of the utmost difficulty to procure domestic servants of any description. The generality of servants that are met with in Philadelphia are emigrant Europeans; they, however, for the most part, only remain in service until they can save a little money, when they constantly quit their masters, being led to do so by that desire for independence which is so natural to the mind of man, and which every person in America may enjoy that will be industrious. The few that remain steady to those who have hired them are retained at most exorbitant wages. As for the Americans, none but those of the most indifferent characters ever enter into service, which they consider as suitable only to negroes; the negroes again, in Pennsylvania and in the other states where steps have been taken for the gradual abolition of slavery, are taught by the Quakers to look upon themselves in every respect as equal to their white brethren, and they endeavour to imitate them by being saucy. It is the same both with males and females. I must here observe, that amongst the generality of the lower sort of people in the United States, and particularly amongst those

those of Philadelphia, there is a want of good manners which excites the surprize of almost every foreigner; I wish also that it may not be thought that this remark has been made, merely because the same deference and the same respectful attention, which we see so commonly paid by the lower orders of people in Great Britain and Ireland to those who are in a situation somewhat superior to themselves, is not also paid in America to persons in the same station; it is the want of common civility I complain of, which it is always desirable to behold between man and man, let their situations in life be what they may, and which is not contrary to the dictates of nature, or to the spirit of genuine liberty, as it is observable in the behaviour of the wild Indians that wander through the forests of this vast continent, the most free and independent of all human beings. In the United States, however, the lower classes of people will return rude and impertinent answers to questions couched in the most civil terms, and will insult a person that bears the appearance of a gentleman, on purpose to shew how much they consider themselves upon an equality with him. Civility cannot be purchased from them on any terms; they seem to think that it is incompatible with freedom, and that there is no other way of convincing a stranger that he

is

is really in a land of liberty, but by being surly and ill mannered in his presence.

LETTER III.

Journey to Baltimore.—Description of the Country about Philadelphia.—Floating Bridges over the Schuylkill, how constructed.—Mills in Brandy-wine Creek.—Improvement in the Machinery of Flour Mills in America.—Town of Wilmington.—Log Houses.— Bad Roads.—Fine Prospects.— How relished by Americans.— Taverns.— Susquehannah River.— Town of Baltimore.— Plan of the Town. — Harbour. — Public and private Buildings.— Inhabitants.— Country between Baltimore and Washington.—Execrable Roads.

MY DEAR SIR,   Washington, November.

ON the 16th of November I left Philadelphia for Baltimore. The only mode of conveyance which offers for a traveller, who is not provided with his own horses or carriage, is the public stage waggon; it is possible, indeed, to procure a private carriage at Philadelphia to go on to Baltimore, for which a great price is always demanded; but there is no such thing as hiring a carriage or horses from stage to stage. The country about Philadelphia is well cultivated, and it abounds with

neat

neat country houſes; but it has a bare appearance, being almoſt totally ſtripped of the trees, which have been cut down without mercy for firing, and to make way for the plough; neither are there any hedges, an idea prevailing that they impoveriſh the land wherever they are planted. The fences are all of the common poſt and rail, or of the angular kind. Theſe laſt are made of rails about eight or nine feet long, roughly ſplit out of trees, and placed horizontally above one another, as the bars of a gate; but each tier of rails, or gate as it were, inſtead of being on a ſtraight line with the one next to it, is put in a different direction, ſo as to form an angle ſufficient to permit the ends of the rails of one tier to reſt ſteadily on thoſe of the next. As theſe fences, from their ſerpentine courſe, occupy at leaſt ſix times as much ground as a common poſt and rail fence, and require alſo a great deal more wood, they are moſtly laid aſide whenever land and timber become objects of importance, as they ſoon do in the neighbourhood of large towns.

The road to Baltimore is over the loweſt of three floating bridges, which have been thrown acroſs the river Schuylkill, in the neighbourhood of Philadelphia. The view on paſſing this river, which is about two hundred and fifty yards wide, is beautiful. The banks on each

each side are high, and for many miles above afford the most delightful situations for villas. A very elegant one, laid out in the English taste, is seen on passing the river just above the bridge. Adjoining to it are public gardens, and a house of entertainment, with several good rooms, to which the citizens of Philadelphia resort in great numbers during the summer season.

The floating bridges are formed of large trees, which are placed in the water transversely, and chained together; beams are then laid lengthways upon these, and the whole boarded over, to render the way convenient for passengers. On each side there is a railing. When very heavy carriages go across these bridges, they sink a few inches below the surface of the water; but the passage is by no means dangerous. They are kept in an even direction across the river, by means of chains and anchors in different parts, and are also strongly secured on both shores. Over that part of the river where the channel lies, they are so contrived that a piece can be removed to allow vessels to pass through. These bridges are frequently damaged, and sometimes entirely carried away, during floods, at the breaking up of winter, especially if there happens to be much ice floating in the river. To guard against this, when danger is apprehended and the flood does not come on too rapidly, they unfaften all the chains by which the bridge is confined in its proper place, and then let the whole float down with the ftream to a convenient part of the fhore, where it can be hauled up and fecured.

The country, after paffing the Schuylkill, is pleafingly diverfified with rifing grounds and woods, and appears to be in a good ftate of cultivation. The firft town of any note which you come to is Chefter, fifteen miles from Philadelphia; this town contains about fixty dwellings, and is remarkable for being the place where the firft colonian affembly fat. From the neighbourhood of this town there is a very grand view of the river Delaware.

About half a mile before you come to Wilmington is Brandy-wine River, remarkable for its mills, no lefs than thirteen being built almoft clofe to each other upon it. The water, juft above the bridge which is thrown over it, comes tumbling down with great violence over a bed of rocks; and feats, at a very trifling expenfe, could be made for three times the number of mills already built. Veffels carrying 1,000 bufhels of wheat can come clofe up to them, and by means of machinery their cargoes are received from, or delivered to them in a very expeditious manner. Among the mills, fome are for flour, fome some for sawing of wood, and others for stone. The improvements which have been made in the machinery of the flour mills in America are very great. The chief of these consist in a new application of the screw, and the introduction of what are called elevators, the idea of which was evidently borrowed from the chain pump. The screw is made by sticking small thin pieces of board, about three inches long and two wide, into a cylinder, so as to form the spiral line. This screw is placed in a horizontal position, and by turning on its axis it forces wheat or flour from one end of a trough to the other. For instance, in the trough which receives the meal immediately coming from the stones, a screw of this kind is placed, by which the meal is forced on, to the distance of six or eight feet perhaps, into a reservoir; from thence, without any manual labour, it is conveyed to the very top of the mill by the elevators, which consist of a number of small buckets of the size of tea-cups, attached to a long band that goes round a wheel at the top, and another at the bottom of the mill. As the band revolves round the wheels, these buckets dip into the reservoir of wheat or flour below, and take their loads up to the top, where they empty themselves as they turn round the upper wheel. The elevators are inclosed in square

square wooden tubes, to prevent them from catching in any thing, and also to prevent dust. By means of these two simple contrivances no manual labour is required from the moment the wheat is taken to the mill till it is converted into flour, and ready to be packed, during the various processes of screening, grinding, sifting, &c.

Wilmington is the capital of the state of Delaware, and contains about six hundred houses, which are chiefly of brick. The streets are laid out on a plan somewhat similar to that of Philadelphia. There is nothing very interesting in this town, and the country round about it is flat and insipid. Elkton, twenty-one miles distant from Wilmington, and the first town in Maryland, contains about ninety indifferent houses, which are built without any regularity; it is a dirty disagreeable place. In this neighbourhood I first took notice of log-houses; those which I had hitherto seen having been built either of brick or stone, or else constructed with wooden frames, sheathed on the outside with boards. The log-houses are cheaper than any others in a country where there is abundance of wood, and generally are the first that are erected on a new settlement in America. The sides consist of trees just squared, and placed horizontally one upon the other; the ends of of the logs of one side resting alternately on the ends of those of the adjoining sides, in notches; the interstices between the logs are stopped with clay; and the roof is covered with boards or with shingles, which are small pieces of wood in the shape of slates or tiles, and which are used for that purpose, with a few exceptions, throughout America. These habitations are not very sightly, but when well built they are warm and comfortable, and last for a long time

A considerable quantity of wheat and Indian corn is raised in this neighbourhood, to the production of which the soil is favourable; but the best cultivated parts of the country are not seen from the road, which passes chiefly over barren and hilly tracts, called " ridges." The reason for carrying the road over these is, because it is found to last longer than if carried over the flat part of the country, where the soil is deep, a circumstance which the people of Maryland always take into consideration; for after a road is once cut, they never take pains to keep it in good repair. The roads in this state are worse than in any one in the union; indeed so very bad are they, that on going from Elkton to the Susquehannah ferry, the driver frequently had to call to the passengers in the stage, to lean out of the carriage first at one side, then at the other, to prevent it from overfetting in the deep ruts with which the road abounds: "Now, gentlemen, to the right;" upon which the paffengers all ftretched their bodies half way out of the carriage to balance it on that fide: "Now, gentlemen, to the left," and fo on. This was found abfolutely neceffary at leaft a dozen times in half the number of miles. Whenever they attempt to mend thefe roads, it is always by filling the ruts with faplings or bufhes, and covering them over with earth. This, however, is done only when there are fields on each fide of the road. If the road runs contiguous to a wood, then, inftead of mending it where it is bad, they open a new paffage through the trees, which they call making a road. It is very common in Maryland to fee fix or feven different roads branching out from one, which all lead to the fame place. A ftranger, before he is acquainted with this circumftance, is frequently puzzled to know which he ought to take. The dexterity with which the drivers of the ftages guide their horfes along thefe new roads, which are full of ftumps of trees, is aftonifhing, yet to appearance they are the moft awkward drivers poffible; it is more by the different noifes which they make, than by their reins, that they manage their horfes.

Charlefton

Charleston stands at a few miles distance from Elkton; there are about twenty houses only in it, which are inhabited chiefly by people who carry on a herring fishery. Beyond it the country is much diversified with hill and dale, and the soil being but of an indifferent quality, the lands are so little cleared, that in many parts the road winds through uninterrupted woods for four or five miles together. The scenery in this neighbourhood is extremely interesting. From the top of the hills you meet with numberless bold and extensive prospects of the Chesapeak Bay and of the river Susquehannah; and scarcely do you cross a valley without beholding in the depths of the wood the waters of some little creek or rivulet rushing over ledges of rock in a beautiful cascade. The generality of Americans stare with astonishment at a person who can feel any delight at passing through such a country as this. To them the sight of a wheat field or a cabbage garden would convey pleasure far greater than that of the most romantic woodland views. They have an unconquerable aversion to trees; and whenever a settlement is made, they cut away all before them without mercy; not one is spared; all share the same fate, and are involved in the general havoc. It appears strange, that in a country where the rays of the sun act with such prodigious

digious power, some few trees near the habitations should not be spared, whose foliage might afford a cooling shade during the parching heats of summer; and I have oftentimes expressed my astonishment that none were ever left for that purpose. In answer I have generally been told, that they could not be left standing near a house without danger. The trees it seems in the American forests have but a very slender hold in the ground, considering their immense height, so that when two or three fully grown are deprived of shelter in consequence of the others which stood around them being cut down, they are very apt to be levelled by the first storm that chances to blow. This, however, would not be the case with trees of a small growth, which might safely be spared, and which would soon afford an agreeable shade if the Americans thought proper to leave them standing: but the fact of the matter is, that from the face of the country being entirely overspread with trees, the eyes of the people become satiated with the sight of them. The ground cannot be tilled, nor can the inhabitants support themselves, till they are removed; they are looked upon as a nuisance, and the man that can cut down the largest number, and have the fields about his house most clear of them, is looked upon as the most industrious citizen, and the one that is

making

making the greatest improvements * in the country.

Every ten or twelve miles upon this road there are taverns, which are all built of wood, and much in the same ſtile, with a porch in front the entire length of the houſe. Few of theſe taverns have any ſigns, and they are only to be diſtinguiſhed from the other houſes by the number of handbills paſted up on the walls near the door. They take their name, not from the ſign, but from the perſon who keeps them, as Jones's, Brown's, &c. &c. All of them are kept nearly in the ſame manner. At each houſe there are regular hours for breakfaſt, dinner, and ſupper, and if a traveller arrives ſomewhat before the time appointed for any one of theſe, it is in vain to call for a ſeparate meal for himſelf; he muſt wait patiently till the appointed hour, and then ſit down with the other gueſts that may happen to be in the houſe. Breakfaſts are generally plentifully ſerved; there is tea, coffee, and different ſorts of bread, cold ſalt meat, and, very commonly beſides, beef ſteaks, fried fiſh,

---

* I have heard of Americans landing on barren parts of the north weſt coaſt of Ireland, and evincing the greateſt ſurpriſe and pleaſure at the beauty and improved ſtate of the country, " ſo clear of trees!!"

&c.

&c. &c †. The charge made for breakfast is nearly the same as that for dinner.

This part of Maryland abounds with iron ore, which is of a quality particularly well adapted for casting. The ore is found in banks so near the surface of the earth that there is never occasion to sink a shaft to get at it. Near Charleston there is a small foundery for cannon. The cannon are bored by water. As I passed by, they were making twenty-four pounders, two of which I was informed they finished every week. The iron is extremely tough; very few of the guns burst on being proved.

The Susquehannah river is crossed, on the way to Baltimore, at a ferry five miles above its entrance into the Chesapeak. The river is here about a mile and quarter wide, and deep enough for any vessels; the banks are high and thickly wooded, and the scenery is grand and picturesque. A small town called Havre de Grace, which contains about forty houses, stands on this river at the ferry. A petition was presented to congress the last year to have it made a port of entry; but at present

---

† The landlady always presides at the head of the table to make the tea, or a female servant attends for that purpose at breakfast and in the evening; and at many taverns in the country the whole of the family sit down to dinner with the guests.

there is very little trade carried on there. A few ships are annually built in the neighbourhood. From hence to Baltimore the country is extremely poor; the soil is of a yellow gravel mixed with clay, and the roads execrable.

Baltimore is supposed to contain about sixteen thousand inhabitants, and though not the capital of the state, is the largest town in Maryland, and the most considerable place of trade in North America, after Philadelphia and New York. The plan of the town is somewhat similar to that of Philadelphia, most of the streets crossing each other at right angles. The main street, which runs east and west nearly, is about eighty feet wide; the others are from forty to sixty feet. The streets are not all paved, so that when it rains heavily they are rendered almost impassable, the soil being a stiff yellow clay, which retains the water a long time. On the south side of the town is a harbour commonly called the Bason, which affords about nine feet water, and is large enough to contain two thousand sail of merchant vessels. There are wharfs and stores along it, the whole length of the town; but as a particular wind is necessary to enable ships to get out of this bason, by far the greater number of those which enter the port of Baltimore stop at a harbour which is formed by
a neck

a neck of land near the mouth of the bafon, called Fell's Point. Here alfo wharfs have been built, alongfide which veffels of fix hundred tons burthen can lie with perfect fafety. Numbers of perfons have been induced to fettle on this Point, in order to be contiguous to the fhipping. Upwards of feven hundred houfes have already been built there, and regular ftreets laid out, with a large market place. Thefe houfes, generally fpeaking, are confidered as a part of Baltimore, but to all appearance they form a feparate town, being upwards of a mile diftant from the other part of the town. In the neighbourhood, Fell's Point and Baltimore are fpoken of as diftinct and feparate places. Fell's Point is chiefly the refidence of feafaring people, and of the younger partners of mercantile houfes, who are ftationed there to attend to the fhipping.

The greater number of private houfes in Baltimore are of brick, but many, particularly in the fkirts of the town, are of wood. In fome of the new ftreets a few appear to be well built, but in general the houfes are fmall, heavy, and inconvenient. As for the public buildings, there are none worthy of being mentioned. The churches and places for public worfhip are ten in number; one refpectively for Epifcopalians, Prefbyterians, German Lutherans, German Calvinifts, Reformed Germans,

mans, Nicolites or New Quakers, Baptists, Roman Catholics, and two for Methodists. The Presbyterian church, which has lately been erected, is the best building among them, and indeed the handsomest building in town. It is of brick, with a portico in front supported by six pillars of stone.

They have no less than three incorporated banks in this town, and the number of notes issued from them is so great, as almost to preclude the circulation of specie. Some of the notes are for as small a sum as a single dollar, and being much more portable than silver, are generally preferred. As for gold, it is very scarce; I hardly ever met with it during two months that I remained in Maryland.

Amongst the inhabitants of Baltimore are to be found English, Irish, Scotch, and French. The Irish appear to be most numerous; and many of the principal merchants in town are in the number. Since the war, a great many French have arrived both from France and from the West India Islands. With a few exceptions the inhabitants are all engaged in trade, which is closely attended to. They are mostly plain people, sociable however amongst themselves, and very friendly and hospitable towards strangers. Cards and dancing are favourite amusements, both in private and at public assemblies, which are held

every

every fortnight. There are two theatres here, in which there are performances occasionally. The oldest of them, which stands in the road to Fell's Point, is most wretched, and appears little better than a heap of loose boards; for a long time it lay quite neglected, but has lately been fitted up for a company of French actors, the only one I ever heard of in the country. Baltimore, like Philadelphia, has suffered from the ravages of the yellow fever. During the autumn it is generally unhealthy, and those who can afford it retire to country seats in the neighbourhood, of which some are most delightfully situated.

From Baltimore to Washington, which is forty miles distant, the country wears but a poor appearance. The soil in some parts consists of a yellow clay mixed with gravel; in other parts it is very sandy. In the neighbourhood of the creeks and between the hills are patches of rich black earth, called Bottoms, the trees upon which grow to a large size; but where there is gravel they are very small. The roads passing over these bottoms are worse than any I ever met with elsewhere. In driving over one of them, near the head waters of a branch of Patuxent river, a few days after a heavy fall of rain, the wheels of a sulky which I was in sunk up to the very boxes. For

For a moment I defpaired of being able to get out without affiftance, when my horfe, which was very powerful, finding himfelf impeded, threw himfelf upon his haunches, and difengaging his fore-feet, made a vigorous plunge forwards, which luckily difengaged both himfelf and the fulky, and freed me from my embarraffment. I was afterwards informed that General Wafhington, as he was going to meet congrefs a fhort time before, was ftopped in the very fame place, his carriage finking fo deep in the mud that it was found neceffary to fend to a neighbouring houfe for ropes and poles to extricate it. Over fome of the bottoms, which were abfolutely impaffable in their natural ftate, caufeways have been thrown, which are made with large trees laid fide by fide acrofs the road. For a time thefe caufeways afford a commodious paffage; but they do not laft long, as many of the trees fink into the foft foil, and others, expofed to the continual attrition of waggon wheels in a particular part, breaking afunder. In this ftate, full of unfeen obftacles, it is abfolutely a matter of danger for a perfon unacquainted with the road to attempt to drive a carriage along it. The bridges over the creeks, covered with loofe boards, are as bad as the caufeways, and totter as a carriage paffes over.

That

That the legiflature of Maryland can be fo inactive, and not take fome fteps to repair this, which is one of the principal roads in the ftate, the great road from north to fouth, and the high road to the City of Wafhington, is moft wonderful!

LETTER IV.

Foundation of the City of Washington.—Not readily agreed to by different States.—Choice of the Ground left to General Washington. —Circumstances to be considered in chusing the Ground.—The Spot fixed upon central to all the States.—Also remarkably advantageously situated for Trade. — Nature of the Back Country Trade.—Summary View of the principal Trading Towns in the United States.— Their Prosperity shewn to depend on the Back Country Trade.—Description of the Patowmac River.—Its Connection with other Rivers pointed out.—Prodigious Extent of the Water Communication from Washington City in all Directions.—Country likely to trade immediately with Washington.—Situation of Washington.—Plan of the City.— Public Buildings.—Some begun, others projected.—Capital President's House.—Hotel. —Stone and other building Materials found in the Neighbourhood.—Private Houses and Inhabitants at present in the City.—Different Opinions respecting the future Greatness of the City.—Impediments thrown in the Way of its Improvement.—What has given rise to this.

MY DEAR SIR,   Washington, November.

THE City of Washington, or the Federal City, as it is indiscriminately called, was laid out in the year 1792, and is expressly prefsly defigned for being the metropolis of the United States, and the feat of the federal government. In the year 1800 the congrefs is to meet there for the firft time. As the foundation of this city has attracted the attention of fo many people in Europe, and as fuch very different opinions are entertained about it, I fhall, in the following pages, give you a brief account of its rife and progrefs.

Shortly after the clofe of the American war, confiderable numbers of the Pennfylvanian line, or of the militia, with arms in their hands, furrounded the hall in which the congrefs was affembled at Philadelphia, and with vehement menaces infifted upon immediate appropriations of money being made to difcharge the large arrears due to them for their paft fervices. The members, alarmed at fuch an outrage, refolved to quit a ftate in which they met with infult inftead of protection, and quickly adjourned to New York, where the feffion was terminated. A fhort time afterwards, the propriety was ftrongly urged in congrefs, of fixing upon fome place for the meeting of the legiflature, and for the feat of the general government, which fhould be fubject to the laws and regulations of the congrefs alone, in order that the members, in future, might not have to depend for their perfonal fafety, and for their freedom of deliberation, upon the good or bad police of any individual

dividual ftate. This idea of making the place, which fhould be chofen for the meeting of the legiflature, independent of the particular ftate to which it might belong, was further-corroborated by the following argument: That as the feveral ftates in the union were in fome meafure rivals to each other, although connected together by certain ties, if any one of them was fixed upon for the feat of the general government in preference, and thus raifed to a ftate of pre-eminence, it might perhaps be the occafion of great jealoufy amongft the others. Every perfon was convinced of the expediency of preferving the union of the ftates entire; it was apparent, therefore, that the greateft precautions ought to be taken to remove every fource of jealoufy from amongft them, which might tend, though remotely, to produce a feparation. In fine, it was abfolutely neceffary that the feat of government fhould be made permanent, as the removal of the public offices and the archives from place to place could not but be attended with many and very great inconveniences.

However, notwithftanding this meafure appeared to be beneficial to the intereft of the union at large, it was not until after the revolution, by which the prefent federal conftitution was eftablifhed, that it was acceded to on the part of all the ftates. Pennfylvania,

vania in particular, confcious of her being a principal and central ftate, and therefore likely to be made the feat of government if this new project was not carried into execution, was foremoft in the oppofition. At laft fhe complied; but it was only on condition that the congrefs fhould meet at Philadelphia until the new city was ready for its reception, flattering herfelf that there would be fo many objections afterwards to the removal of the feat of government, and fo many difficulties in putting the project into execution, that it would finally be relinquifhed. To the difcriminating judgment of General Wafhington, then prefident, it was left to determine upon the fpot beft calculated for the federal city. After mature deliberation he fixed upon a fituation on the banks of the Patowmac River, a fituation which feems to be marked out by nature, not only for a large city, but exprefsly for the feat of the metropolis of the United States.

In the choice of the fpot there were two principal confiderations: Firft, that it fhould be as central as poffible in refpect to every ftate in the union; fecondly, that it fhould be advantageoufly fituated for commerce, without which it could not be expected that the city would ever be diftinguifhed for fize or for fplendour; and it was to be fuppofed, that

the

the people of the United States would be desirous of having the metropolis of the country as magnificent as it possibly could be. These two essential points are most happily combined in the spot which has been chosen.

The northern and southern extremities of the United States are in 46° and 31.° north latitude. The latitude of the new city is 38° 53' north; so that it is within twenty-three minutes of being exactly between the two extremities. In no part of North America either is there a port situated so far up the country to the westward, excepting what belongs to Great Britain on the river St. Lawrence, its distance from the ocean being no less than two hundred and eighty miles. A more central situation could certainly have been fixed upon, by going further to the westward; but had this been done, it must have been an inland one, which would have been very unfavourable for trade. The size of all towns in America has hitherto been proportionate to their trade, and particularly to that carried on with the back settlements. This trade consists in supplying the people of the western parts of the United States, or the back settlements, with certain articles of foreign manufacture, which they do not find any interest in fabricating for themselves at present; nor is it to be supposed that they will, for many years to come, while land remains cheap, and thefe articles can be imported and fent to them on reafonable terms. The articles chiefly in demand confift of hardware, woollen cloths, figured cottons, hofiery, haberdafhery, earthen ware, &c. &c. from England; coffee, rum, fugar*, from the Weft Indies; tea, coarfe muflins, and calicoes, from the Eaft Indies. In return for thefe articles the people of the back fettlements fend down for exportation the various kinds of produce which the country affords: wheat and flour, furs, fkins, rice, indigo, tobacco, pitch, tar, &c. &c. It is very evident, therefore, that the beft fituation for a trading town muft be upon a long navigable river, fo that the town may be open to the fea, and thus enabled to carry on a foreign trade, and at the fame time be enabled, by means of an extenfive water communication in an oppofite direction, to trade with the diftant parts of the country. None of the inland towns have as yet increafed to a great fize. Lancafter, which is the largeft in all America, contains only nine hundred houfes, and it is nearly double the fize of any other inland one. Neither do the fea-port towns flourifh, which are not well fituated for carrying on an inland

---

* Sugar is not fent very far back into the country, as it is procured at much lefs expence from the maple-tree.

trade at the fame time. The truth of this pofition muft appear obvious on taking furvey of the principal towns in the United States.

To begin with Bofton, the largeft town north of New York, and one of the oldeft in the United States. Though it has a moft excellent harbour, and has always been inhabited by an enterprizing induftrious fet of people, yet it is now inferior, both in fize and commerce, to Baltimore, which was little more than the refidence of a few fifhermen thirty years ago; and this, becaufe there is no river in the neighbourhood navigable for more than feven miles, and the weftern parts of the ftate of Maffachufets, of which it is the capital, can be fupplied with commodities carried up the North River on much better terms than if the fame commodities were fent by land carriage from Bofton. Neither does Bofton increafe by any means in the fame proportion as the other towns, which have an extenfive trade with the people of the back fettlements. For the fame caufe we do not find that any of the fea-port or other towns in Rhode Ifland and Connecticut are increafing very faft; on the contrary, Newport, the capital of the ftate of Rhode Ifland, and which has a harbour that is boafted of as being one of the beft throughout the United States, is now falling to decay. Newport contains about one thoufand houfes;

none

none of the other towns between Boston and New York contain more than five hundred.

We now come to New York, which enjoys the double advantages of an excellent harbour and a large navigable river, which opens a communication with the interior parts of the country; and here we find a flourishing city, containing forty thousand * inhabitants, and increasing beyond every calculation. The North or Hudson River, at the mouth of which New York stands, is navigable from thence for one hundred and thirty miles in large vessels, and in sloops of eighty tons burthen as far as Albany; smaller ones go still higher. About nine miles above Albany, the Mohawk River falls into the Hudson, by means of which, Wood Creek, Lake Oneida, and Oswego River, a communication is opened with Lake Ontario. In this route there are several portages, but it is a route which is much frequented, and numbers of boats are kept employed upon it in carrying goods whenever the season is not too dry. In long droughts the waters fall so much that oftentimes there is not sufficient to float an empty boat. All these obstructions however may, and will one day or other, be remedied by the hand of art. Oswego river, before it falls into Lake Ontario, communi-

* Six inhabitants may be reckoned for every house in the United States.

cates with the Seneka river, which affords in succeffion an entrance into the lakes Cayuga, Seneka, and Canadaqua. Lake Seneka, the largeft, is about forty miles in length; upon it there is a fchooner-rigged veffel of feventy tons burthen conftantly employed. The fhores of thefe lakes are more thickly fettled than the other part of the adjacent country, but the population of the whole track lying between the rivers Genefee and Hudfon, which are about two hundred and fifty miles apart, is rapidly increafing. All this country weft of the Hudfon River, together with that to the eaft, comprehending the back parts of the ftates of Maffachufetts and Connecticut, and alfo the entire of the ftate of Vermont, are fupplied with European manufactures and Weft Indian produce, &c. &c. by way of New York; not directly from that city, but from Albany, Hudfon, and other towns on the North River, which trade with New York, and which are intermediate places for the depofit of goods paffing to, and coming from the back country. Albany, indeed, is now beginning herfelf to import goods from the Weft Indies; but ftill the bulk of her trade is with New York. Nothing can ferve more to fhew the advantages which accrue to any town from an intercourfe with the back country, than the fudden progrefs of thefe fecondary places of trade upon

upon the North River. At Albany, the number of houses is increasing as fast as at New York; at present there are upwards of eleven hundred; and in Hudson city which was only laid out in the year 1783, there are now more than three hundred and twenty dwellings. This city is on the east side of the North River, one hundred and thirty miles above its mouth. By means also of the North River and Lake Champlain a trade is carried on with Montreal in Canada.

But to go on with the survey of the towns to the southward. In New Jersey, we find Amboy, situated at the head of Raritan Bay, a bay not inferior to any throughout the United States. The greatest encouragements also have been held out by the state legislature to merchants who would settle there; but the town, notwithstanding, remains nearly in the state it was in at the time of the revolution: sixty houses are all that it contains. New Brunswick, which is built on Raritan River, about fifteen miles above its entrance into the bay, carries on a small inland trade with the adjacent country; but the principal part of New Jersey is naturally supplied with foreign manufactures by New York on the one side, and by Philadelphia on the other, the towns most happily situated for the purpose. There are about two hundred houses in New Brunswick, and

and about the same number in Trenton on Delaware, the capital of the state.

Philadelphia, the largest town in the union, has evidently been raised to that state of pre-eminence by her extensive inland commerce. On one side is the river Delaware, which is navigable in sloops for thirty-five miles above the town, and in boats carrying eight or nine tons one hundred miles further. On the other side is the Schuylkill, navigable, excepting at the falls, for ninety miles. But the country bordering upon these rivers is but a trifling part of that which Philadelphia trades with. Goods are forwarded to Harrisburgh, a town situated on the Susquehannah, and from thence sent up that river, and dispersed throughout the adjoining country. The eastern branch of Susquehannah is navigable for two hundred and fifty miles above Harrisburgh. This place, which in 1786 scarcely deserved the name of a village, now contains upwards of three hundred houses. By land carriage Philadelphia also trades with the western parts of Pennsylvania, as far as Pittsburg itself, which is on the Ohio, with the back of Virginia, and, strange to tell, with Kentucky, seven hundred miles distant.

Philadelphia, however, does not enjoy the exclusive trade to Virginia and Kentucky; Baltimore, which lies more to the south, comes

comes in for a confiderable fhare, if not for the greateft part of it, and to that is indebted for her fudden rife, and her great fuperiority over Annapolis, the capital of Maryland. Annapolis, although it has a good harbour, and was made a port of entry as long ago as the year 1694, has fcarcely any trade now. Baltimore, fituated more in the heart of the country, has gradually drawn it all away from her. From Baltimore nearly the entire of Maryland is furnifhed with European manufactures. The very flourifhing ftate of this place has already been mentioned.

As the Patowmac river, and the towns upon it, are to come more particularly under notice afterwards, we may from hence pafs on to the other towns in Virginia. With regard to Virginia, however, it is to be obferved, that the impolitic laws * which have been enacted in that ftate have thrown a great damp upon trade; the Virginians too have always been more difpofed towards agriculture than trade, fo that the towns in that ftate, fome of which are moft advantageoufly fituated, have never increafed as they would have done had the county been inhabited by a different kind of people, and had different

* For fome account of them fee Letter XIII.

laws

laws confequently exifted; ftill however we shall find that the moft flourifhing towns in the ftate are thofe which are open to the fea, and fituated moft conveniently at the fame time for trading with the people of the back country. On Rappahannock River, for inftance, Tappahannock or Hobb's Hole was laid out at the fame time that Philadelphia was. Frederickfburgh was built many years afterwards on the fame river, but thirty miles higher up, and at the head of that part of it which was navigable for fea veffels; the confequence of this has been, that Frederickfburgh, from being fituated more in the heart of the country, is now four times as large a town as Hobb's Hole.

York River, from running fo clofely to James River on the one fide, and the Rappahannock on the other, does not afford a good fituation for a large town. The largeft town upon it, which is York, only contains feventy houfes.

Williamfburgh was formerly the capital of the ftate, and contains about four hundred houfes; but inftead of increafing, this town is going to ruin, and numbers of the houfes at prefent are uninhabited, which is evidently on account of its inland fituation. There is no navigable ftream nearer to it than one mile and a half, and this is only a fmall creek,

creek, which runs into James River. Richmond, on the contrary, which is the present capital of the state, has increased very fast, because it stands on a large navigable river; yet Richmond is no more than an intermediate place for the deposit of goods passing to and from the back country, vessels drawing more than seven feet water being unable to come up to the town.

The principal place of trade in Virginia is Norfolk. This town has a good harbour, and is enabled to trade with the upper parts of the country, by means of James River, near the mouth of which it stands. By land also a brisk trade is carried on with the back parts of North Carolina, for in that state there are no towns of any importance. The entrance from the sea into the rivers in that state are all impeded by shoals and sand banks, none of which afford more than eleven feet water, and the passage over some of them is very dangerous from the sand shifting. Wilmington, which is the greatest place of trade in it, contains only two hundred and fifty houses. In order to carry on their trade to North Carolina to more advantage, a canal is now cutting across the Dismal Swamp, from Norfolk into Albemarle Sound, by means of the rivers that empty into which, a water communication will be opened to the remote parts of that state. Added to this, Norfolk, from its contiguity to the Dismal Swamp, is enabled to supply the West Indian market with lumber on better terms than any other town in the United States. It is in consequence increasing with wonderful rapidity, notwithstanding the disadvantages it labours under from the laws, which are so inimical to commerce. At present it contains upwards of five hundred houses, which have all been built within the last twenty years, for in the year 1776 the town was totally destroyed by orders of Lord Dunmore, then regal governor of Virginia.

Most of the rivers in South Carolina are obstructed at their mouths, much in the same manner as those in North Carolina; at Charleston, however, there is a safe and commodious harbour. From having such an advantage, this town commands nearly the entire trade of the state in which it is situated, as well as a considerable portion of that of North Carolina. The consequence is, that Charleston ranks as the fourth commercial town in the union. There are two rivers which disembogue on each side of the town, Cooper and Ashley; these are navigable, but not for a very great distance; however, from Cooper River a canal is to be cut to the Santee, a large navigable river which runs

a cona confiderable way up the country. Charlefton has unfortunately been almoft totally deftroyed by fire of late, but it is rebuilding very faft, and will moft probably in a few years be larger than ever.

The view that has been taken fo far is fufficient to demonftrate, that the profperity of the towns in the United States is dependant upon their trade, and principally upon that which is carried on with the interior parts of the country; and alfo, that thofe towns which are moft conveniently fituated for the purpofe of carrying on this inland trade, are thofe which enjoy the greateft fhare of it. It is now time to examine more particularly how far the fituation of the federal city is favourable, or otherwife, for commerce: to do fo, it will be neceffary, in the firft place, to trace the courfe of the Patowmac River, on which it ftands, and alfo that of the rivers with which it is connected.

The Patowmac takes its rife on the northweft fide of Alleghany Mountains, and after running in a meandering direction for upwards of four hundred miles, falls into the Chefapeak Bay. At its confluence with the bay it is feven miles and a half wide; about thirty miles higher, at Nominy Bay, four and a half; at Aquia, three; at Hallowing Point, one and a half; and at Alexandria, and from thence to

the

the federal city, it is one mile and quarter wide. The depth of water at its mouth is seven fathoms; at St. George's Island, five; at Alexandria, four; and from thence to Washington, seven miles distant, three fathoms. The navigation of the Patowmac, from the Chesapeak Bay to the city, one hundred and forty miles distant, is remarkable safe, and so plain that any navigator of common abilities, that has once sailed up the river, might venture to take up a vessel drawing twelve feet water without a pilot. This could not be said of any other river on the continent, from the St. Lawrence to the Mississippi. In its course it receives several large streams, the principal one of which falls in at the federal city. This river is called the Eastern Branch of the Patowmac; but it scarcely deserves that name, as it extends no more than thirty miles up the country. At its mouth it is nearly as wide as the main branch of the river, and close to the city the water is in many places thirty feet deep. Thousands of vessels might lie here, and sheltered from all danger, arising either from freshes, or from ice upon the breaking up of a severe winter. Thus it appears that the federal city is possessed of one essential qualification for making it a place of importance, namely, a good harbour, from which there is a ready passage to the ocean; it will also appear that it is well situated for trading with the interior parts of the country.

The water in the Patowmac continues nearly the same depth that it is opposite to the city for one mile higher, where a large rock rises up in the middle of the river, on each side of which there are sand-banks. It is said that there is a deep channel between this rock and the shore, but it is so intricate that it would be dangerous to attempt to take a large vessel through it. The navigation, however, is safe to the little falls for river craft, five miles further on; here a canal, which extends two miles and a half, the length of these falls or rapids, has been cut and perfected, which opens a free passage for boats as far as the great falls, which are seven miles from the others. The descent of the river at these is seventy-six feet in a mile and quarter; but it is intended to make another canal here also; a part of it is already cut, and every exertion is making to have the whole completed with expedition *. From hence to Fort Cumberland, one hundred and ninety-one miles above the federal city, there is a free navigation, and boats are continually passing up and down. Beyond this, the passage in the river is obstructed in numerous places; but there is

* For a further description of these Falls see Letter XXXI.

a possia possibility of opening it, and as soon as the company formed for the purpose have sufficient funds, it will certainly be done. From the place up to which it is asserted the passage of the Patowmac can be opened, the distance across land to Cheat River is only thirty-seven miles. This last river is not at present navigable for more than fifty miles above its mouth; but it can be rendered so for boats, and so far up that there will only be the short portage that I have mentioned between the navigable waters of the two rivers. Things are only great or small by comparison, and a portage of thirty-seven miles will be thought a very short one, when found to be the only interruption to an inland navigation of upwards of two thousand seven hundred miles, of which two thousand one hundred and eighty-three are down stream. Cheat River is two hundred yards wide at its mouth, and falls into the Monongahela, which runs on to Pittsburgh, and there receives the Alleghany River; united they form the Ohio, which after a course of one thousand one hundred and eighty-three miles, during which it receives twenty-four other considerable rivers, some of them six hundred yards wide at the mouth, and navigable for hundreds of miles up the country, empties itself into the Mississippi.

F 2   If

If we trace the water communication in an oppofite direction, its prodigious extent will be a ftill greater fubject of aftonifhment. By afcending the Alleghany River from Pittfburgh as far as French Creek, and afterwards this latter ftream, you come to Fort le Bœuf. This place is within fifteen miles of Prefqu' Ifle, a town fituated upon Lake Erie, which has a harbour capable of admitting veffels drawing nine feet water. Or you may get upon the lake by afcending the Great Miami River, which falls into the Ohio five hundred and fifty miles below Pittsburgh. From the Great Miami there is a portage of nine miles only to Sandufky River, which runs into Lake Erie. It is moft probable, however, that whatever intercourfe there may be between the lakes and the federal city, it will be kept up by means of the Alleghany River and French Creek, rather than by the Miami, as in the laft cafe it would be neceffary to combat againft the ftream of the Ohio for five hundred and fifty miles, a very ferious object of confideration.

Lake Erie is three hundred miles in length, and ninety in breadth, and there is a free communication between it, Lake Huron, and Lake Michigan. Lake Huron is upwards of one thoufand miles in circumference; Michigan is fomewhat fmaller. Numbers of large rivers

rivers fall into these lakes, after having watered immense tracts of country in various directions. Some of these rivers too are connected in a most singular manner with others, which run in a course totally different. For instance, after passing over the Lakes Erie, St. Clair, and Michigan, to the head of Puan's Bay, you come to Fox River; from hence there is a portage of three miles only to Ouisconsing River, which empties itself into the Mississippi; and in the fall of the year, when the waters are high, and the rivers overflow, it is oftentimes possible to pass from Fox River to Ouisconsing River without ever getting out of a canoe. Thus, excepting a portage of three miles only at the most, it is possible to go the whole way by water from Presqu' Isle, on Lake Erie, to New Orleans, at the mouth of the Mississippi, a distance of near four thousand miles. It would be an endless task to trace the water communication in every direction. By a portage of nine miles at the Falls of Niagara, the navigation of Lake Ontario and the St. Lawrence is opened on one side, and at the other that of Lake Superior, by a still shorter portage at the Falls of St. Mary. This last lake, which is at least fifteen hundred miles in circumference, is supplied by no less than forty rivers; and beyond it the water-communication extends for hundreds of miles farther on, through the Lake of the Woods to Lake Winnipeg, which is still larger than that of Superior.

But suppofing that the immenfe regions bordering upon thefe lakes and rivers were already peopled, it is not to be concluded, that becaufe they are connected by water with the Patowmac, the federal city muft neceffarily be the mart for the various productions of the whole country. There are different fea ports to which the inhabitants will trade, according to the fituation of each particular part of the country. Quebec, on the river St. Lawrence, will be one; New York, connected as has been fhewn with Lake Ontario, another; and New Orleans at the mouth of the Miffiffippi, which by the late treaty with Spain has been made a free port, a third. The federal city will come in alfo for its fhare, and what this fhare will be it now remains to afcertain.

Situated upon the banks of the Patowmac, there are already two towns, and both in the vicinity of the federal city. George Town, which contains about two hundred and fifty houfes; and Alexandria, with double the number. The former of thefe ftands about one mile above the city, nearly oppofite the large rock in the river, which has been fpoken of; the latter, feven miles below it. Confiderable quantities of produce are already fent down the Patowmac

Patowmac to each of these towns, and the people in the country are beginning to look thither in return for a part of their supply of foreign manufactures. It has been maintained, therefore, that these two places, already in the practice of trading with the back settlers, will draw the greater part of the country trade to themselves, to the prejudice of the federal city. Both these towns have as great advantages in point of situation as the city; the interests of the three places therefore must unquestionably for a time clash together. It can hardly be doubted, however, but that the federal city will in a few years completely eclipse the other two. George Town can furnish the people of the back country with foreign manufactures, at second hand only, from Baltimore and Philadelphia; Alexandria imports directly from Europe, but on a very contracted scale: more than two thirds of the goods which are sent from thence to the back country are procured in the same manner as at George Town. In neither place are there merchants with large capitals; nor have the banks, of which there is one in each town, sufficient funds to afford them much assistance; but merchants with large capitals are preparing to move to the city. As soon also as the seat of government is fixed there, the national bank, or at least a large branch of it, will be established at the same time; this circumstance alone will afford the people of the city a decided advantage over those of Alexandria and George Town. Added to all, both these towns are in the territory of Columbia, that is, in the district of ten miles round the city which is to be subject to the laws and regulations of congress alone; it may be, therefore, that encouragements will be held out by congress to those who settle in the city, which will be refused to such as go to any other part of the territory. Although Alexandria and George Town, then, may rival the city while it is in its infancy, yet it cannot be imagined that either of them will be able to cope with it in the end. The probable trade of the city may for this reason be spoken of as if neither of the other places existed.

It may be taken for granted, in the first place, that the whole of the country bordering upon the Patowmac river, and upon those rivers which fall into it, will trade with the city of Washington. In tracing the course of the Patowmac all these rivers were not enumerated; a better idea of them may be had from an inspection of the map. Shenandoah, which is the longest, is not navigable at present; but it has been surveyed, and the company for improving the navigation of the Patowmac have stated that it can be made so for one hundred

dred miles. This would be coming very near to Staunton, behind the Blue Mountains, and which is on the high road from Kentucky, and from the new state of Teneſſee, to the city of Philadelphia. Frankfort, the capital of the former of theſe ſtates, is nearly eight hundred miles from Philadelphia; Knoxville, that of the other, ſeven hundred and twenty-eight. Both theſe towns draw their ſupplies of foreign manufactures from Philadelphia, and by landcarriage. Suppoſing then that the navigation of the Shenandoah ſhould be perfected, there would be a ſaving of four hundred and thirty-ſix miles of land carriage from going to Waſhington by the Shenandoah and Patowmac inſtead of going to Philadelphia; ſuch a ſaving, it might be imagined, would draw the whole of this trade to Waſhington. Whether the two weſtern ſtates, Kentucky and Teneſſee, will trade to New Orleans or not, at a future day, in preference to any of theſe places, will be inveſtigated preſently.

By means of Cheat and Monongahela rivers it has been ſhewn, that an opening may be obtained to Pittſburgh. This will be a route of about four hundred and fifty miles from Waſhington, and in it there will be one portage, from the Patowmac to Cheat River, of thirty-ſeven miles, and perhaps two or three others; but theſe will be all very ſmall. It

has

has been ascertained beyond doubt, that the Pittsburgh merchant can have his goods conveyed from New York, by means of the Hudson and Mohawk rivers, to Oswego, and from thence by the lakes Ontario and Erie, and the Alleghany River, to Pittsburgh, for one third of the sum which it costs him to transport them by land from Philadelphia. He prefers getting them by land, because the route from New York is uncertain; his goods may be lost, or damaged, or delayed months beyond the time he expects them. From Hudson River to the Mohawk is a portage of ten miles, or thereabouts; and before they can get to Oswego are two or three more. At Oswego the goods must be shipped on board a vessel suitable for navigating the lakes, where they are exposed to tempests and contrary winds. At the Falls of Niagara is a portage of nine miles more; the goods must here be shipped again on board a vessel on Lake Erie, and after arriving at Presqu' Isle must be conveyed over another portage preparatory to their being laden in a boat upon the Alleghany River. The whole of this route, from New York to Pittsburgh, is about eight hundred miles; that from the federal city not much more than half the distance; if therefore the merchant at Pittsburgh can get his goods conveyed from New York for one third of what he pays for the carriage

of

WATER CARRIAGE.

of them by land from Philadelphia, he ought not to pay more than one sixth of the sum for their carriage from the federal city; it is to be concluded, therefore, that he will avail himself of the latter route, as there will be no objection to it on account of any uncertainty in the mode of conveyance, arising from storms and contrary winds.

The people in Pittsburgh, and the western country along the waters of the Ohio, draw their supplies from Philadelphia and Baltimore; but they send the productions of the country, which would be too bulky for land carriage, down the Ohio and Mississippi to New Orleans. From Pittsburgh to New Orleans the distance is two thousand one hundred and eighty-three miles. On an average it takes about twenty-eight days to go down there with the stream; but to return by water it takes from sixty days to three months. The passage back is very laborious as well as tedious; on which account they seldom think of bringing back boats which are sent down from Pittsburgh, but on arriving at New Orleans they are broken up, and the plank sold. These boats are built on the cheapest construction, and expressly for the purpose of going down stream. The men get back the best way they can, generally in ships bound from New Orleans to the southern states, and from thence home

home by land. Now, if the paffage from the Ohio to the Patowmac is opened, it cannot be fuppofed that the people in Pittfburgh and the vicinity will continue thus to fend the produce down to Orleans, from whence they cannot bring any thing in return; they will naturally fend to the federal city, from whence they can draw the fupplies they are in want of, and which is fo much nearer to them, that when the navigation is perfected it will be poffible to go there and back again in the fame time that it requires merely to go down to New Orleans.

But although the people of that country which borders upon the Ohio and its waters, in the vicinage of Pittfburgh, may have an intereft in trading to the federal city, yet thofe who live towards the mouth of that river will find an intereft equally great in trading to New Orleans, for the Ohio River is no lefs than eleven hundred and eighty-three miles in length. How far down upon the Ohio a commercial intercourfe will be kept up with the city, will moft probably be determined by other circumftances than that of diftance alone; it may depend upon the demand there may be at one or other port for particular articles, &c. &c.; it may alfo depend upon the feafon; for at regular periods there are floods in the Miffiffippi, and alfo in the Ohio, which make a

great

great difference in the time of afcending and defcending thefe rivers. The floods in the Miffiffippi are occafioned by the diffolution of the immenfe bodies of fnow and ice accumulated during winter in thofe northern regions through which the river paffes; they are alfo very regular, beginning in the month of March and fubfiding in July. Thofe in the Ohio take place between Chriftmas and May; but they are not regular and fteady like thofe of the Miffiffippi, for the water rifes and falls many times in the courfe of the feafon. Thefe floods are occafioned by heavy falls of rain in the beginnning of winter, as well as by the thawing of the ice.

The Miffiffippi has a very winding courfe*, and at every bend there is an eddy in the water. Thefe eddies are always ftrongeft during the inundations, confequently it is then a much lefs difficult tafk to afcend the river. With the Ohio, however, it is directly the re-

* In the year 1722, as a party of Canadians were going down the river, they found at one place fuch a bend in it, that although the diftance acrofs land, from one part of the river to the other, was not more perhaps than two hundred yards, yet by water it was no lefs than forty miles—The Canadians cut a trench acrofs the land for curiofity—The foil bordering upon the Miffiffippi is remarkably rich and foft, and the current being ftrong, the river in a fhort time forced a new paffage for itfelf, and the Canadians took their boat through it. This place is called Pointé Coupée. There are many fimilar bends in the river at prefent, but none fo great.

verfe;

verse; there are no eddies in the river; wherefore floods are found to facilitate the paffage downwards; but to render that againft the ftream difficult.

Suppofing, however, the feafon favourable for the navigation of the Miffiffippi, and alfo for the navigation of the Ohio, which it might well be at the fame time, then Louifville, in Kentucky, is the place through which the line may be drawn that will feparate as nearly as poffible the country naturally connected with Wafhington from that appertaining to New Orleans. It takes twenty days, on an average, at the moft favourable feafon, to go from Louifville to New Orleans, and to return, forty; which in the whole makes fixty days. From the rapids in the Ohio, clofe to which Louifville is fituated, to Pittfburgh, the diftance is feven hundred and three miles; fo that at the rate of thirty miles a day, which is a moderate computation, it would require twenty-four days to go there. From Pittfburgh to the Patowmac the diftance is one hundred and fixty miles againft the ftream, which at the fame rate, and allowing time for the portages, would take feven days more, and two hundred and ninety miles down the Patowmac, at fixty miles per day, would require five days: this is allowing thirty-five days for going, and computing the time for returning at the fame rate,
that

that is thirty miles againſt the ſtream, and fixty miles with the ſtream, each day, it would amount to twenty-five days, which, added to the time of going, makes in the whole fifty-nine days; if the odd day be allowed for contingencies, the paſſage to and from the two places would then be exactly alike. It is fair then to conclude, that if the demand at the federal city for country produce be equally great as at New Orleans, and there is no reaſon to ſay why it ſhould not, the whole of the produce of that country, which lies contiguous to the Ohio, and the rivers falling into it, as far down as Louiſville in Kentucky, will be ſent to the former of theſe places. This tract is ſeven hundred miles in length, and from one hundred to two hundred miles in breadth. Added to this, the whole of that country lying near the Alleghany River, and the ſtreams that run into it, muſt naturally be ſupplied from the city; a great part of the country bordering upon Lake Erie, near Preſqu' Iſle, may likewiſe be included.

Conſidering the vaſtneſs of the territory, which is thus opened to the federal city by means of a water communication; conſidering that it is capable, from the fertility of its ſoil, of maintaining three times the number of inhabitants that are to be found at preſent in all the United States; and that it is advancing at the

the present time more rapidly in population than any other part of the whole continent; there is a good foundation for thinking that the federal city, as soon as the navigation is perfected, will increase most rapidly; and that at a future day, if the affairs of the United States go on as prosperously as they have done, it will become the grand emporium of the west, and rival in magnitude and splendor the cities of the old world.

 The city is laid out on a neck of land between the forks formed by the eastern and western or main branch of Patowmac River. This neck of land, together with an adjacent territory, which is in the whole ten miles square, was ceded to congress by the states of Maryland and Virginia. The ground on which the city immediately stands was the property of private individuals, who readily relinquished their claim to one half of it in favour of congress, conscious that the value of what was left to them would increase, and amply compensate them for their loss. The profits arising from the sale that part of which has thus been ceded to congress will be sufficient, it is expected, to pay for the public buildings, for the watering of the city, and also for paving and lighting of the streets. The plan of the city was drawn by a Frenchman of the name of L'Enfant, and is on a

scale

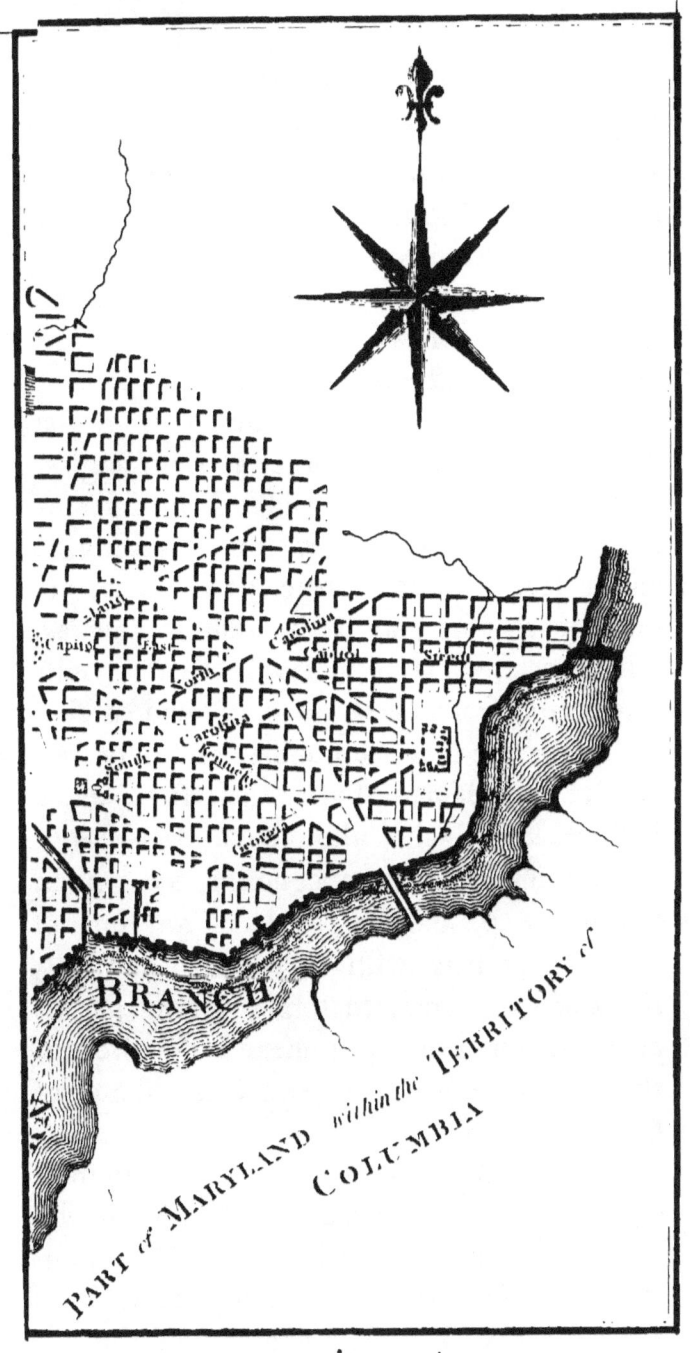

scale well suited to the extent of the country, one thousand two hundred miles in length, and one thousand in breadth, of which it is to be the metropolis; for the ground already marked out for it is no less than fourteen miles in circumference. The streets run north, south, east, and west; but to prevent that sameness necessarily ensuing from the streets all crossing each other at right angles, a number of avenues are laid out in different parts of the city, which run transversely; and in several places, where these avenues intersect each other, are to be hollow squares. The streets, which cross each other at right angles, are from ninety to one hundred feet wide, the avenues one hundred and sixty feet. One of these is named after each state, and a hollow square also allotted to each, as a suitable place for statues, columns, &c. which, at a future period, the people of any one of these states may wish to erect to the memory of great men that may appear in the country. On a small eminence, due west of the capitol, is to be an equestrian statue of General Washington.

The capitol is now building upon the most elevated spot of ground in the city, which happens to be in a very central situation. From this spot there is a complete view of every part of the city, and also of the adjacent

jacent country. In the capitol are to be spacious apartments for the accommodation of congress; in it also are to be the principal public offices in the executive department of the government, together with the courts of justice. The plan on which this building is begun is grand and extensive; the expense of building it is estimated at a million of dollars, equal to two hundred and twenty-five thousand pounds sterling.

The house for the residence of the president stands north-west of the capitol, at the distance of about one mile and a half. It is situated upon a rising ground not far from the Patowmac, and commands a most beautiful prospect of the river, and of the rich country beyond it. One hundred acres of ground, towards the river, are left adjoining to the house for pleasure grounds. South of this there is to be a large park or mall, which is to run in an easterly direction from the river to the capitol. The buildings on either side of this mall are all to be elegant in their kind; amongst the number it is proposed to have houses built at the public expense for the accommodation of the foreign ministers, &c. On the eastern branch a large spot is laid out for a marine hospital and gardens. Various other parts are appointed for churches, theatres, colleges, &c. The ground in general,

neral, within the limits of the city, is agreeably undulated; but none of the risings are so great as to become objects of inconvenience in a town. The soil is chiefly of a yellowish clay mixed with gravel. There are numbers of excellent springs in the city, and water is readily had in most places by digging wells. Here are two streams likewise, which run through the city, Reedy Branch and Tiber Creek.* The perpendicular height of the source of the latter, above the level of the tide, is two hundred and thirty-six feet.

By the regulations published, it was settled that all the houses should be built of brick or stone; the walls to be thirty feet high, and to be built parallel to the line of the street, but either upon it or withdrawn from it, as suited the taste of the builder. However, numbers of wooden habitations have been built; but the different owners have all been cautioned against considering them as permanent. They are to be allowed for a certain term only, and then destroyed. Three com-

---

* Upon the granting possession of waste lands to any person, commonly called the *location* of lands, it is usual to give particular names to different spots, and also to the creeks and rivers. On the original location of the ground now allotted for the seat of the federal city, this creek received the name of Tiber Creek, and the identical spot of ground on which the capitol now stands was called Rome. This anecdote is related by many as a certain prognostic of the future magnificence of this city, which is to be, as it were, a second Rome.

missioners, who reside on the spot, are appointed by the president, with a salary, for the purpose of superintending the public and other buildings, and regulating every thing pertaining to the city.

The only public buildings carrying on as yet, are the president's house, the capitol, and a large hotel. The president's house, which is nearly completed on the outside, is two stories high, and built of free stone. The principal room in it is of an oval form. This is undoubtedly the handsomest building in the country, and the architecture of it is much extolled by the people, who have never seen any thing superior; but it will not bear a critical examination. Many persons find fault with it, as being too large and too splendid for the residence of any one person in a republican country; and certainly it is a ridiculous habitation for a man who receives a salary that amounts to no more than £.5,625 sterling per annum, and in a country where the expences of living are far greater than they are even in London.

The hotel is a large building of brick, ornamented with stone; it stands between the president's house and the capitol. In the beginning of the year 1796, when I last saw it, it was roofed in, and every exertion making to have it finished with the utmost expedition.

It

It is any thing but beautiful. The capitol, at the same period, was raised only a very little way above the foundation.

The stone, which the president's house is built with, and such as will be used for all the public buildings, is very similar in appearance to that found at Portland in England; but I was informed by one of the sculptors, who had frequently worked the Portland stone in England, that it is of a much superior quality, as it will bear to be cut as fine as marble, and is not liable to be injured by rain or frost. On the banks of the Patowmac they have inexhaustible quarries of this stone; good specimens of common marble have also been found; and there is in various parts of the river abundance of excellent slate, paving stone, and lime stone. Good coal may also be had.

The private houses are all plain buildings; most of them have been built on speculation, and still remain empty. The greatest number, at any one place, is at Green Leafs Point, on the main river, just above the entrance of the eastern branch. This spot has been looked upon by many as the most convenient one for trade; but others prefer the shore of the eastern branch, on account of the superiority of the harbour, and the great depth of the water near the shore. There are several other favourite situations, the choice of any one of which is a mere matter of speculation at present. Some build near the capitol, as the most convenient place for the residence of members of congress, some near the president's house; others again prefer the west end of the city, in the neighbourhood of George Town, thinking that as trade is already established in that place, it must be from thence that it will extend into the city. Were the houses that have been built situated in one place all together, they would make a very respectable appearance, but scattered about as they are, a spectator can scarcely perceive any thing like a town. Excepting the streets and avenues, and a small part of the ground adjoining the public buildings, the whole place is covered with trees. To be under the necessity of going through a deep wood for one or two miles, perhaps, in order to see a next door neighbour, and in the same city, is a curious, and, I believe, a novel circumstance. The number of inhabitants in the city, in the spring of 1796, amounted to about five thousand, including artificers, who formed by far the largest part of that number. Numbers of strangers are continually passing and repassing through a place which affords such an extensive field for speculation.

In addition to what has already been said upon the subject, I have only to observe, that

notwith-

notwithstanding all that has been done at the city, and the large sums of money which have been expended, there are numbers of people in the United States, living to the north of the Patowmac, particularly in Philadelphia, who are still very adverse to the removal of the seat of government thither, and are doing all in their power to check the progress of the buildings in the city, and to prevent the congress from meeting there at the appointed time. In the spring of 1796, when I was last on the spot, the building of the capitol was absolutely at a stand for want of money; the public lots were at a very low price, and the commissioners were unwilling to dispose of them; in consequence they made an application to congress, praying the house to guaranty a loan of three hundred thousand dollars, without which they could not go on with the public buildings, except they disposed of the lots to great disadvantage, and to the ultimate injury of the city; so strong, however, was the opposition, that the petition was suffered to lie on the table unattended to for many weeks; nor was the prayer of it complied with until a number of gentlemen, that were very deeply interested in the improvement of the city, went round to the different members, and made interest with them in person to give their assent to the measure. These people, who are opposed to the building of the city of Washington maintain, that it can never become a town of any importance, and that all such as think to the contrary have been led astray by the representations of a few enthusiastic persons; they go so far even as to assert, that the people to the eastward will never submit to see the seat of government removed so far from them, and the congress assembled in a place little better than a forest, where it will be impossible to procure information upon commercial points; finally, they insist, that if the removal from Philadelphia should take place, a separation of the states will inevitably follow. This is the language held forth; but their opposition in reality arises from that jealousy which narrow minded people in trade are but too apt to entertain of each other when their interests clash together. These people wish to crush the city of Washington while it is yet in its infancy, because they know, that if the seat of government is transferred thither, the place will thrive, and enjoy a considerable portion of that trade which is centered at present in Philadelphia, Baltimore, and New York. It is idle, however, to imagine that this will injure their different towns; on the contrary, although a portion of that trade which they enjoy at present should be drawn from them, yet the increase of population in that part of the country, which they must naturally supply, will be

such

such, that their trade on the whole will, in all probability, be found far more extenfive after the federal city is eftablifhed than it ever was before.

A large majority, however, of the people in the United States is defirous that the removal of the feat of government fhould take place; and there is little doubt that it will take place at the appointed time. The difcontents indeed, which an oppofite meafure would give rife to in the fouth could not but be alarming, and if they did not occafion a total feparation of the fouthern from the northern ftates, yet they would certainly materially deftroy that harmony which has hitherto exifted between them.

LETTER V.

Some Account of Alexandria.—Mount Vernon, the Seat of General Washington.—Difficulty of finding the Way thither through the Woods.—Description of the Mount, and of the Views from it.—Description of the House and Grounds.— Slaves at Mount Vernon.— Thoughts thereon.—A Person at Mount Vernon to attend to Strangers.—Return to Washington.

MY DEAR SIR,   Washington, December.

FROM Washington I proceeded to Alexandria, seven miles lower down the river, which is one of the neatest towns in the United States. The houses are mostly brick, and many of them are extremely well built. The streets intersect each other at right angles; they are commodious and well paved. Nine miles below this place, on the banks of the Patowmac, stands Mount Vernon, the seat of General Washington; the way to it, however, from Alexandria, by land, is considerably farther, on account of the numerous creeks which fall into the Patowmac, and the mouths of which it is impossible to pass near to.

Very thick woods remain standing within four or five miles of the place; the roads through

through them are very bad, and so many of them cross one another in different directions, that it is a matter of very great difficulty to find out the right one. I set out from Alexandria with a gentleman who thought himself perfectly well acquainted with the way; had he been so, there was ample time to have reached Mount Vernon before the close of the day, but night overtook us wandering about in the woods. We did not perceive the vestige of a human being to set us right, and we were preparing to pass the night in the carriage, when luckily a light appeared at some distance through the trees; it was from a small farmhouse, the only one in the way for several miles; and having made our way to it, partly in the carriage, partly on foot, we hired a negro for a guide, who conducted us to the place of our destination in about an hour. The next morning I heard of a gentleman, who, a day or two preceding, had been from ten o'clock in the morning till four in the afternoon on horseback, unable to find out the place, although within three or four miles of it the whole time.

The Mount is a high part of the bank of the river, which rises very abruptly about two hundred feet above the level of the water. The river before it is three miles wide, and on the opposite side it forms a bay about the same

same breadth, which extends for a considerable distance up the country. This, at first sight, appears to be a continuation of the river; but the Patowmac takes a very sudden turn to the left, two or three miles above the house, and is quickly lost to the view. Downwards, to the right, there is a prospect of it for twelve miles. The Maryland shore, on the opposite side, is beautifully diversified with hills, which are mostly covered with wood; in many places, however, little patches of cultivated ground appear, ornamented with houses. The scenery altogether is most delightful. The house, which stands about sixty yards from the edge of the Mount, is of wood, cut and painted so as to resemble hewn stone. The rear is towards the river, at which side is a portico of ninety-six feet in length, supported by eight pillars. The front is uniform, and at a distance looks tolerably well. The dwelling house is in the center, and communicates with the wings on either side, by means of covered ways, running in a curved direction. Behind these wings, on the one side, are the different offices belonging to the house, and also to the farm, and on the other, the cabins for the SLAVES*. In front, the breadth of the whole

---

* These are amongst the first of the buildings which are seen on coming to Mount Vernon; and it is not without astonishment

whole building, is a lawn with a gravel walk round it, planted with trees, and separated by hedges

astonishment and regret they are surveyed by the stranger, whose mind has dwelt with admiration upon the inestimable blessings of liberty, whilst approaching the residence of that man who has distinguished himself so gloriously in its cause. Happy would it have been, if the man who stood forth the champion of a nation contending for its freedom, and whose declaration to the whole world was, " That all men were created " equal, and that they were endowed by their Creator with cer- " tain unalienable rights, amongst the first of which were life, " liberty, and the pursuit of happiness;" happy would it have been, if this man could have been the first to wave all interested views, to liberate his own slaves, and thus convince the people he had fought for, that it was their duty, when they had established their own independence, to give freedom to those whom they had themselves held in bondage!!

But material objections, we must suppose, appeared against such a measure, otherwise, doubtless, General Washington would have shewn the glorious example. Perhaps he thought it more for the general good, that the first step for the emancipation of slaves should be taken by the legislative assembly; or perhaps there was reason to apprehend, that the enfranchisement of his own slaves might be the cause of insurrections amongst others who were not liberated, a matter which could not but be attended with evil consequences in a country where the number of slaves exceeded that of freemen; however, it does not appear that any measures have been pursued, either by private individuals or by the legislature in Virginia, for the abolition of slavery; neither have any steps been taken for the purpose in Maryland, much less in the more southern states; but in Pennsylvania and the rest, laws have passed for its gradual abolition. In these states the number of slaves, it is true, was very small, and the measure was therefore easily carried into effect; in the others then it will require more consideration. The plan, however, which has been adopted for the liberation of the few has succeeded well; why then not try it with a larger number? If it does not answer, still I cannot but suppose

hedges on either fide from the farm yard and garden. As for the garden, it wears exactly the appearance of a nurfery, and with every thing about the place indicates that more attention is paid to profit than to pleafure. The ground in the rear of the houfe is alfo laid out in a lawn, and the declivity of the Mount, towards the water, in a deer park.

The rooms in the houfe are very fmall, excepting one, which has been built fince the clofe of the war for the purpofe of entertainments. All of thefe are very plainly furnifhed, and in many of them the furniture is dropping to pieces. Indeed, the clofe attention which General Wafhington has ever paid to public affairs having obliged him to refide principally at Philadelphia, Mount Vernon has confequently fuffered very materially. The houfe and offices, with every other part of the place, are out of repair, and the old part of the building is in fuch a perifhable ftate, that I have been told he wifhes he had pulled it entirely down at firft, and built a new houfe, in-

---

pofe that it might be fo modified as to be rendered applicable to the enfranchifement of the number of ill-fated beings who are enflaved in the fouthern parts of the country, let it be ever fo large. However, that there will be an end to flavery in the United States, on fome day or other, cannot be doubted; negroes will not remain deaf to the inviting call of liberty for ever; and if their avaricious oppreffors do not free them from the galling yoke, they will liberate themfelves with a vengeance.

ftead

stead of making any addition to the old one. The grounds in the neighbourhood are cultivated, but the principal farms are at the distance of two or three miles.

As almost every stranger going through the country makes a point of visiting Mount Vernon, a person is kept at the house during General Washington's absence, whose sole business it is to attend to strangers. Immediately on our arrival every care was taken of our horses, beds were prepared, and an excellent supper provided for us, with claret and other wine, &c.

As the season was now too far advanced to see the country to advantage, I proceeded no farther in Virginia than Mount Vernon, but returned again to the city of Washington.

LETTER VI.

Arrival at Philadelphia.—Some Observations on the Climate of the Middle States.—Public Carriages prevented from plying between Baltimore and Philadelphia by the Badness of the Roads.—Left Baltimore during Frost.—Met with American Travellers on the Road.—Their Behaviour preparatory to setting off from an Inn.—Arrival on the Banks of the Susquehannah.—Passage of that River when frozen over.—Dangerous Situation of the Passengers.—American Travellers at the Tavern on the opposite Side of the River.—Their noisy Disputations.

MY DEAR SIR,   Philadelphia, February.

AFTER having spent some weeks in Washington, George Town, and Baltimore, I set out for this city, where I arrived four days ago.

The months of October and November are the most agreeable, in the middle and southern states, of any in the year; the changes in the weather are then less frequent, and for the most part the air is temperate and the sky serene. During this year the air was so mild, that when I was at George Town, even as late as the second week in December, it

was

was found pleasant to keep the windows up during dinner time. This, however, was an unusual circumstance.

In Maryland, before December was over, there were a few cold days, and during January we had two or three different falls of snow; but for the most part the weather remained very mild until the latter end of January, when a sharp north-west wind set in. The keenness of this wind in winter is prodigious, and surpasses every thing of the kind which we have an idea of in England. Whenever it blows, during the winter months, a frost immediately takes place. In the course of three days, in the present instance, the Susquehannah and Delaware rivers were frozen over; a fall of snow took place, which remained on the ground about two feet deep, and there was every appearance of a severe and tedious winter. Before five days, however, were over, the wind again changed, and so sudden was the thaw that the snow disappeared entirely on the second day, and not a vestige of the frost was to be seen, excepting in the rivers, where large pieces of ice remained floating about.

It was about the middle of December when I reached Baltimore; but I was deterred from going on to Philadelphia until the frosty weather should set in, by the badness of the
Roads;

roads; for they were in such a state, that even the public stages were prevented from plying for the space of ten or twelve days. The frost soon dried them, and rendered them as good as in summer. I set out when it was most severe. At day break, the morning after I left Baltimore, the thermometer, according to Farenheit, stood at 7°. I never observed it so low during any other part of the winter.

Several travellers had stopped at the same house that I did the first night I was on the road, and we all breakfasted together preparatory to setting out the next morning. The American travellers, before they pursued their journey, took a hearty draught each, according to custom, of egg-nog, a mixture composed of new milk, eggs, rum, and sugar, beat up together; they appeared to be at no small pains also in fortifying themselves against the severity of the weather with great coats and wrappers over each other, woollen socks and trowsers over their boots, woollen mittens over their gloves, and silk handkerchiefs tied over their ears and mouths, &c. so that nothing could be seen excepting their noses and their eyes. It was absolutely a subject of diversion to me, and to a young gentleman just arrived from the West Indies, who accompanied me from Baltimore, to see the great care with which they wrapped themselves up,

for

for we both found ourselves sufficiently warm in common clothing. It seems, however, to be a matter generally allowed, that strangers, even from the West Indies, unaccustomed to intense cold, do not suffer so much from the severity of the winter, the first year of their arrival in America, as the white people who have been born in the country. Every person that we met upon the road was wrapped up much in the same manner as the travellers who breakfasted with us, and had silk handkerchiefs tied round their heads, so as to cover their mouths and ears.

About the middle of the day we arrived at the Susquehannah, and, as we expected to find it, the river was frozen entirely over. In what manner we were to get across was now the question. The people at the ferry-house were of opinion that the ice was not sufficiently strong to bear in every part of the river; at the same time they said, it was so very thick near the shores, that it would be impracticable to cut a passage through it before the day was over; however, as a great number of travellers desirous of getting across was collected together, and as all of them were much averse to remaining at the ferry-house till the next morning, by which time it was supposed that the ice would be strong enough to bear in every part, the people were at laſt over-ruled, and every thing was prepared for cutting a way acroſs the river.

The paſſengers were about twelve in number, with four horſes; the boat's crew conſiſted of ſeven blacks; three of whom, with large clubs, ſtood upon the bow of the boat, and broke the ice, whilſt the others, with iron-headed poles, puſhed the boat forwards. So very laborious was the taſk which the men at the bow had to perform, that it was neceſſary for the others to relieve them every ten minutes. At the end of half an hour their hands, arms, faces, and hats, were glazed entirely over with a thick coat of ice, formed from the water which was daſhed up by the reiterated ſtrokes of their clubs. Two hours elapſed before one half of the way was broken; the ice was found much thicker than had been imagined; the clubs were ſhivered to pieces; the men were quite exhauſted; and having ſuffered the boat to remain ſtationary for a minute or two in a part where the ice was remarkably thick, it was frozen up, ſo that the utmoſt exertions of the crew and paſſengers united were unable to extricate it. In this predicament a council was held; it was impoſſible to move either backward or forward; the boat was half a mile from the ſhore; no one would attempt to walk there on the ice; to remain all night in the boat would

would be death. Luckily I had a pair of piſtols in my holſters, and having fired a few ſignals, the attention of the people on ſhore was attracted towards us, and a ſmall batteau, which is a light boat with a flat bottom, was diſpatched for our relief. This was not ſent, however, for the purpoſe of bringing a ſingle perſon back again, but to aſſiſt us in getting to the oppoſite ſhore. It was ſlipped along a-head of the large boat, and two or three men having ſtepped into it, rocked it about from ſide to ſide until the ice was ſufficiently broken for the large boat to follow. The batteau was now in the water, and the men ſeating themſelves as much as poſſible towards the ſtern, by ſo doing raiſed the bow of it conſiderably above the ice; by means of boat hooks it was then pulled on the ice again, and by rocking it about as before a paſſage was as eaſily opened. In this manner we got on, and at the end of three hours and ten minutes found ourſelves again upon dry land, fully prepared for enjoying the pleaſures of a bright fireſide and a good dinner. The people at the tavern had ſeen us coming acroſs, and had accordingly prepared for our reception; and as each individual thought he had travelled quite far enough that day, the paſſengers remained together till the next morning.

At the American taverns, as I before mentioned, all sorts of people, just as they happen to arrive, are crammed together into the one room, where they must reconcile themselves to each other the best way they can. On the present occasion, the company consisted of about thirteen people, amongst whom were some eminent lawyers from Virginia and the southward, together with a judge of the supreme court, who were going to Philadelphia against the approaching sessions: it was not, however, till after I quitted their company that I heard who they were; for these kind of gentlemen in America are so very plain, both in their appearance and manners, that a stranger would not suspect that they were persons of the consequence which they really are in the country. There were also in the company two or three of the neighbouring farmers, boorish, ignorant, and obtrusive fellows. It is scarcely possible for a dozen Americans to sit together without quarrelling about politics, and the British treaty, which had just been ratified, now gave rise to a long and acrimonious debate. The farmers were of one opinion, and gabbled away for a long time; the lawyers and the judge were of another, and in turns they rose to answer their opponents with all the power of rhetoric which they possessed.

Neither

Neither party could say any thing to change the sentiments of the other one; the noisy contest lasted till late at night, when getting heartily tired they withdrew, not to their respective chambers, but to the general one that held five or six beds, and in which they laid down in pairs. Here the conversation was again revived, and pursued with as much noise as below, till at last sleep closed their eyes, and happily their mouths at the same time; for could they have talked in their sleep, I verily believe they would have prated on until morning. Thanks to our stars! my friend and I got the only two-bedded room in the house to ourselves. The next morning I left the banks of the Susquehannah, and the succeeding day reached Philadelphia.

LETTER VII.

Philadelphia gayer in the Winter than at any other Season.—Celebration in that City of General Washington's Birth Day.—Some Account of General Washington's Person and of his Character.—Americans dissatisfied with his Conduct as President.—A Spirit of Dissatisfaction common amongst them.

MY DEAR SIR,   Philadelphia, February.

PHILADELPHIA now wears a very different aspect to what it did when I landed there in the month of November. Both congress and the state assembly are sitting, as well as the supreme federal court. The city is full of strangers; the theatres are open; and a variety of public and private amusements are going forward. On General Washington's birth day, which was a few days ago, this city was unusually gay *; every person

---

* On this day General Washington terminated his sixty-fourth year; but though not an unhealthy man, he seemed considerably older. The innumerable vexations he has met with in his different public capacities have very sensibly impaired the vigour of his constitution, and given him an aged appearance. There is a very material difference, however, in his looks when seen in private and when he appears in public full drest;

son of consequence in it, Quakers alone excepted, made it a point to visit the General on this

dreſt; in the latter caſe the hand of art makes up for the ravages of time, and he ſeems many years younger.

Few perſons find themſelves for the firſt time in the preſence of General Waſhington, a man ſo renowned in the preſent day for his wiſdom and moderation, and whoſe name will be tranſmitted with ſuch honour to poſterity, without being impreſſed with a certain degree of veneration and awe; nor do theſe emotions ſubſide on a cloſer acquaintance; on the contrary, his perſon and deportment are ſuch as rather tend to augment them. There is ſomething very auſtere in his countenance, and in his manners he is uncommonly reſerved. I have heard ſome officers, that ſerved immediately under his command during the American war, ſay, that they never ſaw him ſmile during all the time that they were with him. No man has ever yet been connected with him by the reciprocal and unconſtrained ties of friendſhip; and but a few can boaſt even of having been on an eaſy and familiar footing with him.

The height of his perſon is about five feet eleven; his cheſt is full; and his limbs, though rather ſlender, well ſhaped and muſcular. His head is ſmall, in which reſpect he reſembles the make of a great number of his countrymen. His eyes are of a light grey colour; and, in proportion to the length of his face, his noſe is long. Mr. Stewart, the eminent portrait painter, told me, that there are features in his face totally diferent from what he ever obſerved in that of any other human being; the ſockets for the eyes, for inſtance, are larger than what he ever met with before, and the upper part of the noſe broader. All his features, he obſerved, were indicative of the ſtrongeſt and moſt ungovernable paſſions, and had he been born in the foreſts, it was his opinion that he would have been the fierceſt man amongſt the ſavage tribes. In this Mr. Stewart has given a proof of his great diſcernment and intimate knowledge of the human countenance; for although General Waſhington has been extolled for his great moderation and calmneſs, during the very trying ſituations in which he has ſo often been placed, yet thoſe who have been acquainted with him the longeſt and moſt

this day. As early as eleven o'clock in the morning he was prepared to receive them, and

most intimately say, that he is by nature a man of a fierce and irritable disposition, but that, like Socrates, his judgment and great self-command have always made him appear a man of a different cast in the eyes of the world. He speaks with great diffidence, and sometimes hesitates for a word; but it is always to find one particularly well adapted to his meaning. His language is manly and expressive. At levee, his discourse with strangers turns principally upon the subject of America; and if they have been through any remarkable places, his conversation is free and particularly interesting, as he is intimately acquainted with every part of the country. He is much more open and free in his behaviour at levee than in private, and in the company of ladies still more so than when solely with men.

General Washington gives no public dinners or other entertainments, except to those who are in diplomatic capacities, and to a few families on terms of intimacy with Mrs. Washington. Strangers, with whom he wishes to have some conversation about agriculture, or any such subject, are sometimes invited to tea. This by many is attributed to his saving disposition; but it is more just to ascribe it to his prudence and foresight; for as the salary of the president, as I have before observed, is very small, and totally inadequate by itself to support an expensive style of life, were he to give numerous and splendid entertainments, the same might possibly be expected from subsequent presidents, who, if their private fortunes were not considerable, would be unable to live in the same style, and might be exposed to many ill-natured observations, from the relinquishment of what the people had been accustomed to; it is most likely also that General Washington has been actuated by these motives, because in his private capacity at Mount Vernon every stranger meets with a hospitable reception from him.

General Washington's self-moderation is well known to the world already. It is a remarkable circumstance, which redounds to his eternal honour, that while president of the United States

and the audience lasted till three in the afternoon. The society of the Cincinnati, the clergy, the officers of the militia, and several others, who formed a distinct body of citizens, came by themselves separately. The foreign ministers attended in their richest dresses and most splendid equipages. Two large parlours were open for the reception of the gentlemen, the windows of one of which towards the street were crowded with spectators on the outside. The sideboard was furnished with cake and wines, whereof the visitors partook. I never observed so much cheerfulness before in the countenance of General Washington; but it was impossible for him to remain insensible to the attention and the compliments paid to him on this occasion.

The ladies of the city, equally attentive, paid their respects to Mrs. Washington, who received them in the drawing room up stairs. After having visited the General, most of the gentlemen also waited upon her. A public ball and supper terminated the rejoicings of the day.

Not one town of any importance was there in the whole union, where some meeting did

---

States he never appointed one of his own relations to any office of trust or emolument, although he has several that are men of abilities, and well qualified to fill the most important stations in the government.

not

not take place in honour of this day; yet singular as it may appear, there are people in the country, Americans too, foremost in boasting to other nations of that constitution which has been raised for them by his valour and wisdom, who are either so insensible to his merit, or so totally devoid of every generous sentiment, that they can refuse to join in commendations of those talents to which they are so much indebted; indeed to such a length has this perverse spirit been carried, that I have myself seen numbers of men, in all other points men of respectability, that have peremptorily refused even to pay him the small compliment of drinking to his health after dinner; it is true indeed, that they qualify their conduct partly by asserting, that it is only as president of the United States, and not as General Washington, that they have a dislike to him; but this is only a mean subterfuge, which they are forced to have recourse to, lest their conduct should appear too strongly marked with ingratitude. During the war there were many, and not loyalists either, who were doing all in their power to remove him from that command whereby he so eminently distinguished himself. It is the spirit of dissatisfaction which forms a leading trait in the character of the Americans as a people, which produces this malevolence at present,

§ just

just as it did formerly; and if their public affairs were regulated by a person sent from heaven, I firmly believe his acts, instead of meeting with universal approbation, would by many be considered as deceitful and flagitious.

LETTER VIII.

Singular Mildness of the Winter of 1795-6.—Set out for Lancaster.—Turnpike Road between that Place and Philadelphia.—Summary View of the State of Pennsylvania.—Description of the Farms between Lancaster and Philadelphia.—The Farmers live in a penurious Style.—Greatly inferior to English Farmers.—Bad Taverns on this Road.—Waggons and Waggoners.—Customs of the latter.—Description of Lancaster.—Lately made the Seat of the State Government.—Manufactures carried on there.—Rifle Guns—Great Dexterity with which the Americans use them.—Anecdote of Two Virginian Soldiers belonging to a Rifle Regiment.

MY DEAR SIR, Lancaster, March.

THIS winter has proved one of the mildest that has ever been experienced in the country. During the last month there were two or three slight falls of snow, but in no one

one inſtance did it remain two days on the ground. A ſmart froſt ſat in the firſt week of this month, and ſnow fell to the depth of ſix or ſeven inches; but on the third day a ſudden thaw came on, and it quickly diſappeared: ſince then the weather has remained uncommonly mild. The ſeaſon being ſo fine, and ſo favourable for travelling, I was unwilling to ſtay at Philadelphia; accordingly I ſat out for this place on horſeback, and arrived here laſt night, at the end of the ſecond day's journey. From hence I intend to proceed towards the ſouth, to meet the approaching ſpring.

The road between Philadelphia and Lancaſter has lately undergone a thorough repair, and tolls are levied upon it, to keep it in order, under the direction of a company. Whenever theſe tolls afford a profit of more than fifteen per cent. on the ſtock originally ſubſcribed for making the road, the company is bound, by an act of aſſembly, to leſſen them. This is the firſt attempt to have a turnpike road in Pennſylvania, and it is by no means reliſhed by the people at large, particularly by the waggoners, who go in great numbers by this route to Philadelphia from the back parts of the ſtate.

The ſtate of Pennſylvania lies nearly in the form of a parallelogram, whoſe greateſt length is is from east to west. This parallelogram is crossed diagonally from the north-east to the south-west by several different ridges of mountains, which are about one hundred miles in breadth. The valleys between these ridges contain a rich black soil, and in the south-west and north-east angles also, at the outside of the mountains, the soil is very good. The northern parts of this state are but very thinly inhabited as yet, but towards the south, the whole way from Philadelphia to Pittsburg, it is well settled. The most populous part of it is the south-east corner, which lies between the mountains and the river Delaware; through this part the turnpike road passes which leads to Lancaster. The country on each side of the road is pleasingly diversified with hill and dale. Cultivation is chiefly confined to the low lands, which are the richest; the hills are all left covered with wood, and afford a pleasing variety to the eye. The further you go from Philadelphia the more fertile is the country, and the more picturesque at the same time.

On the whole road from Philadelphia to Lancaster there are not any two dwellings standing together, excepting at a small place called Downing's Town, which lies about midway; numbers of farm houses, however, are scattered over the country as far as the eye can

can reach. These houses are mostly built of stone, and are about as good as those usually met with on an arable farm of fifty acres in a well cultivated part of England. The farms attached to these houses contain about two hundred acres each, and are, with a few exceptions only, the property of the persons who cultivate them. In the cultivated parts of Pennsylvania the farms rarely exceed three hundred acres; towards the north, however, where the settlements are but few, large tracts of land are in the hands of individuals, who are speculators and land jobbers. Adjoining to the houses there is generally a peach or an apple orchard. With the fruit they make cyder and brandy; the people have a method also of drying the peaches and apples, after having sliced them, in the sun, and thus cured they last all the year round. They are used for pies and puddings, but they have a very acrid taste, and scarcely any of the original flavour of the fruit. The peaches in their best state are but indifferent, being small and dry; I never eat any that were good, excepting such as were raised with care in gardens. It is said that the climate is so much altered that they will not grow now as they formerly did. In April and May nightly frosts are very common, which were totally unknown formerly, and frequently the peaches are entirely blighted.

Gardens

Gardens are very rare in the country parts of Pennsylvania, for the farmers think the labour which they require does not afford sufficient profit; in the neighbourhood of towns, however, they are common, and the culinary vegetables raised in them are equal to any of their respective kinds in the world, *potatoes* excepted, which generally have an earthy unpleasant taste.

Though the south-east part of the state of Pennsylvania is better cultivated than any other part of America, yet the style of farming is on the whole very slovenly. I venture, indeed, to assert, that the farmers do not raise more on their two hundred acres than a skilful farmer in Norfolk, Suffolk, or Essex, or in any well cultivated part of England, would do on fifty acres of good land there. The farmer also, who rents fifty acres of arable land in England, lives far more comfortably in every respect than the farmer in Pennsylvania, or in any other of the middle states, who owns two hundred acres of land, his house will be found better furnished, and his table more plentifully covered. That the farmers do not live better in America, I hardly know whether to ascribe to their love of making money, or to their real indifference about better fare; perhaps it may be owing, in some measure,

measure, to both; certain it is however, that their mode of living is most wretched.

The taverns throughout this part of the country are kept by farmers, and they are all very indifferent. If the traveller can procure a few eggs with a little bacon he ought to rest satisfied; it is twenty to one that a bit of fresh meat is to be had, or any salted meat except pork. Vegetables seem also to be very scarce, and when you do get any, they generally consist of turnips, or turnip tops boiled by way of greens. The bread is heavy and four, though they have as fine flour as any in the world; this is owing to their method of making of it; they raise it with what they call *sots*; hops and water boiled together. No dependance is to be placed upon getting a man at these taverns to rub down your horse, or even to give him his food, frequently therefore you will have to do every thing of the kind for yourself if you do not travel with a servant; and indeed, even where men are kept for the purpose of attending to travellers, which at some of the taverns is the case, they are so sullen and disobliging that you feel inclined to do every thing with your own hands rather than be indebted to them for their assistance: they always appear doubtful whether they should do any thing for you or not,

and

and to be reasoning within themselves, whether it is not too great a departure from the rules of equality to take the horse of another man, and whether it would not be a pleasing sight to see a gentleman strip off his coat, and go to work for himself; nor will money make them alter their conduct; civility, as I before said, is not to be purchased at any expence in America; nevertheless the people will pocket your money with the utmost readiness, though without thanking you for it. Of all beings on the earth, Americans are the most interested and covetous.

It is scarcely possible to go one mile on this road without meeting numbers of waggons passing and repassing between the back parts of the state and Philadelphia. These waggons are commonly drawn by four or five horses, four of which are yoked in pairs. The waggons are heavy, the horses small, and the driver unmerciful; the consequence of which is, that in every team, nearly, there is a horse either lame or blind. The Pennsylvanians are notorious for the bad care which they take of their horses. Excepting the night be tempestuous, the waggoners never put their horses under shelter, and then it is only under a shed; each tavern is usually provided with a large one for the purpose. Market or High-street, in Philadelphia, the street by which these people

ple come into the town, is always crowded with waggons and horses, that are left standing there all night. This is to save money; the expence of putting them into a stable would be too great, in the opinion of these people. Food for the horses is always carried in the waggon, and the moment they stop they are unyoked, and fed whilst they are warm. By this treatment half the poor animals are foundered. The horses are fed out of a large trough carried for the purpose, and fixed on the pole of the waggon by means of iron pins.

Lancaster is the largest inland town in North America, and contains about nine hundred houses, built chiefly of brick and stone, together with six churches, a court house, and gaol. Of the churches, there is one respectively for German Lutherans, German Calvinists, Moravians, English Episcopalians, and Roman Catholics. The streets are laid out regularly, and cross each other at right angles.

An act of assembly has been passed, for making this town the seat of the state government instead of Philadelphia, and the assembly was to meet in the year 1797. This circumstance is much in favour of the improvement of the town. The Philadelphians, inimical to the measure, talked of it much in the same
style

style that they do now of the removal of the seat of the federal government, saying, that it must be again changed to Philadelphia; but the necessity of having the seat of the legislature as central as possible in each state is obvious, and if a change does take place again, it is most likely that it will only be to remove the seat still farther from Philadelphia. On the same principle, the assembly of Virginia meets now at Richmond instead of Williamsburgh, and that of New York state at Albany instead of the city of New York.

Several different kinds of articles are manufactured at Lancaster by German mechanics, individually, principally for the people of the town and the neighbourhood. Rifled barrel guns however are to be excepted, which, although not as handsome as those imported from England, are more esteemed by the hunters, and are sent to every part of the country.

The rifled barrel guns, commonly used in America, are nearly of the length of a musket, and carry leaden balls from the size of thirty to sixty in the pound. Some hunters prefer those of a small bore, because they require but little ammunition; others prefer such as have a wide bore, because the wound which they inflict is more certainly attended with death; the wound, however, made by a ball discharged

charged from one of thefe guns is always very dangerous. The infide of the barrel is fluted, and the grooves run in a fpiral direction from one end of the barrel to the other, confequently when the ball comes out it has a whirling motion round its own axis, at the fame time that it moves forward, and when it enters into the body of an animal, it tears up the flefh in a dreadful manner. The beft of powder is chofen for a rifled barrel gun, and after a proper portion of it is put down the barrel, the ball is inclofed in a fmall bit of linen rag, well greafed at the outfide, and then forced down with a thick ramrod. The greafe and the bits of rag, which are called patches, are carried in a little box at the butend of the gun. The beft rifles are furnifhed with two triggers, one of which being firft pulled fets the other, that is, alters the fpring, fo that it will yield even to the flight touch of a feather. They are alfo furnifhed with double fights along the barrel, as fine as thofe of a furveying inftrument. An experienced markfman, with one of thefe guns, will hit an object not larger than a crown piece, to a certainty, at the diftance of one hundred yards. Two men belonging to the Virginia rifle regiment, a large divifion of which was quartered in this town during the war, had fuch a

dependance

dependance on each other's dexterity, that the one would hold a piece of board, not more than nine inches square, between his knees, whilst the other shot at it with a ball at the distance of one hundred paces. This they used to do alternately, for the amusement of the town's people, as often as they were called upon. Numbers of people in Lancaster can vouch for the truth of this fact. Were I, however, to tell you all the stories I have heard of the performances of riflemen, you would think the people were most abominably addicted to lying. A rifle gun will not carry shot, nor will it carry a ball much farther than one hundred yards with certainty.

LETTER IX.

Number of Germans in the Neighbourhood of York and Lancaster.—How brought over.—White Slave Trade.—Cruelty frequently practised in the carrying it on.—Character of the German Settlers contrasted with that of the Americans.—Passage of the Susquehannah between York and Lancaster.—Great Beauty of the Prospects along the River.—Description of York.—Courts of Justice there.—Of the Pennsylvanian System of Judicature.

MY DEAR SIR,   York, March.

I Arrived at this place, which is about twenty miles distant from Lancaster, yesterday. The inhabitants of this town, as well as those of Lancaster and of the adjoining country, consist principally of Dutch and German emigrants, and their descendants. Great numbers of these people emigrate to America every year, and the importation of them forms a very considerable branch of commerce. They are for the most part brought from the Hanse Towns and from Rotterdam. The vessels sail thither from America, laden with different kinds of produce, and the masters of them, on arriving there, entice on board as many of these people as they can persuade to leave their

their native country, without demanding any money for their paſſage. When the veſſel arrives in America, an advertiſement is put into the paper, mentioning the different kinds of men on board, whether ſmiths, tailors, carpenters, labourers, or the like, and the people that are in want of ſuch men flock down to the veſſel; theſe poor Germans are then ſold to the higheſt bidder, and the captain of the veſſel, or the ſhip holder, puts the money into his pocket *.

There have been many very ſhocking inſtances of cruelty in the carrying on of this trade, vulgarly called "The white ſlave "trade." I ſhall tell you but of one. While the yellow fever was raging in Philadelphia in the year 1793, at which time few veſſels would venture to approach nearer to the city than Fort Mifflin, four miles below it, a captain in the trade arrived in the river, and hearing that ſuch was the fatal nature of the infection, that a ſufficient number of nurſes could not be procured to attend the ſick for any ſum whatever, he conceived the philanthropic idea of ſupplying this deficiency from amongſt his paſſengers; accordingly he boldly ſailed up to the city, and advertiſed his cargo for ſale:

* Thouſands of people were brought from the north of Ireland in the ſame way before the war with France.

"A few

"A few healthy servants, generally between seventeen and eighteen years of age, are just arrived in the brig ―――, their times will be disposed of by applying on board." The cargo, as you may suppose, did not remain long unsold. This anecdote was communicated to me by a gentleman who has the original advertisement in his possession.

When I tell you that people are sold in this manner, it is not to be understood that they are sold for ever, but only for a certain number of years; for two, three, four, or five years, according to their respective merits. A good mechanic, that understands a particular kind of trade, for which men are much wanted in America, has to serve a shorter time than a mere labourer, as more money will be given for his time, and the expence of his passage does not exceed that of any other man. During their servitude, these people are liable to be resold at the caprice of their masters; they are as much under dominion as negro slaves, and if they attempt to run away, they may be imprisoned like felons. The laws respecting "redemptioners," so are the men called that are brought over in this manner, were grounded on those formed for the English convicts before the revolution, and they are very severe.

The Germans are a quiet, sober, and industrious set of people, and are most valuable citizens.

citizens. They generally settle a good many together in one place, and, as may be supposed, in consequence keep up many of the customs of their native country as well as their own language. In Lancaster and the neighbourhood German is the prevailing language, and numbers of people living there are ignorant of any other. The Germans are some of the best farmers in the United States, and they seldom are to be found but where the land is particularly good; wherever they settle they build churches, and are wonderfully attentive to the duties of religion. In these and many other respects the Germans and their descendants differ widely from the Americans, that is, from the descendants of the English, Scotch, Irish, and other nations, who, from having lived in the country for many generations, and from having mingled together, now form one people, whose manners and habits are very much the same.

The Germans are a plodding race of men, wholly intent upon their own business, and indifferent about that of others: a stranger is never molested as he passes through their settlements with inquisitive and idle questions. On arriving amongst the Americans*, how-

---

* In speaking of the Americans here, and in the following lines, it is those of the lower and middling classes of the people which I allude to, such as are met with in the country parts of Pennsylvania.

ever,

ever, a stranger must tell where he came from, where he is going, what his name is, what his business is; and until he gratifies their curiosity on these points, and many others of equal importance, he is never suffered to remain quiet for a moment. In a tavern he must satisfy every fresh set that comes in, in the same manner, or involve himself in a quarrel, especially if it is found out that he is not a native, which it does not require much sagacity to discover.

The Germans give themselves but little trouble about politics; they elect their representatives to serve in congress and the state assemblies; and satisfied that deserving men have been chosen by the people at large, they trust that these men do what is best for the public good, and therefore abide patiently by their decisions: they revere the constitution, conscious that they live happily under it, and express no wishes to have it altered. The Americans, however, are for ever cavilling at some of the public measures; something or other is always wrong, and they never appear perfectly satisfied. If any great measure is before congress for discussion, seemingly distrustful of the abilities or the integrity of the men they have elected, they meet together in their towns or districts, canvass the matter themselves, and then send forward instructions

to

to their representatives how to act. They never consider that any important question is more likely to meet with a fair discussion in an assembly where able men are collected together from all parts of the states than in an obscure corner, where a few individuals are assembled, who have no opportunity of getting general information on the subject. Party spirit is for ever creating dissentions amongst them, and one man is continually endeavouring to obtrude his political creed upon another. If it is found out that a stranger is from Great Britain or Ireland, they immediately begin to boast of their own constitution and freedom, and give him to understand, that they think every Englishman a slave, because he submits to be called a subject. Their opinions are for the most part crude and dogmatical, and principally borrowed from newspapers, which are wretchedly compiled from the pamphlets of the day, having read a few of which, they think themselves arrived at the summit of intellectual excellence, and qualified for making the deepest political researches.

The Germans, as I have said, are fond of settling near each other: when the young men of a family are grown up, they generally endeavour to get a piece of land in the neighbourhood of their relations, and by their industry soon make it valuable; the American, on the contrary, is of a roving difpofition, and wholly regardlefs of the ties of confanguinity; he takes his wife with him, goes to a diftant part of the country, and buries himfelf in the woods, hundreds of miles diftant from the reft of his family, never perhaps to fee them again. In the back parts of the country you always meet numbers of men prowling about to try and buy cheap land; having found what they like, they immediately remove; nor having once removed, are thefe people fatisfied; reftlefs and difcontented with what they poffefs, they are for ever changing. It is fcarcely poffible in any part of the continent to find a man, amongft the middling and lower claffes of Americans, who has not changed his farm and his refidence many different times. Thus it is, that though there are not more than four millions of people in the United States, yet they are fcattered from the confines of Canada to the fartheft extremity of Georgia, and from the Atlantic to the banks of the Miffiffippi. Thoufands of acres of wafte land are annually taken up in unhealthy and unfruitful parts of the country, notwithftanding that the beft fettled and healthy parts of the middle ftates would maintain five times the number of inhabitants that they do at prefent. The American, however, does not change about from place to place in this manner merely to gratify a wandering difpofition; in every change he hopes to make money. By the defire of making money, both the Germans and Americans of every clafs and defcription are actuated in all their movements; felf-intereft is always uppermoft in their thoughts; it is the idol which they worfhip, and at its fhrine thoufands and thoufands would be found, in all parts of the country, ready to make a facrifice of every noble and generous fentiment that can adorn the human mind.

In coming to this place from Lancafter I croffed the Sufquehannah River, which runs nearly midway between the two towns, at the fmall village of Columbia, as better boats are kept there than at either of the ferries higher up or lower down the river. The Sufquehannah is here fomewhat more than a quarter of a mile wide, and for a confiderable diftance, both above and below the ferry, it abounds with iflands and large rocks, over which laft the water runs with prodigious velocity: the roaring noife that it makes is heard a great way off. The banks rife very boldly on each fide, and are thickly wooded; the iflands alfo are covered with fmall trees, which, interfperfed with the rocks, produce a very fine effect. The fcenery in every point of view is wild and romantic. In croffing the river it is neceffary to row up againft the ftream

under

under the shore, and then to strike over to the oppofite fide, under the shelter of some of the largeft iflands. As thefe rapids continue for many miles, they totally impede the navigation, excepting when there are floods in the river, at which time large rafts may be conducted down the ftream, carrying several hundred barrels of flour. It is faid that the river could be rendered navigable in this neighbourhood, but the expence of fuch an undertaking would be enormous, and there is little likelihood indeed that it will ever be attempted, as the Pennfylvanians are already engaged in cutting a canal below Harrifburgh, which will connect the navigable part of the river with the Schuylkill, and alfo another canal from the Schuylkill to the Delaware, by means of which a vent will be opened for the produce of the country bordering upon the Sufquehannah at Philadelphia. Thefe canals would have been finifhed by this time if the fubfcribers had all paid their refpective fhares, but at prefent they are almoft at a ftand for want of money.

The quantity of wild fowl that is feen on every part of the Sufquehannah is immenfe. Throughout America the wild fowl is excellent and plentiful; but there is one duck in particular found on this river, and alfo on Patowmac and James rivers, which furpaffes all others:

others: it is called the white or canvass-back duck, from the feathers between the wings being somewhat of the colour of canvass. This duck is held in such estimation in America, that it is sent frequently as a present for hundreds of miles—indeed it would be a dainty morsel for the greatest epicure in any country.

York contains about five hundred houses and six churches, and is much such another town as Lancaster. It is inhabited by Germans, by whom the same manufactures are carried on as at Lancaster.

The courts of common pleas, and those of general quarter sessions, were holding when I reached this place; I found it difficult, therefore, at first, to procure accommodation, but at last I got admission in a house principally taken up by lawyers. To behold the strange assemblage of persons that was brought together this morning in the one poor apartment which was allotted to all the lodgers, was really a subject of diversion. Here one lawyer had his clients in a corner of the room; there another had his; a third was shaving; a fourth powdering his own hair; a fifth noting his brief; and the table standing in the middle of the room, between a clamorous set of old men on one side, and three or four women in tears on the other; I and the rest of the company, who were not lawyers, were left to eat our breakfast.

On entering into the courts a stranger is apt to smile at the grotesque appearance of the judges who preside in them, and at their manners on the bench; but this smile must be suppressed when it is recollected, that there is no country, perhaps, in the world, where justice is more impartially administered, or more easily obtained by those who have been injured. The judges in the country parts of Pennsylvania are no more than plain farmers, who from their infancy have been accustomed to little else than following the plough. The laws expresly declare that there must be, at least, three judges resident in every county; now as the salary allowed is but a mere trifle, no lawyer would accept of the office, which of course must be filled from amongst the inhabitants *, who are all in a happy state of mediocrity, and on a perfect equality with each other. The district judge, however, who presides in the district or circuit, has a larger salary, and is a man of a different cast. The district or circuit consists of at least three, but not more than six counties. The county judges, which I have mentioned, are, " judges of the court of common pleas, and by virtue of their offices " also justices of oyer and terminer, and ge-

---

* This is also the case in Philadelphia, where we find practising physicians and surgeons sitting on the bench as judges in a court of justice.

" neral

"neral gaol delivery, for the trial of capital and other offenders therein." Any two judges compose the court of quarter sessions. Under certain regulations, established by law, the accused party has the power of removing the proceedings into the supreme court, which has jurisdiction over every part of the state. This short account of the courts relates only to Pennsylvania: every state in the union has a separate code of laws for itself, and a distinct judicature.

LETTER X.

Of the Country near York.—Of the Soil of the Country on each Side of the Blue Mountains.—Frederic-town.—Change in the Inhabitants and in the Country as you proceed towards the Sea.—Numbers of Slaves.—Tobacco chiefly cultivated.—Inquisitiveness of the People at the Taverns.—Observations thereon.—Description of the Great Falls of the Patowmac River.—George Town.—Of the Country between that Place and Hoe's Ferry.—Poisonous Vines.—Port Tobacco.—Wretched Appearance of the Country bordering upon the Ferry.—Slaves neglected.—Passage of the Patowmac very dangerous.—Freſh Water Oyſters.—Landed on a deſerted Part of the Virginian Shore.—Great Hoſpitality of the Virginians.

Stratford, March.

IN the neighbourhood of York and Lancaſter, the ſoil conſiſts of a rich, brown, loamy earth; and if you proceed in a ſouth weſterly courſe, parallel to the Blue Mountains, you meet with the ſame kind of ſoil as far as Frederic in Maryland. Here it changes gradually to a deep reddiſh colour, and continues much the ſame along the eaſtern ſide of the mountains, all the way down to North Carolina. On croſſing over the mountains, however, directly from Frederic, the ſame fertile brown ſoil, which is common in the neighbourhood of York and Lancaſter, is again met with, and it is found throughout the Shenandoah Valley, and as far down as the Carolinas, on the weſt ſide of the mountains.

Between York and Frederic in Maryland there are two or three ſmall towns; viz. Hanover, Peterſburgh, and Woodſburg, but there is nothing worthy of mention in any of them. Frederic contains about ſeven hundred houſes and five churches, two of which are for German Lutherans, one for Preſbyterians, one for Calviniſts, and one for Baptiſts. It is a flouriſh-
ing

ing town, and carries on a brisk inland trade. The arsenal of the state of Maryland is placed here, the situation being secure and central.

From Frederic I proceeded in a southerly course through Montgomery county in Maryland. In this direction the soil changes to a yellowish sort of clay mixed with gravel, and continues much the same until you come to the federal city, beyond which, as I have before mentioned, it becomes more and more sandy as you approach the sea coast. The change in the face of the country after leaving Frederic is gradual, but at the end of a day's journey a striking difference is perceptible. Instead of well cultivated fields, green with wheat, such as are met with along that rich track which runs contiguous to the mountains, large pieces of land, which have been worn out with the culture of tobacco, are here seen lying waste, with scarcely an herb to cover them. Instead of the furrows of the plough, the marks of the hoe appear on the ground; the fields are overspread with little hillocks for the reception of tobacco plants, and the eye is assailed in every direction with the unpleasant sight of gangs of male and female slaves toiling under the harsh commands of the overseer. The difference in the manners of the inhabitants is also great: Instead of being amongst the phlegmatic Germans, a traveller finds himself again in the midst of an inquisitive and prying set of Americans, to gratify whose curiosity it is always necessary to devote a certain portion of time after alighting at a tavern.

A traveller on arriving in America may possibly imagine, that it is the desire of obtaining useful information which leads the people, wherever he stops, to accost him; and that the particular enquiries respecting the object of his pursuits, the place of his abode, and that of his destination, &c. are made to prepare the way for questions of a more general nature, and for conversation that may be attended with some amusement to him; he therefore readily answers them, hoping in return to gain information about the country through which he passes; but when it is found that these questions are asked merely through an idle and impertinent curiosity, and that by far the greater part of the people who ask them are ignorant, boorish fellows; when it is found that those who can keep up some little conversation immediately begin to talk upon politics, and to abuse every country excepting their own; when, lastly, it is found that the people scarcely ever give satisfactory answers at first to the enquiries which are made by a stranger respecting their country, but always hesitate, as if suspicious that he was asking these questions to procure some local

information

information, in order to enable him to overreach them in a bargain, or to make some speculation in land to their injury; the traveller then loses all patience at this disagreeable and prying disposition, and feels disposed to turn from them with disgust; still, however, if he wishes to go through the country peaceably, and without quarrelling at every place where he stops, it is absolutely necessary to answer some few of their questions.

Having followed the high way as far as Montgomery court-house, which is about thirty miles from Frederic, I turned off along a bye road running through the woods, in order to see the great falls of Patowmac River. The view of them from the Maryland shore is very pleasing, but not so much so as that from the opposite side. Having reached the river therefore close to the falls, I rode along through the woods, with which its banks are covered, for some distance higher up, to a place where there was a ferry, and where I crossed into Virginia. From the place where I landed to the Falls, which is a distance of about three miles, there is a wild romantic path running along the margin of the river, and winding at the same time round the base of a high hill covered with lofty trees and rocks. Near to the shore, almost the whole way, there are clusters of small islands covered with trees,

which

which suddenly opposing the rapid course of the stream, form very dangerous eddies, in which boats are frequently lost when navigated by men who are not active and careful. On the shore prodigious heaps of white sand are washed up by the waves, and in many places the path is rendered almost impassable by piles of large trees, which have been brought down from the upper country by floods, and drifted together.

The river, at the ferry which I mentioned, is about one mile and a quarter wide, and it continues much the same breadth as far as the falls, where it is considerably contracted and confined in its channel by immense rocks on either side. There also its course is very suddenly altered, so much so indeed, that below the falls for a short distance it runs in an opposite direction from what it did above, but soon after it resumes its former course. The water does not descend perpendicularly, excepting in one part close to the Virginian shore, where the height is about thirty feet, but comes rushing down with tremendous impetuosity over a ledge of rocks in several different falls. The best view of the cataract is from the top of a pile of rocks about sixty feet above the level of the water, and which, owing to the bend in the river, is situated nearly opposite to the falls. The river comes from

the

the right, then gradually turning, precipitates itself down the falls, and winds along at the foot of the rocks on which you stand with great velocity. The rocks are of a slate colour, and lie in strata; the surface of them in many places is glossy and sparkling.

From hence I followed the course of the river downwards as far as George Town, where I again crossed it; and after passing through the federal city, proceeded along the Maryland shore of the river to Piscatoway, and afterwards to Port Tobacco, two small towns situated on creeks of their own name, which run into the Patowmac. In the neighbourhood of Piscatoway there are several very fine views of the Virginian shore; Mount Vernon in particular appears to great advantage.

I observed here great numbers of the poisonous vines which grow about the large trees, and are extremely like the common grape vines. If handled in the morning, when the branches are moist with the dew, they infallibly raise blisters on the hands, which it is sometimes difficult to get rid of.

Port Tobacco contains about eighty houses, most of which are of wood, and very poor. There is a large English episcopalian church on the border of the town, built of stone, which formerly was an ornament to the place, but

but it is now entirely out of repair; the windows are all broken, and the road is carried through the church-yard over the graves, the paling that surrounded it having been torn down. Near the town is Mount Misery, towards the top of which is a medicinal spring, remarkable in summer for the coldness of the water.

From Port Tobacco to Hoe's Ferry, on the Patowmac River, the country is flat and sandy, and wears a most dreary aspect. Nothing is to be seen here for miles together but extensive plains, that have been worn out by the culture of tobacco, overgrown with yellow sedge,* and interspersed with groves of pine and cedar trees, the dark green colour of which forms a curious contrast with the yellow of the sedge. In the midst of these plains are the remains of several good houses, which shew that the country was once very different to what it is now. These were the houses, most probably, of people who originally settled in Maryland with Lord Baltimore, but which have now been suffered

---

* This sedge, as it is called, is a sort of coarse grass, so hard that cattle will not eat it, which springs up spontaneously, in this part of the country, on the ground that has been left waste; it commonly grows about two feet high; towards winter it turns yellow, and remains standing until the ensuing summer, when a new growth displaces that of the former year. At its first springing up it is of a bright green colour.

to go to decay, as the land around them is worn out, and the people find it more to their intereſt to remove to another part of the country, and clear a piece of rich land, than to attempt to reclaim theſe exhauſted plains. In conſequence of this, the country in many of the lower parts of Maryland appears as if it had been deſerted by one half of its inhabitants.

Such a number of roads in different directions croſs over theſe flats, upon none of which there is any thing like a direction poſt, and the face of a human being is ſo rarely met with, that it is ſcarcely poſſible for a traveller to find out the direct way at once. Inſtead of twelve miles, the diſtance by the ſtraight road from Port Tobacco to the ferry, my horſe had certainly travelled twice the number before we got there. The ferry-houſe was one of thoſe old dilapidated manſions that formerly was the reſidence perhaps of ſome wealthy planter, and at the time when the fields yielded their rich crops of tobacco would have afforded ſome refreſhment to the weary traveller; but in the ſtate I found it, it was the picture of wretchedneſs and poverty. After having waited for two hours and a half for my breakfaſt, the moſt I could procure was two eggs, a pint of milk, and a bit of cake bread, ſcarcely as big as my hand, and but little

tle better than dough. This I had alfo to divide with my fervant, who came to inform me, that there was abfolutely nothing to eat in the houfe but what had been brought to me. I could not but mention this circumftance to feveral perfons when I got into Virginia, and many of them informed me, that they had experienced the fame treatment themfelves at this houfe; yet this houfe had the name of a tavern. What the white people who inhabited it lived upon I could not difcover, but it was evident that they took care of themfelves. As for the poor flaves, however, of which there were many in the huts adjoining the tavern, they had a moft wretched appearance, and feemed to be half ftarved. The men and women were covered with rags, and the children were running about ftark naked.

After having got into the ferry boat, the man of the houfe, as if confcious that he had given me very bad fare, told me that there was a bank of oyfters in the river, clofe to which it was neceffary to pafs, and that if I chofe to ftop the men would procure abundance of them for me. The curiofity of getting oyfters in frefh water tempted me to ftop, and the men got near a bufhel of them in a very few minutes. Thefe oyfters are extremely good when cooked, but very difagreeable eaten raw; indeed all the

oyfters

oyſters found in America, not excepting what are taken at New York, ſo cloſe to the ocean, are, in the opinion of moſt Europeans, very indifferent and taſteleſs when raw. The Americans, on their part, find ſtill greater fault with our oyſters, which they ſay are not fit to be eat in any ſhape, becauſe they taſte of copper. The Patowmac, as well as the reſt of the rivers in Virginia, abounds with excellent fiſh of many different kinds, as ſturgeon, ſhad, roach, herrings, &c. which form a very principal part of the food of the people living in the neighbourhood of them.

The river at the ferry is about three miles wide, and with particular winds the waves riſe very high; in theſe caſes they always tie the horſes, for fear of accidents, before they ſet out; indeed, with the ſmall open boats which they make uſe of, it is what ought always to be done, for in this country guſts of wind riſe ſuddenly, and frequently when they are not at all expected: having omitted to take this precaution, the boat was on the point of being overſet two or three different times as I croſſed over.

On the Virginian ſhore, oppoſite to the ferry houſe from whence I ſailed, there are ſeveral large creeks, which fall into the Patowmac, and it is impoſſible to croſs theſe on horſeback, without riding thirty or forty miles up a ſandy

unin-

uninteresting part of the country to the fords or bridges. As I wished to go beyond these creeks, I therefore hired the boatmen to carry me ten miles down the Patowmac River in the ferry boat, past the mouths of them all; this they accordingly did, and in the afternoon I landed on the beach, not a little pleased at finding that I had reached the shore without having been under the necessity of swimming any part of the way, for during the last hour the horses had not remained quiet for two minutes together, and on one or two occasions, having got both to the same side of the boat, the trim of it was very nearly destroyed, and it was with the utmost difficulty that we prevented it from being overset.

The part of the country where I landed appeared to be a perfect wilderness; no traces of a road or pathway were visible on the loose white sand, and the cedar and pine trees grew so closely together on all sides, that it was scarcely possible to see farther forward in any direction than one hundred yards. Taking a course, however, as nearly as I could guess, in a direct line from the river up the country, at the end of an hour I came upon a narrow road, which led to a large old brick house, somewhat similar to those I had met with on the Maryland shore. On enquiring here, from two blacks, for a tavern, I was told there was
no

no such thing in this part of the country; that in the house before me no part of the family was at home; but that if I rode on a little farther, I should come to some other gentlemen's houses, where I could readily get accommodation. In the course of five or six miles I saw several more of the same sort of old brick houses, and the evening now drawing towards a close, I began to feel the necessity of going to some one of them. I had seen no person for several miles to tell me who any of the owners were, and I was considering within myself which house I should visit, when a lively old negro, mounted on a little horse, came galloping after me. On applying to him for information on the subject, he took great pains to assure me, that I should be well received at any one of the houses I might stop at; he said there were no taverns in this part of the country, and strongly recommended me to proceed under his guidance to his master's house, which was but a mile farther on; "Masser will be so glad "to see to you," added he, "nothing can be like." Having been apprized beforehand, that it was customary in Virginia for a traveller to go without ceremony to a gentleman's house, when there was no tavern at hand, I accordingly took the negro's advice, and rode to the dwelling of his master, made him acquainted with my situation, and begged I might be

allowed

allowed to put my horses in his stable for the night. The reception, however, which this gentleman gave me, differed so materially from what I had been led to expect, that I was happy at hearing from him, that there was a *good* tavern at the distance of two miles. I apologised for the liberty I had taken, and made the best of my way to it. Instead of two miles, however, this tavern proved to be about three times as far off, and when I came to it, I found it to be a most wretched hovel; but any place was preferable to the house of a man so thoroughly devoid of hospitality.

The next day I arrived at this place, the residence of a gentleman, who, when at Philadelphia, had invited me to pass some time with him whenever I visited Virginia. Some of the neighbouring gentlemen yesterday dined here together, and having related to them my adventures on arriving in Virginia, the whole company expressed the greatest astonishment, and assured me that it was never known before, in that part of Virginia, that a stranger had been suffered to go away from a gentleman's house, where he stopped, to a tavern, although it was close by. Every one seemed eager to know the name of the person who had given me such a reception, and begged me to tell it. I did so, and the Virginians were satisfied, for the person was a — Scotchman, and

and had, it seems, removed from some town or other to the plantation on which I found him but a short time before. The Virginians in the lower parts of the state are celebrated for their politeness and hospitality towards strangers; beyond the mountains there is a great difference in the manners of the inhabitants.

LETTER XI.

Of the Northern Neck of Virginia.—First settled by the English.—Houses built by them remaining.—Disparity of Condition amongst the Inhabitants.—Estates worked by Negroes.—Condition of the Slaves.—Worse in the Carolinas.—Lands worn out by Cultivation of Tobacco.—Mode of cultivating and curing Tobacco.—Houses in Virginia.—Those of Wood preferred.—Lower Classes of People in Virginia.—Their unhealthy Appearance.

Stratford, April.

THIS part of Virginia, situated between the Patowmac and Rappahannock rivers, is called the Northern Neck, and is remarkable for having been the birth place of many of the principal characters, which distinguished themselves in America, during the war, by their great talents, General Washington at their

their head. It was here that numbers of English gentlemen, who migrated when Virginia was a young colony, fixed their refidence; and feveral of the houfes which they built, exactly fimilar to the old manor houfes in England, are ftill remaining, particularly in the counties of Richmond and Weftmoreland. Some of thefe, like the houfes in Maryland, are quite in ruins; others are kept in good repair by the prefent occupiers, who live in a ftyle which approaches nearer to that of Englifh country gentlemen than what is to be met with any where elfe on the continent, fome other parts of Virginia alone excepted.

Amongft the inhabitants here and in the lower parts of Virginia there is a difparity unknown elfewhere in America, excepting in the large towns. Inftead of the lands being equally divided, immenfe eftates are held by a few individuals, who derive large incomes from them, whilft the generality of the people are but in a ftate of mediocrity. Moft of the men alfo, who poffefs thefe large eftates, having received liberal educations, which the others have not, the diftinction between them is ftill more obfervable. I met with feveral in this neighbourhood, who had been brought up at the public fchools and univerfities in England, where, until the unfortunate war which feparated the colonies from her, the young men were

were very generally educated; and even still a few are sent there, as the veneration for that country from whence their anceſtors came, and with which they were themſelves for a long time afterwards connected, is by no means yet extinguiſhed.

There is by no means ſo great a diſparity now, however, amongſt the inhabitants of the Northern Neck, as was formerly, and it is becoming leſs and leſs perceptible every year, many of the large eſtates having been divided in conſequence of the removal of the proprietors to other parts of the country that were more healthy, and many more on account of the preſent laws of Virginia, which do not permit any one ſon to inherit the landed eſtates of the father to the excluſion of his brothers.

The principal planters in Virginia have nearly every thing they can want on their own eſtates Amongſt their ſlaves are found taylors, ſhoemakers, carpenters, ſmiths, turners, wheelwrights, weavers, tanners, &c. I have ſeen patterns of excellent coarſe woollen cloth made in the country by ſlaves, and a variety of cotton manufactures, amongſt the reſt good nankeen. Cotton grows here extremely well; the plants are often killed by froſt in winter, but they always produce abundantly the firſt year in which they are ſown. The cotton from which

which nankeen is made is of a particular kind, naturally of a yellowish colour.

The large estates are managed by stewards and overseers, the proprietors just amusing themselves with seeing what is going forward. The work is done wholly by slaves, whose numbers are in this part of the country more than double that of white persons. The slaves on the large plantations are in general very well provided for, and treated with mildness. During three months nearly, that I was in Virginia, but two or three instances of ill treatment towards them came under my observation. Their quarters, the name whereby their habitations are called, are usually situated one or two hundred yards from the dwelling house, which gives the appearance of a village to the residence of every planter in Virginia; when the estate, however, is so large as to be divided into several farms, then separate quarters are attached to the house of the overseer on each farm. Adjoining their little habitations, the slaves commonly have small gardens and yards for poultry, which are all their own property; they have ample time to attend to their own concerns, and their gardens are generally found well stocked, and their flocks of poultry numerous. Besides the food they raise for themselves, they are allowed liberal rations of salted pork and Indian corn. Many

of

of their little huts are comfortably furnished, and they are themselves, in general, extremely well clothed. In short, their condition is by no means so wretched as might be imagined. They are forced to work certain hours in the day; but in return they are clothed, dieted, and lodged comfortably, and saved all anxiety about provision for their offspring. Still, however, let the condition of a slave be made ever so comfortable, as long as he is conscious of being the property of another man, who has it in his power to dispose of him according to the dictates of caprice; as long as he hears people around him talking of the blessings of liberty, and considers that he is in a state of bondage, it is not to be supposed that he can feel equally happy with the freeman. It is immaterial under what form slavery presents itself, whenever it appears there is ample cause for humanity to weep at the sight, and to lament that men can be found so forgetful of their own situations, as to live regardless of the feelings of their fellow creatures.

With respect to the policy of holding slaves in any country, on account of the depravity of morals which it necessarily occasions, besides the many other evil consequences attendant upon it, so much has already been said by others, that it is needless here to make any comments on the subject.

The number of the flaves increafes moft rapidly, fo that there is fcarcely any eftate but what is overftocked. This is a circumftance complained of by every planter, as the maintenance of more than are requifite for the culture of the eftate is attended with great expence. Motives of humanity deter them from felling the poor creatures, or turning them adrift from the fpot where they have been born and brought up, in the midft of friends and relations.

What I have here faid, refpecting the condition and treatment of flaves, appertains, it muft be remembered, to thofe only who are upon the large plantations in Virginia; the lot of fuch as are unfortunate enough to fall into the hands of the lower clafs of white people, and of hard tafk-mafters in the towns, is very different. In the Carolinas and Georgia again, flavery prefents itfelf in very different colours from what it does even in its worft form in Virginia. I am told, that it is no uncommon thing there, to fee gangs of negroes ftaked at a horfe race, and to fee thefe unfortunate beings bandied about from one fet of drunken gamblers to another for days together. How much to be deprecated are the laws which fuffer fuch abufes to exift! yet thefe are the laws enacted by people who boaft of their love of liberty and independence

dence, and who presume to say, that it is in the breasts of Americans alone that the blessings of freedom are held in just estimation.

The Northern Neck, with the exception of some few spots only, is flat and sandy, and abounds with pine and cedar trees. Some parts of it are well cultivated, and afford good crops; but these are so intermixed with extensive tracts of waste land, worn out by the culture of tobacco, and which are almost destitute of verdure, that on the whole the country has the appearance of barrenness.

This is the case wherever tobacco has been made the principal object of cultivation. It is not, however, so much owing to the great share of nutriment which the tobacco plant requires, that the land is impoverished, as to the particular mode of cultivating it, which renders it necessary for people to be continually walking between the plants from the moment they are set out, so that the ground about each plant is left exposed to the burning rays of the sun all the summer, and becomes at the end of the season a hard beaten pathway. A ruinous system has prevailed also of working the same piece of land year after year, till it was totally exhausted; after this it was left neglected, and a fresh piece of land was cleared, that always produced good crops for one or two seasons; but this in its turn was worn out and afterwards left waſte. Many of the planters are at length beginning to ſee the abſurdity of wearing out their lands in this manner, and now raiſe only one crop of tobacco upon a piece of new land, then they ſow wheat for two years, and afterwards clover. They put on from twelve to fifteen hundred buſhels of manure per acre at firſt, which is found to be ſufficient both for the tobacco and wheat; the latter is produced at the rate of about twenty buſhels per acre.

In ſome parts of Virginia, the lands left waſte in this manner throw up, in a very ſhort time, a ſpontaneous growth of pines and cedars; in which caſe, being ſhaded from the powerful influence of the ſun, they recover their former fertility at the end of fifteen or twenty years; but in other parts many years elapſe before any verdure appears upon them. The trees ſpringing up in this ſpontaneous manner uſually grow very cloſe to each other; they attain the height of fifteen or twenty feet, perhaps, in the ſame number of years; there is, however, but very little ſap in them, and in a ſhort time after they are cut down they decay.

Tobacco is raiſed and manufactured in the following manner: When the ſpring is ſo far advanced that every apprehenſion of the return of froſt is baniſhed, a convenient ſpot of ground

ground is chosen, from twenty to one hundred feet square, whereon they burn prodigious piles of wood, in order to destroy the weeds and insects. The warm ashes are then dug in with the earth, and the seed, which is black, and remarkably small, sown. The whole is next covered over with bushes, to prevent birds and flies, if possible, from getting to it; but this, in general, proves very ineffectual; for the plant scarcely appears above ground, when it is attacked by a large black fly of the beetle kind, which destroys the leaves. Persons are repeatedly sent to pick off these flies; but sometimes, notwithstanding all their attention, so much mischief is done that very few plants are left alive. As I passed through Virginia, I heard universal complaints of the depredations they had committed; the beds were almost wholly destroyed.

As soon as the young plants are sufficiently grown, which is generally in the beginning of May, they are transplanted into fields, and set out in hillocks, at the distance of three or four feet from each other. Here again they have other enemies to contend with; the roots are attacked by worms, and between the leaves and stem different flies deposit their eggs, to the infallible ruin of the plant if not quickly removed; it is absolutely necessary, therefore,

therefore, as I have said, for persons to be continually walking between the plants in order to watch, and also to trim them at the proper periods. The tops are broken off at a certain height, and the suckers, which spring out between the leaves, are removed as soon as discovered. According also to the particular kind of tobacco which the planter wishes to have, the lower, the middle, or the upper leaves are suffered to remain. The lower leaves grow the largest; they are also milder, and more inclined to a yellow colour than those growing towards the top of the plant.

When arrived at maturity, which is generally about the month of August, the plants are cut down, pegs are driven into the stems, and they are hung up in large houses, built for the purpose, to dry. If the weather is not favourable for drying the leaves, fires are then lighted, and the smoke is suffered to circulate between the plants; this is also sometimes done to give the leaves a browner colour than what they have naturally. After this they are tied up in bundles of six or seven leaves each, and thrown in heaps to sweat; then they are again dried. When sufficiently cured, the bundles are packed, by means of presses, in hogsheads capable of containing eight hundred or one thousand pounds weight. The planters send the tobacco thus packed to the

the nearest shipping town, where, before exportation, it is examined by an inspector appointed for the purpose, who gives a certificate to warrant the shipping of it if it is sound and merchantable, if not, he sends it back to the owner. Some of the warehouses to which the tobacco is sent for inspection are very extensive, and skilful merchants can accurately tell the quality of the tobacco from knowing the warehouse at which it has been inspected*. Where the roads are good and dry, tobacco is sent to the warehouses in a singular manner: Two large pins of wood are driven into either end of the hogshead by way of axles; a pair of shafts, made for the purpose, are attached to these, and the hogshead is thus drawn along by one or two horses; when this is done great care is taken to have the hoops very strong.

Tobacco is not near so much cultivated now as it was formerly, the great demand for wheat having induced most of the planters to raise that grain in preference. Those who raise to-

---

* By the laws of America, no produce which has undergone any sort of manufacture, as flour, potash, tobacco, rice, &c. can be exported without inspection, nor even put into a boat to be conveyed down a river to a sea port. The inspectors are all sworn, are paid by the states, and not suffered to take fees from any individual. This is a most politic measure; for as none but the best of each article can be sent out of the country, it enhances the price of American produce in foreign markets, and increases the demand.

bacco

bacco and Indian corn are called planters, and those who cultivate small grain, farmers.

Though many of the houses in the Northern Neck are built, as I have said, of brick and stone, in the style of the old English manor houses, yet the greater number there, and throughout Virginia, are of wood; amongst which are all those that have been built of late years. This is chiefly owing to a prevailing, though absurd opinion, that wooden houses are the healthiest, because the inside walls never appear damp, like' those of brick and stone, in rainy weather. In front of every house is a porch or pent-house, commonly extending the whole length of the building; very often there is one also in the rear, and sometimes all round. These porches afford an agreeable shade from the sun during summer. The hall, or saloon as it is called, is always a favourite apartment, during the hot weather, in a Virginian house, on account of the draught of air through it, and it is usually furnished similar to a parlour, with sofas, &c.

The common people in the lower parts of Virginia have very sallow complexions, owing to the burning rays of the sun in summer, and the bilious complaints to which they are subject in the fall of the year. The women are far from being comely, and the dresses, which they wear out of doors to guard them

from

from the sun, make them appear still more ugly than nature has formed them. There is a kind of bonnet very commonly worn, which, in particular, disfigures them amazingly; it is made with a caul, fitting close on the back part of the head, and a front stiffened with small pieces of cane, which projects nearly two feet from the head in a horizontal direction. To look at a person at one side, it is necessary for a woman wearing a bonnet of this kind to turn her whole body round.

In the upper parts of the country, towards the mountains, the women are totally different, having a healthy comely appearance.

LETTER XII.

Town of Tappahannock.—Rappahannock River.—Sharks found in it.—Country bordering upon Urbanna.—Fires common in the Woods.—Manner of stopping their dreadful Progress.—Mode of getting Turpentine from Trees.—Gloucester.—York Town.—Remains of the Fortifications erected here during the American War.—Houses shattered by Balls still remaining.—Cave in the Bank of the River.—Williamsburgh.—State House in Ruins.—Statue of Lord Bottetourt.—College of William and Mary.—Condition of the Students.

Williamsburgh, April.

SINCE I last wrote, the greater part of my time has been spent at the houses of different gentlemen in the Northern Neck. Four days ago I crossed the Rappahannock River, which bounds the Northern Neck on one side, to a small town called Tappahannock, or Hobb's Hole, containing about one hundred houses. Before the war this town was in a much more flourishing state than at present; that unfortunate contest ruined the trade of this little place, as it did that of most of the sea-port towns in Virginia. The Rappahannock is about three quarters of
a mile

a mile wide oppofite the town, which is feventy miles above its mouth. Sharks are very often feen in this river. What is very remarkable, the fifh are all found on the fide of the river next to the town.

From Tappahannock to Urbanna, another fmall town on the Rappahannock River, fituated about twenty-five miles lower down, the country wears but a poor afpect.

The road, which is level and very fandy, runs through woods for miles together. The habitations that are feen from it are but few, and they are of the pooreft defcription. The woods chiefly confift of black oak, pine, and cedar trees, which grow on land of the worft quality only.

On this road there are many creeks to be croffed, which empty themfelves into the Rappahannock River, in the neighbourhood of which there are extenfive marfhes, that render the adjacent country, as may be fuppofed, very unhealthy. Such a quantity of fnipes are feen in thefe marfhes continually, that it would be hardly poffible to fire a gun in a horizontal direction, and not kill many at one fhot.

As I paffed through this part of the country, I obferved many traces of fires in the woods, which are frequent, it feems, in the fpring of the year. They ufually proceed from the

negligence

negligence of people who are burning brush-wood to clear the lands, and considering how often they happen, it is wonderful that they are not attended with more serious consequences than commonly follow. I was a witness myself to one of these fires, that happened in the Northern Neck. The day had been remarkably serene, and appearing favourable for the purpose, large quantities of brushwood had been fired in different places; in the afternoon, however, it became sultry, and streams of hot air were perceptible now and then, the usual tokens of a gust. About five o'clock, the horizon towards the north became dark, and a terrible whirlwind arose. I was standing with some gentlemen on an eminence at the time, and perceived it gradually advancing. It carried with it a cloud of dust, dried leaves, and pieces of rotten wood, and in many places, as it came along, it levelled the fence rails and unroofed the sheds for the cattle. We made every endeavour, but in vain, to get to a place of shelter; in the course of two minutes the whirlwind overtook us; the shock was violent; it was hardly possible to stand, and difficult to breathe; the whirlwind passed over in about three minutes, but a storm, accompanied by heavy thunder and lightning, succeeded, which lasted for more than half an hour. On looking

ing round immediately after the whirlwind had paffed, a prodigious column of fire now appeared in a part of the wood where fome brufhwood had been burning; in many places the flames rofe confiderably above the fummit of the trees, which were of a large growth. It was a tremendous, and at the fame time fublime fight. The negroes on the furrounding plantations were all affembled with their hoes, and watches were ftationed at every corner to give the alarm if the fire appeared elfewhere, left the conflagration fhould become general. To one plantation a fpark was carried by the wind more than half a mile; happily, however, a torrent of rain in a fhort time afterwards came pouring down, and enabled the people to extinguifh the flames in every quarter.

When thefe fires do not receive a timely check, they fometimes increafe to a moft alarming height; and if the grafs and dead leaves happen to be very dry, and the wind brifk, proceed with fo great velocity that the fwifteft runners are often overtaken in endeavouring to efcape from the flames. Indeed I have met with people, on whofe veracity the greateft dependance might be placed, that have affured me they have found it a difficult tafk, at times, to get out of the reach of them, though mounted on good horfes.

There is but one mode of ftopping a fire of this kind, which makes fuch a rapid progrefs along the ground. A number of other fires are kindled at fome diftance a head of that which they wifh to extinguifh, fo as to form a line acrofs the courfe, which, from the direction of the wind, it is likely to take. Thefe are carefully watched by a fufficient number of men furnifhed with hoes and rakes, and they are prevented from fpreading, except on that fide which is towards the large fire, a matter eafily accomplifhed when attended to in the beginning. Thus the fires in a few minutes meet, and of confequence they muft ceafe, as there is nothing left to feed them, the grafs and leaves being burnt on all fides. In general there is but very little brufhwood in the woods of America, fo that thefe fires chiefly run along the ground; the trees, however, are often fcorched, but it is very rare for any of them to be entirely confumed.

The country between Urbanna and Gloucefter, a town fituated upon York River, is neither fo fandy nor fo flat as that bordering upon the Rappahannock. The trees, chiefly pines, are of a very large fize, and afford abundance of turpentine, which is extracted from them in great quantities by the inhabitants, principally, however, for home confumption. The turpentine is got by cutting

GLOUCESTER AND YORK.

ting a large gash in the tree, and setting a trough underneath to receive the resinous matter distilled from the wound. The trees thus drained last but a short time after they are cut down. In this neighbourhood there are numbers of ponds or small lakes, surrounded by woods, along some of which the views are very pleasing. From most of them are falls of water into some creek or river, which afford excellent seats for mills.

Gloucester contains only ten or twelve houses; it is situated on a neck of land nearly opposite to the town of York, which is at the other side of the river. There are remains here of one or two redoubts thrown up during the war. The river between the two places is about one mile and a half wide, and affords four fathom and a half of water.

The town of York consists of about seventy houses, an episcopalian church, and a gaol. It is not now more than one third of the size it was before the war, and it does not appear likely soon to recover its former flourishing state. Great quantities of tobacco were formerly inspected here; very little, however, is now raised in the neighbourhood, the people having got into a habit of cultivating wheat in preference. The little that is sent for inspection is reckoned to be of the very best quality,

quality, and is all engaged for the London market.

York is remarkable for having been the place where Lord Cornwallis furrendered his army to the combined forces of the Americans and French. A few of the redoubts, which were erected by each army, are still remaining, but the principal fortifications are almoſt quite obliterated; the plough has paſſed over ſome of them, and groves of pine trees ſprung up about others, though, during the ſiege, every tree near the town was deſtroyed. The firſt and ſecond parallels can juſt be traced, when pointed out by a perſon acquainted with them in a more perfect ſtate.

In the town the houſes bear evident marks of the ſiege, and the inhabitants will not, on any account, ſuffer the holes perforated by the cannon balls to be repaired on the outſide. There is one houſe in particular, which ſtands in the ſkirt of the town, that is in a moſt ſhattered condition. It was the habitation of a Mr. Neilſon, a ſecretary under the regal government, and was made the head quarters of Lord Cornwallis when he firſt came to the town; but it ſtood ſo much expoſed, and afforded ſo good a mark to the enemy, that he was ſoon forced to quit it. Neilſon, however, it ſeems, was determined to ſtay there

till

till the last, and absolutely remained till his negro servant, the only person that would live with him in such a house, had his brains dashed out by a cannon shot while he stood by his side; he then thought it time to retire, but the house was still continually fired at, as if it had been head quarters. The walls and roof are pierced in innumerable places, and at one corner a large piece of the wall is torn away; in this state, however, it is still inhabited in one room by some person or other equally fanciful as the old secretary. There are trenches thrown up round it, and on every side are deep hollows made by the bombs that fell near it. Till within a year or two the broken shells themselves remained; but the New England men that traded to York finding they would sell well as old iron, dug them up, and carried them away in their ships.

The banks of the river, where the town stands, are high and inaccessible, excepting in a few places; the principal part of the town is built on the top of them; a few fishing huts and storehouses merely stand at the bottom. A cave is shewn here in the banks, described by the people as having been the place of head-quarters during the siege, after the cannonade of the enemy became warm; but in reality it was formed and hung with green

green baize for a lady, either the wife or acquaintance of an officer, who was terrified with the idea of remaining in the town, and died of fright after her removal down to the cave.

Twelve miles from York, to the westward, stands Williamsburgh, formerly the seat of government in Virginia. Richmond was fixed upon during the war as a more secure place, being farther removed from the sea coast, and not so much exposed to depredations if an enemy were to land unexpectedly. Richmond also had the advantage of being situated at the head of a navigable river, and was therefore likely to increase to a size which the other never could attain. It is wonderful, indeed, what could have induced people to fix upon the spot where Williamsburgh stands for a town, in the middle of a plain, and one mile and a half removed from any navigable stream, when there were so many noble rivers in the neighbourhood.

The town consists of one principal street, and two others which run parallel to it. At one end of the main street stands the college, and at the other end the old capitol or statehouse, a capacious building of brick, now crumbling to pieces from negligence. The houses around it are mostly uninhabited, and present a melancholy picture. In the hall of the capitol stands a maimed statue of lord Botetourt,

Botetourt, one of the regal governors of Virginia, erected at the public expence, in memory of his lordship's equitable and popular administration. During the war, when party rage was at its highest pitch, and every thing pertaining to royalty obnoxious, the head and one arm of the statue were knocked off; it now remains quite exposed, and is more and more defaced every day. Whether the motto, "*Resurgo rege favente,*" inscribed under the coat of arms, did or did not help to bring upon it its present fate, I cannot pretend to say; as it is, it certainly remains a monument of the extinction of monarchical power in America.

The college of William and Mary, as it is still called, stands at the opposite end of the main street; it is a heavy pile, which bears, as Mr. Jefferson, I think, says, " a very close resemblance to a large brick kiln, excepting that it has a roof." The students were about thirty in number when I was there: from their appearance one would imagine that the seminary ought rather to be termed a grammar school than a college; yet I understand the visiters, since the present revolution, finding it full of young boys just learning the rudiments of Greek and Latin, a circumstance which consequently deterred others more advanced

vanced from going there, dropped the professorships for these two languages, and established others in their place. The professorships, as they now stand, are for law, medicine, natural and moral philosophy, mathematics, and modern languages. The bishop of Virginia is president of the college, and has apartments in the buildings. Half a dozen or more of the students, the eldest about twelve years old, dined at his table one day that I was there; some were without shoes or stockings, others without coats. During dinner they constantly rose to help themselves at the side board. A couple of dishes of salted meat, and some oyster soup, formed the whole of the dinner. I only mention this, as it may convey some little idea of American colleges and American dignitaries.

The episcopalian church, the only one in the place, stands in the middle of the main street; it is much out of repair. On either side of it is an extensive green, surrounded with neat looking houses, which bring to mind an English village.

The town contains about twelve hundred inhabitants, and the society in it is thought to be more extensive and more genteel at the same time than what is to be met with in any other place of its size in America. No
manufactures

mnufactures are carried on here, and scarcely any trade.

There is an hospital here for lunatics, but it does not appear to be well regulated.

LETTER XIII.

Hampton.— Ferry to Norfolk.— Danger in crossing the numerous Ferries in Virginia.— Norfolk.— Laws of Virginia injurious to the Trading Interest.— Streets narrow and dirty in Norfolk.— Yellow Fever there.— Observations on this Disorder.— Violent Party Spirit amongst the Inhabitants.— Few Churches in Virginia.— Several in Ruins.— Private Grave Yards.

Norfolk, April.

FROM Williamsburgh to Hampton the country is flat and uninteresting. Hampton is a small town, situated at the head of a bay, near the mouth of James River, which contains about thirty houses and an episcopalian church. A few sea boats are annually built here; and corn and lumber are exported annually to the value of about forty-two thousand dollars. It is a dirty disagreeable place, always

always infested by a shocking stench from a muddy shore when the tide is out.

From this town there is a regular ferry to Norfolk, across Hampton roads, eighteen miles over. I was forced to leave my horses here behind me for several days, as all the flats belonging to the place had been sent up a creek some miles for staves, &c. and they had no other method of getting horses into the ferry boats, which were too large to come close into shore, excepting by carrying them out in these flats, and then making them leap on board. It is a most irksome piece of business to cross the ferries in Virginia; there is not one in six where the boats are good and well manned, and it is necessary to employ great circumspection in order to guard against accidents, which are but too common. As I passed along I heard of numberless recent instances of horses being drowned, killed, and having their legs broken, by getting in and out of the boats.

Norfolk stands nearly at the mouth of the eastern branch of Elizabeth River, the most southern of those which empty themselves into the Chesapeak Bay. It is the largest commercial town in Virginia, and carries on a flourishing trade to the West Indies. The exports consist principally of tobacco, flour, and corn, and various kinds of lumber; of the latter it derives an inexhaustible supply from the Dismal

mal Swamp, immediately in the neighbourhood.

Norfolk would be a place of much greater trade than it is at prefent, were it not for the impolicy of fome laws which have exifted in the ftate of Virginia. One of thefe laws, fo injurious to commerce, was paffed during the war. By this law it was enacted, that all merchants and planters in Virginia, who owed money to Britifh merchants, fhould be exonerated from their debts if they paid the money due into the public treafury inftead of fending it to Great Britain; and all fuch as ftood indebted were invited to come forward, and give their money in this manner, towards the fupport of the conteft in which America was then engaged.

The treafury at firft did not become much richer in confequence of this law; for the Virginian debtor, individually, could gain nothing by paying the money that he owed into the treafury, as he had to pay the full fum which was due to the Britifh merchant; on the contrary, he might lofe confiderably: his credit would be ruined in the eyes of the Britifh merchant by fuch a meafure, and it would be a great impediment to the renewal of a commercial intercourfe between them after the conclufion of the war.

However,

However, when the continental paper money became so much depreciated, that one hundred paper dollars were not worth one in silver, many of the people, who stood deeply indebted to the merchants in Great Britain, began to look upon the measure in a different point of view; they now saw a positive advantage in paying their debts into the treasury in these paper dollars, which were a legal tender; accordingly they did so, and in consequence were exonerated of their debts by the laws of their country, though in reality they had not paid more than one hundredth part of them. In vain did the British merchant sue for his money when hostilities were terminated; he could obtain no redress in any court of justice in Virginia. Thus juggled out of his property he naturally became distrustful of the Virginians; he refused to trade with them on the same terms as with the people of the other states, and the Virginians have consequently reaped the fruits of their very dishonourable conduct *.

Another law, baneful in the highest degree to the trading interest, is one which renders

* In February 1796, this nefarious business was at last brought before the supreme court of the United States in Philadelphia, by the agents of the British merchants, and the decision of the judges was such as redounded to their honour; for, they declared that these debts should all be paid over again, bona fide, to the British merchant.

all

all landed property inviolable. This law has induced numbers to run into debt; and as long as it exists foreigners will be cautious of giving credit to a large amount to men who, if they chuse to purchase a tract of land with the goods or money entrusted to their care, may sit down upon it securely, out of the reach of all their creditors, under protection of the laws of the country. Owing to this law they have not yet been enabled to get a bank established in Norfolk, though it would be of the utmost importance to the traders. The directors of the bank of the United States have always peremptorily refused to let a branch of it be fixed in any part of Virginia whilst this law remains. In Boston, New York, Baltimore, Charleston, &c. there are branches of the bank of the United States, besides other banks, established under the sanction of the state legislature.

Repeated attempts have been made in the state assembly to get this last mentioned law repealed, but they have all proved ineffectual. The debates have been very warm on the business, and the names of the majority, who voted for the continuation of it, have been published, to expose them if possible to infamy; but so many have sheltered themselves under its sanction, and so many still find an interest in its continuance, that it is not likely to be speedily repealed.

The

The houses in Norfolk are about five hundred in number; by far the greater part of them are of wood, and but meanly built. These have all been erected since the year 1776, when the town was totally destroyed by fire, by the order of Lord Dunmore, then regal governor of Virginia. The losses sustained on that occasion were estimated at £.300,000 sterling. Towards the harbour the streets are narrow and irregular; in the other parts of the town they are tolerably wide; none of them are paved, and all are filthy; indeed, in the hot months of summer, the stench that proceeds from some of them is horrid. That people can be thus inattentive to cleanliness, which is so conducive to health, and in a town where a sixth part of the people died in one year of a pestilential disorder, is most wonderful!! *

Amongst

---

* The yellow fever, which has committed such dreadful ravages of late years in America, is certainly to be considered as a sort of plague. It first appeared at Philadelphia in the year 1793; in 1794 it appeared at Baltimore; in 1795, at New York and Norfolk; and in 1796, though the matter was hushed up as much as possible, in order to prevent an alarm, similar to that which had injured the city so much the preceding year, yet in New York a far greater number of deaths than usual were heard of during the summer and autumn, strongly supposed to have been occasioned by the same malignant disorder.

The accounts given of the calamitous consequences attendant upon it, in these different places, are all much alike, and nearly

Amongst the inhabitants are great numbers of Scotch and French. The latter are almost entirely

nearly similar to those given of the plague:—The people dying suddenly, and under the most shocking circumstances—such as were well flying away—the sick abandoned, and perishing for want of common necessaries—the dead buried in heaps together without any ceremony—charity at an end—the ties of friendship and consanguinity disregarded by many—others, on the contrary, nobly coming forward, and at the hazard of their own lives doing all in their power to relieve their fellow citizens, and avert the general woe.——At Philadelphia, in the space of about three months, no less than four thousand inhabitants were swept off by this dreadful malady, a number, at that time, amounting to about one tenth of the whole. Baltimore and New York did not suffer so severely; but at Norfolk, which is computed to contain about three thousand people, no less than five hundred fell victims to it.

The disorder has been treated very differently by different physicians, and as some few have survived under each system that has been tried, no general one has yet been adopted. I was told, however, by several people in Norfolk, who resided in the most sickly part of the town during the whole time the fever lasted, that as a preventative medicine, a strong mercurial purge was very generally administered, and afterwards Peruvian bark; and that few of those who had taken this medicine were attacked by the fever. All however that can be done by medicine to stop the progress of the disorder, when it has broke out in a town, seems to be of no very great effect; for as long as the excessive hot weather lasts the fever rages, but it regularly disappears on the approach of cold weather. With regard to its origin there have been also various opinions; some have contended that it was imported into every place where it appeared from the West Indies; others, that it was generated in the country. These opinions have been ably supported on either side of the question by medical men, who resided at the different places where the fever has appeared. There are a few notorious circumstances, however, which lead me, as an individual,

entirely from the West Indies, and principally from St. Domingo. In such prodigious numbers did they flock over after the British forces had got footing in the French islands, that between two and three thousand were in Norfolk at one time; most of them, however, afterwards dispersed themselves throughout different parts of the country; those who staid in the town opened little shops of different kinds, and amongst them I found many who had been in affluent circumstances before they were driven from their homes.

A strong party spirit has always been prevalent amongst the American inhabitants of this town; so much so that a few years ago,

dual, to think that the fever has been generated on the American continent. In the first place, the fever has always broken out in those parts of towns which were most closely built, and where the streets have been suffered through negligence to remain foul and nasty; in the second place, it has regularly broken out during the hottest time of the year, in the months of July and August, when the air on the American coast is for the most part stagnant and sultry, and when vegetable and animal matter becomes putrid in an incredible short space of time; thirdly, numbers of people died of the disorder in New York, in the year 1796, notwithstanding that every West Indian vessel which entered the port that season was examined by the health officer, a regular bred physician, and that every one suspected was obliged to perform quarantine. The people in New York are so fully persuaded that the fever originates in America from putrid matter, that they have stopped up one or two docks, which were receptacles for the filth of the neighbourhood, and which contaminated the air when the tide was out.

when

when some English and French vessels of war were lying in Hampton roads, and the sailors, from each, on shore, the whole people were up and ready to join them, on the one side or the other, in open contest; but the mayor drew out the militia, and sent them to their respective homes.

Here are two churches, one for episcopalians, the other for methodists. In the former, service is not performed more than once in two or three weeks, and very little regard is paid by the people in general to Sunday. Indeed, throughout the lower parts of Virginia, that is, between the mountains and the sea, the people have scarcely any sense of religion, and in the country parts the churches are all falling into decay. As I rode along, I scarcely observed one that was not in a ruinous condition, with the windows broken, and doors dropping off the hinges, and lying open to the pigs and cattle wandering about the woods; yet many of these were not past repair. The churches in Virginia, excepting such as are in towns, stand for the most part in the woods, retired from any houses, and it does not appear that any persons are appointed to pay the smallest attention to them.

A custom prevails in Norfolk, of private individuals holding grave yards, which are looked upon as a very lucrative kind of property, the owners

owners receiving confiderable fees annually for giving permiffion to people to bury their dead in them. It is very common alfo to fee, in the large plantations in Virginia, and not far from the dwelling houfe, cemeteries walled in, where the people of the family are all buried. Thefe cemeteries are generally built adjoining the garden.

LETTER XIV.

Defcription of Difmal Swamp.—Wild Men found in it.—Bears, Wolves, &c.—Country between Swamp and Richmond.—Mode of making Tar and Pitch.—Poor Soil.—Wretched Taverns.—Corn Bread.—Difficulty of getting Food for Horfes.—Peterfburgh.—Horfe Races there.—Defcription of Virginian Horfes. —Stile of Riding in America.—Defcription of Richmond, Capital of Virginia.—Singular Bridge acrofs James River.—State Houfe. —Falls of James River.—Gambling common in Richmond.—Lower Claffes of People very quarrelfome.— Their Mode of Fighting.— Gouging.

Richmond, May.

FROM Norfolk I went to look at the great Difmal Swamp, which commences at the diftance of nine miles from the town, and extends

tends into North Carolina, occupying in the whole, about one hundred and fifty thousand acres. This great tract is entirely covered with trees; juniper and cypress trees grow where there is moſt moiſture, and on the dry parts, white and red oaks and a variety of pines.

These trees grow to a moſt enormous ſize, and between them the bruſhwood ſprings up ſo thick that the ſwamp in many parts is abſolutely impervious. In this reſpect it differs totally from the common woods in the country. It abounds alſo with cane reeds, and with long rich graſs, upon which cattle feed with great avidity, and become fat in a very ſhort ſpace of time; the canes, indeed, are conſidered to be the very beſt green food that can be given to them. The people who live on the borders of the ſwamp drive all their cattle into it to feed; care however is taken to train them to come back regularly to the farms every night by themſelves, otherwiſe it would be impoſſible to find them. This is effected by turning into the ſwamp with them, for the firſt few weeks they are ſent thither to feed, two or three old milch cows accuſtomed to the place, round whoſe necks are faſtened ſmall bells. The cows come back every evening to be milked; the reſt of the cattle herd with theſe, following the noiſe of the bells, and when they return to the farm a handful of ſalt, or ſomething of which they are equally fond, is given to each as an inducement for them to return again. In a fhort time the cattle become familiar with the place, and having been accuftomed from the firft day to return, they regularly walk to the farms every evening.

In the interior parts of the fwamp large herds of wild cattle are found, moft probably originally loft on being turned in to feed. Bears, wolves, deer, and other wild indigenous animals are alfo met with there. Stories are common in the neighbourhood of wild men having been found in it, who were loft, it is fuppofed, in the fwamp when children.

The fwamp varies very much in different parts; in fome the furface of it is quite dry, and firm enough to bear a horfe; in others it is overflowed with water; and elfewhere fo miry that a man would fink up to his neck if he attempted to walk upon it; in the drieft part, if a trench is cut only a few feet deep, the water gufhes in, and it is filled immediately. Where the canal to connect the water of Albemarle Sound with Norfolk is cut, the water in many places flows in from the fides, at the depth of three feet from the furface, in large ftreams, without intermiffion; in its colour it exactly refembles brandy, which is fuppofed to be occafioned by the roots of the juniper trees; it is perfectly clear however,

however, and by no means unpalatable; it is said to possess a diuretic quality, and the people in the neighbourhood, who think it very wholesome, prefer it to any other. Certainly there is something very uncommon in the nature of this swamp, for the people living upon the borders of it do not suffer by fever and ague, or bilious complaints, as is generally the case with those resident in the neighbourhood of other swamps and marshes. Whether it is the medicinal quality of the water, however, which keeps them in better health or not, I do not pretend to determine.

As the Dismal Swamp lies so very near to Norfolk, where there is a constant demand for shingles, staves, &c. for exportation, and as the very best of these different articles are made from the trees growing upon the swamp, it of course becomes a very valuable species of property. The canal which is now cutting through it will also enhance its value, as when it is completed, lumber can then be readily sent from the remotest parts. The more southern parts of it, when cleared, answer uncommonly well for the culture of rice; but in the neighbourhood of Norfolk, as far as ten feet deep from the surface, there seems to be nothing but roots and fibres of different herbs mixed with a whitish sand, which would not answer for the purpose, as rice requires

requires a very rich foil. The trees, however, that grow upon it, are a moſt profitable crop, and inſtead of cutting them all down promiſcuouſly, as commonly is done, they only fell ſuch as have attained a large ſize, by which means they have a continued ſucceſſion for the manufacture of thoſe articles I mentioned. Eighty thouſand acres of the ſwamp are the property of a company incorporated under the title of " The Diſmal Swamp Company." Before the war broke out a large number of negroes was conſtantly employed by the company in cutting and manufacturing ſtaves, &c. and their affairs were going on very proſperouſly; but at the time that Norfolk was burnt they loſt all their negroes, and very little has been done by them ſince. The lumber that is now ſent to Norfolk is taken principally off thoſe parts of the ſwamp which are private property.

From the Diſmal Swamp to Richmond, a diſtance of about one hundred and forty miles, along the ſouth ſide of James River, the country is flat and ſandy, and for miles together entirely covered with pine trees. In Nanſemonde county, bordering on the Swamp, the ſoil is ſo poor that but very little corn or grain is raiſed; it anſwers well however for peach orchards, which are found to be very profitable. From the peaches they make brandy,

brandy, and when properly matured it is an excellent liquor, and much efteemed; they give it a very delicious flavour in this part of the country by infufing dried pears in it. Spirit and water is the univerfal beverage throughout Virginia. They alfo make confiderable quantities of tar and pitch from the pine trees. For this purpofe a fort of pit is dug, in which they burn large piles of the trees. The tar runs out, and is depofited at the bottom of the pit, from whence it is taken, cleared of the bits of charcoal that may be mixed with it and put into barrels. The tar, infpiffated by boiling, makes pitch.

The accommodation at the taverns along this road I found moft wretched; nothing was to be had but rancid fifh, fat falt pork, and bread made of Indian corn. For this indifferent fare alfo I had to wait oftentimes an hour or two. Indian corn bread, if well made, is tolerably good, but very few people can relifh it on the firft trial; it is a coarfe, ftrong kind of bread, which has fomething of the tafte of that made from oats. The beft way of preparing it is in cakes; the large loaves made of it are always like dough in the middle. There is a difh alfo which they make of Indian corn, very common in Virginia and Maryland, called "hominy." It confifts of pounded Indian corn and beans boiled

boiled together with milk till the whole mafs becomes firm. This is eat, either hot or cold, with bacon, or with other meat.

As for my horfes, they were almoft ftarved. Hay is fcarcely ever made ufe of in this part of the country, but in place of it they feed their cattle upon fodder, that is, the leaves of the Indian corn plant. Not a bit of fodder, however, was to be had on the whole road from Norfolk to Richmond, excepting at two places; and the feafon having been remarkably dry, the little grafs that had fprung up had been eat down every where by the cattle in the country. Oats were not to be had on any terms; and Indian corn was fo fcarce, that I had frequently to fend to one or two different houfes before I could get even fufficient to give one feed each to my horfes. The people in the country endeavoured to account for this fcarcity from the badnefs of the harveft the preceding year; but the fact, I believe, was, that corn for exportation having been in great demand, and a moft enormous price offered for it, the people had been tempted to difpofe of a great deal more than they could well fpare. Each perfon was eager to fell his own corn to fuch advantage, and depended upon getting fupplied by his neighbour, fo that they were all reduced to want.

Peterfburgh ftands at the head of the navigable

vigable part of Appamatox River, and is the only place of consequence south of James River, between Norfolk and Richmond. The rest of the towns, which are but very small, seem to be fast on the decline, and present a miserable and melancholy appearance. The houses in Petersburgh amount to about three hundred; they are built without any regularity. The people who inhabit them are mostly foreigners; ten families are not to be found in the town that have been born in it. A very flourishing trade is carried on in this place. About two thousand four hundred hogsheads of tobacco are inspected annually at the warehouses; and at the falls of the Appamatox River, at the upper end of the town, are some of the best flour mills in the state.

Great crowds were assembled at this place, as I passed through, attracted to it by the horse races, which take place four or five times in the year. Horse racing is a favourite amusement in Virginia; and it is carried on with spirit in different parts of the state. The best bred horses which they have are imported from England; but still some of those raised at home are very good. They usually run for purses made up by subscription. The only particular circumstance in their mode of carrying on their races in Virginia is, that they always

always run to the left; the horses are commonly rode by negro boys, some of whom are really good jockies.

The horses in common use in Virginia are all of a light description, chiefly adapted for the saddle; some of them are handsome, but they are for the most part spoiled by the false gaits which they are taught. The Virginians are wretched horsemen, as indeed are all the Americans I ever met with, excepting some few in the neighbourhood of New York. They sit with their toes just under the horse's nose, their stirrups being left extremely long, and the saddle put about three or four inches forward on the mane. As for the management of the reins, it is what they have no conception of. A trot is odious to them, and they express the utmost astonishment at a person who can like that uneasy gait, as they call it. The favourite gaits which all their horses are taught, are a pace and a *wrack*. In the first, the animal moves his two feet on one side at the same time, and gets on with a sort of shuffling motion, being unable to spring from the ground on these two feet as in a trot. We should call this an unnatural gait, as none of our horses would ever move in that manner without a rider; but the Americans insist upon it that it is otherwise, because many of their foals pace as soon as born.

These

These kind of horses are called "natural pacers," and it is a matter of the utmost difficulty to make them move in any other manner; but it is not one horse in five hundred that would pace without being taught. In the wrack, the horse gallops with his fore feet, and trots with those behind. This is a gait equally devoid of grace with the other, and equally contrary to nature; it is very fatiguing also to the horse; but the Virginian finds it more conducive to his ease than a fair gallop, and this circumstance banishes every other consideration.

The people in this part of the country, bordering upon James River, are extremely fond of an entertainment which they call a barbacue. It consists in a large party meeting together, either under some trees, or in a house, to partake of a sturgeon or pig roasted in the open air, on a sort of hurdle, over a slow fire; this, however, is an entertainment chiefly confined to the lower ranks, and, like most others of the same nature, it generally ends in intoxication.

Richmond, the capital of Virginia, is situated immediately below the falls of James River, on the north side. The river opposite to the town is about four hundred yards wide, and is crossed by means of two bridges, which are separated by an island that lies nearly in the middle of the

the river. The bridge, leading from the south shore to the island, is built upon fifteen large flat bottomed boats, kept stationary in the river by strong chains and anchors. The bows of them, which are very sharp, are put against the stream, and fore and aft there is a strong beam, upon which the piers of the bridge rest. Between the island and the town, the water being shallower, the bridge is built upon piers formed of square casements of logs filled with stones. To this there is no railing, and the boards with which it is covered are so loose, that it is dangerous to ride a horse across it that is not accustomed to it. The bridges thrown across this river, opposite the town, have repeatedly been carried away; it is thought idle, therefore, to go to the expence of a better one than what exists at present. The strongest stone bridge could hardly resist the bodies of ice that are hurried down the falls by the floods on the breaking up of a severe winter.

Though the houses in Richmond are not more than seven hundred in number, yet they extend nearly one mile and a half along the banks of the river. The lower part of the town, according to the course of the river, is built close to the water, and opposite to it lies the shipping; this is connected with the upper town by a long street, which runs parallel to the course of the river, about fifty yards removed from

from the banks. The situation of the upper town is very pleasing; it stands on an elevated spot, and commands a fine prospect of the falls of the river, and of the adjacent country on the opposite side. The best houses stand here, and also the capitol or statehouse. From the opposite side of the river this building appears extremely well, as its defects cannot be observed at that distance, but on a closer inspection it proves to be a clumsy ill shapen pile. The original plan was sent over from France by Mr. Jefferson, and had great merit; but his ingenious countrymen thought they could improve it, and to do so placed what was intended for the attic story, in the plan, at the bottom, and put the columns on the top of it. In many other respects, likewise, the plan was inverted. This building is finished entirely with red brick; even the columns themselves are formed of brick; but to make them appear like stone, they have been partially whitened with common whitewash. The inside of the building is but very little better than its exterior part. The principal room is for the house of representatives; this is used also for divine service, as there is no such thing as a church in the town. The vestibule is circular, and very dark; it is to be ornamented with a statue of General Washington, executed by an eminent artist in France, which arrived while I

was

was in the town. Ugly and ill contrived as this building is, a stranger must not attempt to find fault with any part of it, for it is looked upon by the inhabitants as a most elegant fabric.

The falls in the river, or the rapids, as they should be called, extend six miles above the city, in the course of which there is a descent of about eighty feet. The river is here full of large rocks, and the water rushes over them in some places with great impetuosity. A canal is completed at the north side of these falls, which renders the navigation complete from Richmond to the Blue Mountains, and at particular times of the year, boats with light burthens can proceed still higher up. In the river, opposite the town, are no more than seven feet water, but ten miles lower down about twelve feet. Most of the vessels trading to Richmond unlade the greater part of their cargoes at this place into river craft, and then proceed up to the town. Trade is carried on here chiefly by foreigners, as the Virginians have but little inclination for it, and are too fond of amusement to pursue it with much success.

Richmond contains about four thousand inhabitants, one half of whom are slaves. Amongst the freemen are numbers of lawyers, who, with the officers of the state government, and several

hat

that live retired on their fortunes, reside in the upper town; the other part is inhabited principally by the traders.

Perhaps in no place of the same size in the world is there more gambling going forward than in Richmond. I had scarcely alighted from my horse at the tavern, when the landlord came to ask what game I was most partial to, as in such a room there was a faro table, in another a hazard table, in a third a billiard table, to any one of which he was ready to conduct me. Not the smallest secrecy is employed in keeping these tables; they are always crowded with people, and the doors of the apartment are only shut to prevent the rabble from coming in. Indeed, throughout the lower parts of the country in Virginia, and also in that part of Maryland next to it, there is scarcely a petty tavern without a billiard room, and this is always full of a set of idle low-lived fellows, drinking spirits or playing cards, if not engaged at the table. Cockfighting is also another favourite diversion. It is chiefly, however, the lower class of people that partake of these amusements at the taverns; in private there is, perhaps, as little gambling in Virginia as in any other part of America. The circumstance of having the taverns thus infested by such a set of people renders travelling extremely unpleasant. Many times I have been

forced

forced to proceed much farther in a day than I have wished, in order to avoid the scenes of rioting and quarrelling that I have met with at the taverns, which it is impossible to escape as long as you remain in the same house where they are carried on, for every apartment is considered as common, and that room in which a stranger sits down is sure to be the most frequented.

Whenever these people come to blows, they fight just like wild beasts, biting, kicking, and endeavouring to tear each other's eyes out with their nails. It is by no means uncommon to meet with those who have lost an eye in a combat, and there are men who pride themselves upon the dexterity with which they can scoop one out. This is called *gouging*. To perform the horrid operation, the combatant twists his forefingers in the side locks of his adversary's hair, and then applies his thumbs to the bottom of the eye, to force it out of the socket. If ever there is a battle, in which neither of those engaged loses an eye, their faces are however generally cut in a shocking manner with the thumb nails, in the many attempts which are made at gouging. But what is worse than all, these wretches in their combat endeavour to their utmost to tear out each other's testicles. Four or five instances came within my own observation, as I passed through

through Maryland and Virginia, of men being confined in their beds from the injuries which they had received of this nature in a fight. In the Carolinas and Georgia, I have been credibly assured, that the people are still more depraved in this respect than in Virginia, and that in some particular parts of these states, every third or fourth man appears with one eye.

LETTER XV.

Description of Virginia between Richmond and the Mountains.—Fragrance of Flowers and Shrubs in the Woods.—Melody of the Birds.— Of the Birds of Virginia.—Mocking Bird— Blue Bird—Red Bird, &c.—Singular Noises of the Frogs.—Columbia.—Magazine there. —Fire Flies in the Woods.—Green Springs.— Wretchedness of the Accommodation there.— Difficulty of finding the Way through the Woods.—Serpents.—Rattle-Snake.—Copper-Snake.—Black Snake.—South-west, or Green Mountains.— Soil of them.—Mountain Torrents do great Damage.—Salubrity of the Climate.—Great Beauty of the Peasantry.— Many Gentlemen of Property living here.— Monticello,

Monticello, the Seat of Mr. Jefferson.—Vineyards.—Observations on the Culture of the Grape, and the Manufacture of Wine.

Monticello, May.

HAVING staid at Richmond somewhat longer than a week, which I found absolutely necessary, if it had only been to recruit the strength of my horses, that had been half starved in coming from Norfolk, I proceeded in a north-westerly direction towards the South-west or Green Mountains.

The country about Richmond is sandy, but not so much so, nor as flat as on the south side of James River towards the sea. It now wore a most pleasing aspect. The first week in May had arrived; the trees had obtained a considerable part of their foliage, and the air in the woods was perfumed with the fragrant smell of numberless flowers and flowering shrubs, which sprang up on all sides. The music of the birds was also delightful. It is thought that in Virginia the singing birds are finer than what are to be met with on any other part of the continent, as the climate is more congenial to them, being neither so intensely hot in summer as that of the Carolinas, nor so cold in winter as that of the more northern states. The notes of the mocking bird or Virginian nightingale are in particular most melodious.

This

This bird is of the colour and about the size of a thrush, but more slender; it imitates the song of every other bird, but with increased strength and sweetness. The bird whose song it mocks generally flies away, as if conscious of being excelled by the other, and dissatisfied with its own powers. It is a remark, however, made by Catesby, and which appears to be a very just one, that the birds in America are much inferior to those in Europe in the melody of their notes, but that they are superior in point of plumage. I know of no American bird that has the rich mellow note of our black-bird, the sprightly note of the skylark, or the sweet and plaintive one of the nightingale.

After having listened to the mocking bird, there is no novelty in hearing the song of any other bird in the country; and indeed their songs are for the most part but very simple in themselves, though combined they are pleasing.

The most remarkable for their plumage of those commonly met with are, the blue bird and the red bird. The first is about the size of a linnet; its back, head, and wings are of dark yet bright blue; when flying the plumage appears to the greatest advantage. The red bird is larger than a sky lark, though smaller than a thrush; it is of a vermilion colour, and has a small tuft on its head. A few humming birds make their appearance in summer, but their plumage is not so beautiful as those found more to the southward.

Of the other common birds there are but few worth notice. Doves and quails, or partridges as they are sometimes called, afford good diversion for the sportsman. These last birds in their habits are exactly similar to European partridges, excepting that they alight sometimes upon trees; their size is that of the quail, but they are neither the same as the English quail or the English partridge. It is the same with many other birds, as jays, robins, larks, pheasants, &c. which were called by the English settlers after the birds of the same name in England, because they bore some resemblance to them, though in fact they are materially different. In the lower parts of Virginia, and to the southward, are great numbers of large birds, called turkey buzzards, which, when mounted aloft on the wing, look like eagles. In Carolina there is a law prohibiting the killing these birds, as they feed upon putrid carcases, and therefore contribute to keep the air wholesome. There is only one bird more which I shall mention, the whipperwill, or whip-poor-will, as it is sometimes called, from the plaintive noise that it makes; to my ear it sounded wȳp-ŏ-īl. It begins to make

make this noise, which is heard a great way off, about dusk, and continues it through the greater part of the night. This bird is so very wary, and so few instances have occurred of its being seen, much less taken, that many have imagined the noise does not proceed from a bird, but from a frog, especially as it is heard most frequently in the neighbourhood of low grounds.

The frogs in America, it must here be observed, make a most singular noise, some of them absolutely whistling, whilst others croak so loudly, that it is difficult at times to tell whether the sound proceeds from a calf or a frog: I have more than once been deceived by the noise when walking in a meadow. These last frogs are called bull frogs; they mostly keep in pairs, and are never found but where there is good water; their bodies are from four to seven inches long, and their legs are in proportion; they are extremely active, and take prodigious leaps.

The first town I reached on going towards the mountains was Columbia, or Point of Fork, as it is called in the neighbourhood. It is situated about sixty miles above Richmond, at the confluence of Rivanna and Fluvanna rivers, which united form James River. This is a flourishing little place, containing about forty houses, and a warehouse for the inspection of tobacco.

tobacco. On the neck of land between the two rivers, juft oppofite to the town, is the magazine of the ftate, in which are kept twelve thoufand ftand of arms, and about thirty tons of powder. The low lands bordering upon the river in this neighbourhood are extremely valuable.

From Columbia to the Green Springs, about twenty miles farther on, the road runs almoft wholly through a pine foreft, and is very lonely. Night came on before I got to the end of it, and, as very commonly happens with travellers in this part of the world, I foon loft my way. A light, however, feen through the trees, feemed to indicate that a houfe was not far off; my fervant eagerly rode up to it, but the poor fellow's confternation was great indeed when he obferved it moving from him, prefently coming back, and then with fwiftnefs departing again into the woods. I was at a lofs for a time myfelf to account for the appearance, but after proceeding a little farther, I obferved the fame fort of light in many other places, and difmounting from my horfe to examine a bufh where one of thefe fparks appeared to have fallen, I found it proceeded from the fire fly. As the fummer came on, thefe flies appeared every night: after a light fhower in the afternoon, I have feen the woods fparkling with them in every quarter. The light

light is emitted from the tail, and the animal has the power of emitting it or not at pleasure.

After wandering about till it was near eleven o'clock, a plantation at laſt appeared, and having got freſh information reſpecting the road from the negroes in the quarter, who generally ſit up half the night, and over a fire in all ſeaſons, I again ſet out for the Green Springs. With ſome difficulty I at laſt found the way, and arrived there about midnight. The hour was ſo unſeaſonable, that the people at the tavern were very unwilling to open their doors; and it was not till I had related the hiſtory of my adventures from the laſt ſtage two or three times that they could be prevailed upon to let me in. At laſt a tall fellow in his ſhirt came grumbling to the door, and told me I might come in if I would. I had now a parley for another quarter of an hour to perſuade him to give me ſome corn for my horſes, which he was very unwilling to do; but at laſt he complied, though much againſt his inclination, and unlocked the ſtable door. Returning to the houſe, I was ſhewn into a room about ten feet ſquare, in which were two filthy beds ſwarming with bugs; the ceiling had mouldered away, and the walls admitted light in various places; it was a happy circumſtance, however, that theſe apertures were in the wall, for the window of the apartment was infufficient in itfelf to admit either light or frefh air. Here I would fain have got fomething to eat, if poffible, but not even fo much as a piece of bread was to be had; indeed, in this part of the country they feldom think of keeping bread ready made, but juft prepare fufficient for the meal about half an hour before it is wanted, and then ferve it hot. Unable therefore to procure any food, and fatigued with a long journey during a parching day, I threw myfelf down on one of the beds in my clothes, and enjoyed a profound repofe, notwithftanding the repeated onfets of the bugs and other vermin with which I was molefted.

Befides the tavern and the quarters of the flaves, there is but one more building at this place. This is a large farm houfe, where people that refort to the fprings are accommodated with lodgings, about as good as thofe at the tavern. Thefe habitations ftand in the center of a cleared fpot of land of about fifty acres, furrounded entirely with wood. The fprings are juft on the margin of the wood, at the bottom of a flope, which begins at the houfes, and are covered with a few boards, merely to keep the leaves from falling in. The waters are chalybeate, and are drank chiefly by perfons from the low country, whofe conftitutions

tions have been relaxed by the heats of summer.

Having breakfasted in the morning at this miserable little place, I proceeded on my journey up the South-west Mountain. In the course of this day's ride I observed a great number of snakes, which were now beginning to come forth from their holes. I killed a black one, that I found sleeping, stretched across the road; it was five feet in length. The black snake is more commonly met with than any other in this part of America, and is usually from four to six feet in length. In proportion to the length it is extremely slender; the back is perfectly black, the belly lead colour, inclining to white towards the throat. The bite of this snake is not poisonous, and the people in that country are not generally inclined to kill it, from its great utility in destroying rats and mice. It is wonderfully fond of milk, and is frequently found in the dairies, which in Virginia are for the most part in low situations, like cellars, as the milk could not otherwise be kept sweet for two hours together in summer time. The black snake, at the time of copulation, immediately pursues any person who comes in sight, and with such swiftness, that the best runner cannot escape from him upon even ground. Many other sorts of harmless snakes are found here, some of which are

beautifully

beautifully variegated, as the garter, the ribbon, the blueish green snake, &c. &c. Of the venomous kind, the most common are the rattle snake, and the copper or moccassin snake. The former is found chiefly on the mountains; but although frequently met with, it is very rarely that people are bitten by it; scarcely a summer, however, passes over without several being bit by the copper snake. The poison of the latter is not so subtile as that of the rattle snake, but it is very injurious, and if not attended to in time, death will certainly ensue. The rattle snake is very dull, and never attacks a person that does not molest him; but, at the same time, he will not turn out of the way to avoid any one; before he bites, he always gives notice by shaking his rattles, so that a person that hears them can readily get out of his way. The copper snake, on the contrary, is more active and treacherous, and, it is said, will absolutely put himself in the way of a person to bite him. Snakes are neither so numerous nor so venomous in the northern as in the southern states. Horses, cows, dogs, and fowl seem to have an innate sense of the danger they are exposed to from these poisonous reptiles, and will shew evident symptoms of fear on approaching near them, although they are dead; but what is remarkable, hogs, so far from being afraid of them, pursue and devour them

them with the greatest avidity, totally regardless of their bites. It is supposed that the great quantity of fat, with which they are furnished, prevents the poison from operating on their bodies as on those of other animals. Hog's lard, it might therefore reasonably be conjectured, would be a good remedy for the bite of a snake: however, I never heard of its being tried; the people generally apply herbs to the wound, the specific qualities of which are well known. It is a remarkable instance of the bounty of providence, that in all those parts of the country where these venomous reptiles abound, those herbs which are the most certain antidote to the poison are found in the greatest plenty.

The South-west Mountains run nearly parallel to the Blue Ridge, and are the first which you come to on going up the country from the sea-coast in Virginia. These mountains are not lofty, and ought indeed rather to be called hills than mountains; they are not seen till you come within a very few miles of them, and the ascent is so gradual, that you get upon their top almost without perceiving it.

The soil here changes to a deep argilaceous earth, particularly well suited to the culture of small grain and clover, and produces abundant crops. As this earth, however, does not

not absorb the water very quickly, the farmer is exposed to great losses from heavy falls of rain; the seed is liable to be washed out of the ground, so that sometimes it is found necessary to sow a field two or three different times before it becomes green; and if great care be not taken to guard such fields as lie on a declivity by proper trenches, the crops are sometimes entirely destroyed, even after they arrive at maturity; indeed, very often, notwithstanding the utmost precautions, the water departs from its usual channel, and sweeps away all before it. After heavy torrents of rain I have frequently seen all the negroes in a farm dispatched with hoes and spades to different fields, to be ready to turn the course of the water, in case it should take an improper direction. On the sides of the mountain, where the ground has been worn out with the culture of tobacco, and left waste, and the water has been suffered to run in the same channel for a length of time, it is surprising to see the depth of the ravines or gullies, as they are called, which it has formed. They are just like so many precipices, and are insurmountable barriers to the passage from one side of the mountain to the other.

Notwithstanding such disadvantages, however, the country in the neighbourhood of these mountains is far more populous than that

that which lies towards Richmond; and there are many persons that even consider it to be the garden of the United States. All the productions of the lower part of Virginia may be had here, at the same time that the heat is never found to be so oppressive; for in the hottest months in the year there is a freshness and elasticity in the air unknown in the low country. The extremes of heat and cold are found to be 90° and 60° above cipher, but it is not often that the thermometer rises above 84°, and the winters are so mild in general, that it is a very rare circumstance for the snow to lie for three days together upon the ground.

The salubrity of the climate is equal also to that of any part of the United States; and the inhabitants have in consequence a healthy ruddy appearance. The female part of the peasantry in particular is totally different from that in the low country. Instead of the pale, sickly, debilitated beings, whom you meet with there, you find amongst these mountains many a one that would be a fit subject to be painted for a Lavinia. It is really delightful to behold the groups of females, assembled here, at times, to gather the cherries and other fruits which grow in the greatest abundance in the neighbourhood of almost every habitation. Their shapes and complexions

ions are charming; and the carelessness of their dresses, which consist of little more, in common, than a simple bodice and petticoat, makes them appear even still more engaging.

The common people in this neighbourhood appeared to me to be of a more frank and open disposition, more inclined to hospitality, and to live more contentedly on what they possessed, than the people of the same class in any other part of the United States I passed through. From being able, however, to procure the necessaries of life upon very easy terms, they are rather of an indolent habit, and inclined to dissipation. Intoxication is very prevalent, and it is scarcely possible to meet with a man who does not begin the day with taking one, two, or more drams as soon as he rises. Brandy is the liquor which they principally use, and having the greatest abundance of peaches, they make it at a very trifling expence. There is hardly a house to be found with two rooms in it, but where the inhabitants have a still. The females do not fall into the habit of intoxication like the men, but in other respects they are equally disposed to pleasure, and their morals are in like manner relaxed.

Along these mountains live several gentlemen of large landed property, who farm their own estates, as in the lower parts of Virginia;

among

among the number is Mr. Jefferson*, from whose seat I date this letter. His house is about three miles distant from Charlottesville and two from Milton, which is on the head waters of Rivanna River. It is most singularly situated, being built upon the top of a small mountain, the apex of which has been cut off, so as to leave an area of about an acre and half. At present it is in an unfinished state; but if carried on according to the plan laid down, it will be one of the most elegant private habitations in the United States. A large apartment is laid out for a library and museum, meant to extend the entire breadth of the house, the windows of which are to open into an extensive green house and aviary. In the center is another very spacious apartment, of an octagon form, reaching from the front to the rear of the house, the large folding glass doors of which, at each end, open under a portico. An apartment like this, extending from front to back, is very common in a Virginian house; it is called the saloon, and during summer is the one generally preferred by the family, on account of its being more airy and spacious than any other. The house commands a magnificent prospect on one side of the blue ridge of mountains for nearly forty miles, and on the

---

* Vice-president of the United States.

opposite

oppofite one, of the low country, in appearance like an extended heath covered with trees, the tops alone of which are vifible. The mifts and vapours arifing from the low grounds give a continual variety to the fcene. The mountain whereon the houfe ftands is thickly wooded on one fide, and walks are carried round it, with different degrees of obliquity, running into each other. On the fouth fide is the garden and a large vineyard, that produces abundance of fine fruit.

Several attempts have been made in this neighbourhood to bring the manufacture of wine to perfection; none of them however have fucceeded to the wifh of the parties. A fet of gentlemen once went to the expence even of getting fix Italians over for the purpofe, but the vines which the Italians found growing here were different, as well as the foil, from what they had been in the habit of cultivating, and they were not much more fuccefsful in the bufinefs than the people of the country. We muft not, however, from hence conclude that good wine can never be manufactured upon thefe mountains. It is well known that the vines, and the mode of cultivating them, vary as much in different parts of Europe as the foil in one country differs from that in another. It will require fome time, therefore, and different experiments, to afcertain the particular kind

kind of vine, and the mode of cultivating it, beſt adapted to the ſoil of theſe mountains. This, however, having been once aſcertained, there is every reaſon to ſuppoſe that the grape may be cultivated to the greateſt perfection, as the climate is as favourable for the purpoſe as that of any country in Europe. By experiments alſo it is by no means improbable, that they will in proceſs of time learn the beſt method of converting the juice of the fruit into wine.

LETTER XVI.

Of the Country between the South-weſt and Blue Mountains. — Copper and Iron Mines. — Lynchburgh. — New London. — Armoury here. — Deſcription of the Road over the Blue Mountains. — Peaks of Otter, higheſt of the Mountains. — Suppoſed Height. — Much overrated. — German Settlers numerous beyond the Blue Mountains. — Singular Contraſt between the Country and the Inhabitants on each Side of the Mountains. — Of the Weevil. — Of the Heſſian Fly. — Bottetourt County. — Its Soil. — Salubrity of the Climate. — Medicinal Springs here. — Much frequented.

Fincaſtle, May.

THE country between the South-weſt Mountains and the Blue Ridge is very fertile, and it is much more thickly inhabited than

than the lower parts of Virginia. The climate is good, and the people have a healthy and robuſt appearance. Several valuable mines of iron and copper have been diſcovered here, for the working of ſome of which works have been eſtabliſhed; but till the country becomes more populous it cannot be expected that they will be carried on with much ſpirit.

Having croſſed the South-weſt Mountains, I paſſed along through this county to Lynchburgh, a town ſituated on the ſouth ſide of Fluvanna River, one hundred and fifty miles above Richmond. This town contains about one hundred houſes, and a warehouſe for the inſpection of tobacco, where about two thouſand hogſheads are annually inſpected. It has been built entirely within the laſt fifteen years, and is rapidly increaſing, from its advantageous ſituation for carrying on trade with the adjacent country. The boats, in which the produce is conveyed down the river, are from forty-eight to fifty-four feet long, but very narrow in proportion to their breadth. Three men are ſufficient to navigate one of theſe boats, and they can go to Richmond and back again in ten days. They fall down with the ſtream, but work their way back again with poles. The cargo carried in theſe boats is always proportionate to the depth of water in the river, which varies very much. When I paſſed it

to

to Lynchburgh, there was no difficulty in riding acrofs, yet when I got upon the oppofite banks I obferved great quantities of weeds hanging upon the trees, confiderably above my head though on horfeback, evidently left there by a flood. This flood happened in the preceding September, when the waters rofe fifteen feet above their ufual level.

A few miles from Lynchburgh, towards the Blue Mountains, is a fmall town called New London, in which there is a magazine, and alfo an armoury, erected during the war. About fifteen men were here employed, as I paffed through, repairing old arms and furbifhing up others; and indeed, from the flovenly manner in which they keep their arms, I fhould imagine that the fame number muft be conftantly employed all the year round. At one end of the room lay the mufquets, to the amount of about five thoufand, all together in a large heap, and at the oppofite end lay a pile of leathern accoutrements, abfolutely rotting for want of common attention. All the armouries throughout the United States are kept much in the fame ftyle.

Between this place and the Blue Mountains the country is rough and hilly, and but very thinly inhabited. The few inhabitants, however, met with here are, uncommonly robuft

and

and tall; it is rare to see a man amongst them who is not six feet high. These people entertain a high opinion of their own superiority in point of bodily strength over the inhabitants of the low country. A similar race of men is found all along the Blue Mountains.

The Blue Ridge is thickly covered with large trees to the very summit; some of the mountains are rugged and extremely stony, others are not so, and on these last the soil is found to be rich and fertile. It is only in particular places that this ridge of mountains can be crossed, and at some of the gaps the ascent is steep and difficult; but at the place where I crossed it, which was near the Peak of Otter, on the south side, instead of one great mountain to pass over, as might be imagined from an inspection of the map, there is a succession of small hills, rising imperceptibly one above the other, so that you get upon the top of the ridge before you are aware of it.

The Peaks of Otter are the highest mountains in the Blue Ridge, and, measured from their bases, are supposed to be more lofty than any others in North America. According to Mr. Jefferson, whose authority has been quoted nearly by every person that has written on the subject since the publication of his Notes on Virginia, the principal peak is about

four

four thousand feet in perpendicular height; but it must be observed, that Mr. Jefferson does not say that he measured the height himself; on the contrary, he acknowledges that the height of the mountains in America has never yet been ascertained with any degree of exactness; it is only from certain data, from which he says a tolerable conjecture may be formed, that he supposes this to be the height of the loftiest peak. Positively to assert that this peak is not so high, without having measured it in any manner, would be absurd; as I did not measure it, I do not therefore pretend to contradict Mr. Jefferson; I have only to say, that the most elevated of the peaks of Otter appeared to me but a very insignificant mountain in comparison with Snowden, in Wales; and every person that I conversed with that had seen both, and I conversed with many, made the same remark. Now the highest peak of Snowden is found by triangular admeasurement to be no more than three thousand five hundred and sixty-eight feet high, reckoning from the quay at Carnarvon. None of the other mountains in the Blue Ridge are supposed, from the same data, to be more than two thousand feet in perpendicular height.

Beyond the Blue Ridge, after crossing by this route near the Peaks of Otter, I met with but very few settlements till I drew near to Fincastle, in Bottetourt County. This town stands about twenty miles distant from the mountain, and about fifteen south of Fluvanna River. It was only begun about the year 1790, yet it already contains sixty houses, and is most rapidly increasing. The improvement of the adjacent country has likewise been very rapid, and land now bears nearly the same price that it does in the neighbourhood of York and Lancaster, in Pennsylvania. The inhabitants consist principally of Germans, who have extended their settlements from Pennsylvania along the whole of that rich track of land which runs through the upper part of Maryland, and from thence behind the Blue Mountains to the most southern parts of Virginia. These people, as I before mentioned, keep very much together, and are never to be found but where the land is remarkably good. It is singular, that although they form three fourths of the inhabitants on the western side of the Blue Ridge, yet not one of them is to be met with on the eastern side, notwithstanding that land is to be purchased in the neighbourhood of the South-west Mountains for one fourth of what is paid for it in Bottetourt County. They have many times, I am told, crossed the Blue Ridge to examine the land, but the red soil which they

they found there was different from what they had been accustomed to, and the injury it was exposed to from the mountain torrents always appeared to them an insuperable objection to settling in that part of the country. The difference indeed between the country on the eastern and on the western side of the Blue Ridge, in Bottetourt County, is astonishing, when it is considered that both are under the same latitude, and that this difference is perceptible within the short distance of thirty miles.

On the eastern side of the ridge cotton grows extremely well; and in winter the snow scarcely ever remains more than a day or two upon the ground. On the other side cotton never comes to perfection, the winters are severe, and the fields covered with snow for weeks together. In every farm yard you see sleighs or sledges, carriages used to run upon the snow. Wherever these carriages are met with, it may be taken for granted that the winter lasts in that part of the country for a considerable length of time, for the people would never go to the expence of building them, without being tolerably certain that they would be useful. On the eastern side of the Blue Ridge, in Virginia, not one of these carriages is to be met with.

It has already been mentioned, that the

predominant soil to the eastward of the Blue Ridge is a red earth, and that it is always a matter of some difficulty to lay down a piece of land in grass, on account of the rains, which are apt to wash away the seeds, together with the mould on the surface. In Bottetourt County, on the contrary, the soil consists chiefly of a rich brown mould, and throws up white clover spontaneously. To have a rich meadow, it is only necessary to leave a piece of ground to the hand of nature for one year. Again, on the eastern side of the Blue Mountains, scarcely any limestone is to be met with; on the opposite one, a bed of it runs entirely through the country, so that by some it is emphatically called the limestone county. In sinking wells, they have always to dig fifteen or twenty feet through a solid rock to get at the water.

Another circumstance may also be mentioned, as making a material difference between the country on one side of the Blue Ridge and that on the other, namely, that behind the mountains the weevil is unknown. The weevil is a small insect of the moth kind, which deposits its eggs in the cavity of the grain, and particularly in that of wheat; and if the crops are stacked or laid up in the barn in sheaves, these eggs are there hatched, and the grain is in consequence totally destroyed.

ſtroyed. To guard againſt this in the lower parts of Virginia, and the other ſtates where the weevil is common, they always threſh out the grain as ſoon as the crops are brought in, and leave it in the chaff, which creates a degree of heat ſufficient to deſtroy the inſect, at the ſame time that it does not injure the wheat. This inſect has been known in America but a very few years; according to the general opinion, it originated on the eaſtern ſhore of Maryland, where a perſon, in expectation of a great riſe in the price of wheat, kept over all his crops for the ſpace of ſix years, when they were found full of theſe inſects; from thence they have ſpread gradually over different parts of the country. For a conſiderable time the Patowmac River formed a barrier to their progreſs, and while the crops were entirely deſtroyed in Maryland, they remained ſecure in Virginia; but theſe inſects at laſt found their way acroſs the river. The Blue Mountains at preſent ſerve as a barrier, and ſecure the country to the weſtward from their depredations *.

Botte-

* There is another inſect, which in a ſimilar manner made its appearance, and afterwards ſpread through a great part of the country, very injurious alſo to the crops. It is called the Heſſian fly, from having been brought over, as is ſuppoſed, in ſome forage belonging to the Heſſian troops, during the war. This inſect lodges itſelf in different parts of the ſtalk, while green,

Bottetourt County is entirely surrounded by mountains; it is also crossed by various ridges of mountains in different directions, a circumstance which renders the climate particuarly agreeable. It appears to me, that there is no part of America where the climate would be more congenial to the constitution of a native of Great Britain or Ireland. The frost in winter is more regular, but not severer than commonly takes place in those islands. In summer the heat is, perhaps, somewhat greater; but there is not a night in the year that a blanket is not found very comfortable. Before ten o'clock in the morning the heat is greatest; at that hour a breeze generally springs up from the mountains, and renders the air agreeable the whole day. Fever and ague are disorders unknown here, and the air is so salu-

green, and makes such rapid devastations, that a crop which appears in the best possible state will, perhaps, be totally destroyed in the course of two or three days. In Maryland, they say, that if the land is very highly manured, the Hessian fly never attacks the grain; they also say, that crops raised upon land that has been worked for a long time are much less exposed to injury from these insects than the crops raised upon new land. If this is really the case, the appearance of the Hessian fly should be considered as a circumstance rather beneficial than otherwise to the country, as it will induce the inhabitants to relinquish that ruinous practice of working the same piece of ground year after year till it is entirely worn out, and then leaving it waste, instead of taking some pains to improve it by manure. This fly is not known at present south of the Patowmac River, nor behind the Blue Ridge.

brious

brious, that perfons who come hither afflicted with it from the low country, towards the fea, get rid of it in a very fhort time.

In the weftern part of the county are feveral medicinal fprings, whereto numbers of people refort towards the latter end of fummer, as much for the fake of efcaping the heat in the low country, as for drinking the waters. Thofe moft frequented are called the Sweet Springs, and are fituated at the foot of the Alleghany Mountains. During the laft feafon upwards of two hundred perfons reforted to them with fervants and horfes. The accommodations at the fprings are moft wretched at prefent; but a fet of gentlemen from South Carolina have, I underftand, fince I was there, purchafed the place, and are going to erect feveral commodious dwellings in the neighbourhood, for the reception of company. Befides thefe fprings there are others in Jackfon's Mountains, a ridge which runs between the Blue Mountains and the Alleghany. One of the fprings here is warm, and another quite hot; a few paces from the latter a fpring of common water iffues from the earth, but which, from the contraft, is generally thought to be as remarkable for its coldnefs as the water of the adjoining one is for its heat: there is alfo a fulphur fpring near thefe; leaves of trees falling into it become thickly incrufted with fulphur sulphur in a very short time, aud silver is turned black almost immediately. At a future period the medicinal qualities of all these springs will probably be accurately ascertained; at present they are but very little known. As for the relief obtained by those persons that frequent the Sweet Springs in particular, it is strongly conjectured that they are more indebted for it to the change of the climate than to the rare qualities of the water.

LETTER XVII.

Description of the celebrated Rock Bridge, and of an immense Cavern.—Description of the Shenandoa Valley.—Inhabitants mostly Germans.—Soil and Climate.—Observations on American Landscapes.—Mode of cutting down Trees.—High Road to Kentucky, behind Blue Mountains.— Much frequented.—Uncouth, inquisitive People.—Lexington.—Staunton.— Military Titles very common in America.— Causes thereof.—Winchester.

Winchester, May.

AFTER remaining a considerable time in Bottetourt County, I again crossed Fluvanna River into the county of Rockbridge, so called from the remarkable natural bridge of

of rock that is in it. This bridge ſtands about ten miles from Fluvanna River, and nearly the ſame diſtance from the Blue Ridge. It extends acroſs a deep cleft in a mountain, which, by ſome great convulſion of nature, has been ſplit aſunder from top to bottom, and it ſeems to have been left there purpoſely to afford a paſſage from one ſide of the chaſm to the other. The cleft or chaſm is about two miles long, and is in ſome places upwards of three hundred feet deep; the depth varies according to the height of the mountain, being deepeſt where the mountain is moſt lofty. The breadth of the chaſm alſo varies in different places; but in every part it is uniformly wider at top than towards the bottom. That the two ſides of the chaſm were once united appears very evident, not only from projecting rocks on the one ſide correſponding with ſuitable cavities on the other, but alſo from the different ſtrata of earth, ſand, clay, &c. being exactly ſimilar from top to bottom on both ſides; but by what great agent they were ſeparated, whether by fire or by water, remains hidden amongſt thoſe arcana of nature which we vainly endeavour to develope.

The arch conſiſts of a ſolid maſs of ſtone, or of ſeveral ſtones cemented ſo ſtrongly together, that they appear but as one. This
maſs,

mass, it is to be supposed, at the time that the hill was rent asunder, was drawn across the fissure from adhering closely to one side, and being loosened from its bed of earth at the opposite one. It seems as probable, I think, that the mass of stone forming the arch was thus forcibly plucked from one side, and drawn across the fissure, as that the hill should have remained disunited at this one spot from top to bottom, and that a passage should afterwards have been forced through it by water. The road leading to the bridge runs through a thick wood, and up a hill, having ascended which, nearly to the top, you pause for a moment at finding a sudden discontinuance of the trees at one side; but the amazement which fills the mind is great indeed, when, on going a few paces towards the part which appears thus open, you find yourself on the brink of a tremendous precipice. You involuntarily draw back, stare around, then again come forward to satisfy yourself that what you have seen is real, and not the illusions of fancy. You now perceive, that you are upon the top of the bridge, to the very edge of which, on one side, you may approach with safety, and look down into the abyss, being protected from falling by a parapet of fixed rocks. The walls, as it were, of the bridge at this side are so perpendicular, that a person a person leaning over the parapet of rock might let fall a plummet from the hand to the very bottom of the chasm. On the opposite side this is not the case, nor is there any parapet; but from the edge of the road, which runs over the bridge, is a gradual slope to the brink of the chasm, upon which it is somewhat dangerous to venture. This slope is thickly covered with large trees, principally cedars and pines. The opposite side was also well furnished with trees formerly, but all those that grew near the edge of the bridge have been cut down by different people, for the sake of seeing them tumble to the bottom. Before the trees were destroyed in this manner, you might have passed over the bridge, without having had any idea of being upon it; for the breadth of it is no less than eighty feet. The road runs nearly in the middle, and is frequented daily by waggons.

At the distance of a few yards from the bridge, a narrow path appears, winding along the sides of the fissure, amidst immense rocks and trees, down to the bottom of the bridge. Here the stupendous arch appears in all its glory, and seems to touch the very skies. To behold it without rapture, indeed, is impossible; and the more critically it is examined, the more beautiful and the more surprising does it appear. The height of the bridge to the

the top of the parapet is two hundred and thirteen feet by admeasurement with a line, the thickness of the arch forty feet, the span of the arch at top ninety feet, and the distance between the abutments at bottom fifty feet. The abutments consist of a solid mass of limestone on either side, and, together with the arch, seem as if they had been chiseled out by the hand of art. A small stream, called Cedar Creek, running at the bottom of the fissure, over bed of rocks, adds much to the beauty of the scene.

The fissure takes a very sudden turn just above the bridge, according to the course of the stream, so that when you stand below, and look under the arch, the view is intercepted at the distance of about fifty yards from the bridge. Mr. Jefferson's statement, in his Notes, that the fissure continues strait, terminating with a pleasing view of the North Mountains, is quite erroneous. The sides of the chasm are thickly covered in every part with trees, excepting where the huge rocks of limestone appear.

Besides this view from below, the bridge is seen to very great advantage from a pinnacle of rocks, about fifty feet below the top of the fissure; for here not only the arch is seen in all its beauty, but the spectator is impressed in the most forcible manner with ideas of its

grandeur

grandeur, from being enabled at the same time to look down into the profound gulph over which it passes.

About fifty miles to the northward of the Rock Bridge, and also behind the Blue Mountains, there is another very remarkable natural curiosity; this is a large cavern, known in the neighbourhood by the name of Maddison's Cave. It is in the heart of a mountain, about two hundred feet high, and which is so steep on one side, that a person standing on the top of it, might easily throw a pebble into the river, which flows round the base; the opposite side of it is, however, very easy of ascent, and on this side the path leading to the cavern runs, excepting for the last twenty yards, when it suddenly turns along the steep part of the mountain, which is extremely rugged, and covered with immense rocks and trees from top to bottom. The mouth of the cavern, on this steep side, about two thirds of the way up, is guarded by a huge pendent stone, which seems ready to drop every instant, and it is hardly possible to stoop under it, without reflecting with a certain degree of awe, that were it to drop, nothing could save you from perishing within the dreary walls of that mansion to which it affords an entrance.

Preparatory to entering, the guide, whom I had procured from a neighbouring houfe, lighted the ends of three or four fplinters of pitch pine, a large bundle of which he had brought with him: they burn out very faft, but while they laft are moft excellent torches. The fire he brought along with him, by means of a bit of green hiccory wood, which, when once lighted, will burn flowly without any blaze till the whole is confumed.

The firft apartment you enter is about twenty-five feet high, and fifteen broad, and extends a confiderable way to the right and left, the floor afcending towards the former; here it is very moift, from the quantity of water continually trickling from the roof. Fahrenheit's thermometer, which ftood at 67° in the air, fell to 61° in this room. A few yards to the left, on the fide oppofite to you on entering, a paffage prefents itfelf, which leads to a fort of anti-chamber as it were, from whence you proceed into the found room, fo named from the prodigious reverberation of the found of a voice or mufical inftrument at the infide. This room is about twenty feet fquare; it is arched at top, and the fides of it, as well as of that apartment which you firft enter, are beautifully ornamented with ftalactites. Returning from hence
into

into the antichamber, and afterwards taking two or three turns to the right and left, you enter a long paſſage about thirteen feet wide, and perhaps about fifteen in height perpendicularly; but if it was meaſured from the floor to the higheſt part of the roof obliquely, the diſtance would be found much greater, as the walls on both ſides ſlope very conſiderably, and finally meet at top. This paſſage deſcends very rapidly, and is, I ſhould ſuppoſe, about ſixty yards long. Towards the end it narrows conſiderably, and terminates in a pool of clear water, about three or four feet deep. How far this pool extends it is impoſſible to ſay. A canoe was once brought down by a party, for the purpoſe of examination, but they ſaid, that after proceeding a little way upon the water the canoe would not float, and they were forced to return. Their fears, moſt probably, led them to fancy it was ſo. I fired a piſtol with a ball over the water, but the report was echoed from the after part of the cavern, and not from that part beyond the water, ſo that I ſhould not ſuppoſe the paſſage extended much farther than could be traced with the eye. The walls of this paſſage conſiſt of a ſolid rock of limeſtone on each ſide, which appears to have been ſeparated by ſome convulſion. The floor is of a deep ſandy earth, and it has repeatedly been dug up for

the

the purpofe of getting falt-petre, with which the earth is ftrongly impregnated. The earth, after being dug up, is mixed with water, and when the groffer particles fall to the bottom, the water is drawn off and evaporated; from the refidue the faltpetre is procured. There are many other caverns in this neighbourhood, and alfo farther to the weftward, in Virginia; from all of them great quantities of faltpetre are thus obtained. The gunpowder made with it, in the back country, forms a principal article of commerce, and is fent to Philadelphia in exchange for European manufactures.

About two thirds of the way down this long paffage, juft defcribed, is a large aperture in the wall on the right, leading to another apartment, the bottom of which is about ten feet below the floor of the paffage, and it is no eafy matter to get down into it, as the fides are very fteep and extremely flippery. This is the largeft and moft beautiful room in the whole cavern; it is fomewhat of an oval form, about fixty feet in length, thirty in breadth, and in fome parts nearly fifty feet high. The petrifactions formed by the water dropping from above are moft beautiful, and hang down from the ceiling in the form of elegant drapery, the folds of which are fimilar to what thofe of large blankets or carpets would

would be if suspended by one corner in a lofty room. If struck with a stick a deep hollow sound is produced, which echoes through the vaults of the cavern. In other parts of this room the petrifactions have commenced at the bottom, and formed in pillars of different heights; some of them reach nearly to the roof. If you go to a remote part of this apartment, and leave a person with a lighted torch moving about amidst these pillars, a thousand imaginary forms present themselves, and you might almost fancy yourself in the infernal regions, with spectres and monsters on every side. The floor of this room slopes down gradually from one end to the other, and terminates in a pool of water, which appears to be on a level with that at the end of the long passage; from their situation it is most probable that they communicate together. The thermometer which I had with me stood, in the remotest part of this chamber, at 55°. From hence we returned to the mouth of the cavern, and on coming into the light it appeared as if we really had been in the infernal regions, for our faces, hands, and clothes were smutted all over, every part of the cave being covered with soot from the smoke of the pine torches which are so often carried in. The smoke from the pitch pine is particularly thick and heavy. Before this cave was much visited,

visited, and the walls blackened by the smoke, its beauty, I was told by some of the old inhabitants, was great indeed, for the petrifactions on the roof and walls are all of the dead white kind.

The country immediately behind the Blue Mountains, between Bottetourt County and the Patowmac River, is agreeably diversified with hill and dale, and abounds with extensive tracts of rich land. The low grounds bordering upon the Shenandoah River, which runs contiguous to the Blue Ridge for upwards of one hundred miles, are in particular distinguished for their fertility. These low grounds are those which, strictly speaking, constitute the Shenandoah Valley, though in general the country lying for several miles distant from the river, and in some parts very hilly, goes under that name. The natural herbage is not so fine here as in Bottetourt County, but when clover is once sown it grows most luxuriantly; wheat also is produced in as plentiful crops as in any part of the United States. Tobacco is not raised excepting for private use, and but little Indian corn is sown, as it is liable to be injured by the nightly frosts, which are common in the spring.

The climate here is not so warm as in the lower parts of the country, on the eastern side
of

of the mountains; but it is by no means so temperate as in Bottetourt County, which, from being environed with ridges of mountains, is constantly refreshed with cooling breezes during summer, and in the winter is sheltered from the keen blasts from the north west.

The whole of this country, to the west of the mountains, is increasing most rapidly in population. In the neighbourhood of Winchester it is so thickly settled, and consequently so much cleared, that wood is now beginning to be thought valuable; the farmers are obliged frequently to send ten or fifteen miles even for their fence rails. It is only, however, in this particular neighbourhood that the country is so much improved; in other places there are immense tracts of woodlands still remaining, and in general the hills are all left uncleared. The hills being thus left covered with trees is a circumstance which adds much to the beauty of the country, and intermixed with extensive fields clothed with the richest verdure, and watered by the numerous branches of the Shenandoah River, a variety of pleasing landscapes are presented to the eye in almost every part of the route from Bottetourt to the Patowmac, many of which are considerably heightened by the appearance of the Blue Mountains in the back ground.

With regard to these landscapes however, and to American landscapes in general, it is to be observed, that their beauty is much impaired by the unpicturesque appearance of the angular fences, and of the stiff wooden houses, which have at a little distance a heavy, dull, and gloomy aspect. The stumps of the trees also, on land newly cleared, are most disagreeable objects, wherewith the eye is continually assailed. When trees are felled in America, they are never cut down close to the ground, but the trunks are left standing two or three feet high; for it is found that a woodman can cut down many more in a day, standing with a gentle inclination of the body, than if he were to stoop so as to apply his axe to the bottom of the tree; it does not make any difference either to the farmer, whether the stump is left two or three feet high, or whether it is cut down level with the ground, as in each case it would equally be a hindrance to the plough. These stumps usually decay in the course of seven or eight years; sometimes however sooner, sometimes later, according to the quality of the timber. They never throw up suckers, as stumps of trees would do in England if left in that manner.

The cultivated lands in this country are mostly parcelled out in small portions; there are no persons here, as on the other side of the mountains,

mountains, poffeffing large farms; nor are there any eminently diftinguifhed by their education or knowledge from the reft of their fellow citizens. Poverty alfo is as much unknown in this country as great wealth. Each man owns the houfe he lives in and the land which he cultivates, and every one appears to be in a happy ftate of mediocrity, and unambitious of a more elevated fituation than what he himfelf enjoys.

The free inhabitants confift for the moft part of Germans, who here maintain the fame character as in Pennfylvania and the other ftates where they have fettled. About one fixth of the people, on an average, are flaves, but in fome of the counties the proportion is much lefs; in Rockbridge the flaves do not amount to more than an eleventh, and in Shenandoah County not to more than a twentieth part of the whole.

Between Fincaftle and the Patowmac there are feveral towns, as Lexington, Staunton, Newmarket, Woodftock, Winchefter, Strafburgh, and fome others. Thefe towns all ftand on the great road, running north and fouth behind the Blue Mountains, and which is the high road from the northern ftates to Kentucky.

As I paffed along it, I met with great numbers of people from Kentucky and the new ftate ſtate of Tenaſſee going towards Philadelphia and Baltimore, and with many others going in a contrary direction, "to explore," as they call it, that is, to ſearch for lands conveniently ſituated for new ſettlements in the weſtern country. Theſe people all travel on horſeback, with piſtols or ſwords, and a large blanket folded up under their ſaddle, which laſt they uſe for ſleeping in when obliged to paſs the night in the woods. There is but little occaſion for arms now that peace has been made with the Indians; but formerly it uſed to be a very ſerious undertaking to go by this route to Kentucky, and travellers were always obliged to go forty or fifty in a party, and well prepared for defence. It would be ſtill dangerous for any perſon to venture ſingly; but if five or ſix travel together, they are perfectly ſecure. There are houſes now ſcattered along nearly the whole way from Fincaſtle to Lexington in Kentucky, ſo that it is not neceſſary to ſleep more than two or three nights in the woods in going there. Of all the uncouth human beings I met with in America, theſe people from the weſtern country were the moſt ſo; their curioſity was boundleſs. Frequently have I been ſtopped abruptly by one of them in a ſolitary part of the road, and in ſuch a manner, that had it been in another country, I ſhould have imagined it was a highwayman

LEXINGTON.

that was going to demand my purse, and without any further preface, asked where I came from? if I was acquainted with any news? where bound to? and finally, my name? —" Stop, Mister! why I guess now you be "coming from the new state." " No, Sir,"— " Why then I guess as how you be coming "from Kentuc*." " No, Sir."—" Oh! why "then, pray now where might you be coming "from?" " From the low country."—" Why "you must have heard all the news then; pray "now, Mister, what might the price of bacon "be in those parts?" " Upon my word, my "friend, I can't inform you."—" Aye, aye; I "see, Mister, you be'n't one of us; pray now, "Mister, what might your name be?"— A stranger going the same way is sure of having the company of these worthy people, so desirous of information, as far as the next tavern, where he is seldom suffered to remain for five minutes, till he is again assailed by a fresh set with the same questions.

The first town you come to, going northward from Bottetourt County, is Lexington, a neat little place, that did contain about one hundred houses, a court-house, and gaol; but the greater part of it was destroyed by fire just before I got there. Great numbers of Irish are

* Kentucky.

settled

settled in this place. Thirty miles farther on stands Staunton. This town carries on a considerable trade with the back country, and contains nearly two hundred dwellings, mostly built of stone, together with a church. This was the first place on the entire road from Lynchburgh, one hundred and fifty miles distant, and which I was about ten days in travelling, where I was not able to get a bit of fresh meat, excepting indeed on passing the Blue Mountains, where they brought me some venison that had been just killed. I went on fifty miles further, from Staunton, before I got any again. Salted pork, boiled with turnip tops by way of greens, or fried bacon, or fried salted fish, with warm sallad, dressed with vinegar and the melted fat which remains in the frying-pan after dressing the bacon, is the only food to be got at most of the taverns in this country; in spring it is the constant food of the people in the country; and indeed, throughout the whole year, I am told, salted meat is what they most generally use.

In every part of America a European is surprised at finding so many men with military titles, and still more so at seeing such numbers of them employed in capacities apparently so inconsistent with their rank; for it is nothing uncommon to see a captain in the shape of a waggoner, a colonel the driver of a stage

stage coach, or a general dealing out penny ribbon behind his counter; but no where, I believe, is there such a superfluity of these military personages as in the little town of Staunton; there is hardly a decent person in it, excepting lawyers and medical men, but what is a colonel, a major, or a captain. This is to be accounted for as follows: in America, every freeman from the age of sixteen to fifty years, whose occupation does not absolutely forbid it, must enrol himself in the militia. In Virginia alone, the militia amounts to about sixty-two thousand men, and it is divided into four divisions and seventeen brigades, to each of which there is a general and other officers. Were there no officers therefore, excepting those actually belonging to the militia, the number must be very great; but independent of the militia, there are also volunteer corps in most of the towns, which have likewise their respective officers. In Staunton there are two of these corps, one of cavalry, the other of artillery. These are formed chiefly of men who find a certain degree of amusement in exercising as soldiers, and who are also induced to associate, by the vanity of appearing in regimentals. The militia is not assembled oftener than once in two or three months, and as it rests with every individual to provide himself with arms and accoutrements, and no

stress

ſtreſs being laid upon coming in uniform, the appearance of the men is not very military. Numbers alſo of the officers of theſe volunteer corps, and of the militia, are reſigning every day; and if a man has been a captain or a colonel but one day either in the one body or the other, it ſeems to be an eſtabliſhed rule that he is to have nominal rank the reſt of his life. Added to all, there are ſeveral officers of the old continental army neither in the militia nor in the volunteer corps.

Wincheſter ſtands one hundred miles to the northward of Staunton, and is the largeſt town in the United States on the weſtern ſide of the Blue Mountains. The houſes are eſtimated at three hundred and fifty, and the inhabitants at two thouſand. There are four churches in this town, which, as well as the houſes, are plainly built. The ſtreets are regular, but very narrow. There is nothing particularly deſerving of attention in this place, nor indeed in any of the other ſmall towns which have been mentioned, none of them containing more than ſeventy houſes each.

LETTER XVIII.

Description of the Passage of Patowmac and Shenandoah Rivers through a Break in the Blue Mountains.—Some Observations on Mr. Jefferson's Account of the Scene.—Summary Account of Maryland.—Arrival at Philadelphia.—Remarks on the Climate of the United States.—State of the City of Philadelphia during the Heat of Summer.—Difficulty of preserving Butter, Milk, Meat, Fish, &c.—General Use of Ice.—Of the Winds.—State of Weather in America depends greatly upon them.

Philadelphia, June.

HAVING traversed, in various directions, the country to the west of the Blue Mountains in Virginia, I came to the Patowmac, at the place where that river passes through the Blue Ridge, which Mr. Jefferson, in his Notes upon Virginia, has represented as one of the most "stupendous scenes in nature, and worth "a voyage across the Atlantic." The approach towards the place is wild and romantic. After crossing a number of small hills, which rise one above the other in succession, you at last perceive the break in the Blue Ridge; at the same time the road suddenly turning, winds

down

down a long and steep hill, shaded with lofty trees, whose branches unite over your head. On one side of the road there are large heaps of rocks above you, which seem to threaten destruction to any one that passes under them; on the other, a deep precipice presents itself, at the bottom of which is heard the roaring of the waters, that are concealed from the eye by the thickness of the foliage. Towards the end of this hill, about sixty feet above the level of the water, stands a tavern and a few houses, and from some fields in the rear of them the passage of the river through the mountain is, I think, seen to the best advantage.

The Patowmac on the left comes winding along through a fertile country towards the mountain; on the right flows the Shenandoah: uniting together at the foot of the mountain, they roll on through the gap; then suddenly expanding to the breadth of about four hundred yards, they pass on towards the sea, and are finally lost to the view amidst surrounding hills. The rugged appearance of the sides of the mountain towards the river, and the large rocks that lie scattered about at the bottom, many of which have evidently been split asunder by some great convulsion, " are monuments," as Mr. Jefferson observes, of the " war that has taken place at this spot be-
" tween

"tween rivers and mountains; and at first "sight they lead us into an opinion that "mountains were created before rivers be- "gan to flow; that the waters of the Pa- "towmac and Shenandoah were dammed up "for a time by the Blue Ridge, but continu- "ing to rife, that they at length broke through "at this spot, and tore the mountain asunder "from its summit to its base." Certain it is, that if the Blue Ridge could be again made entire, an immense body of water would be formed on the western side of it, by the Shenandoah and Patowmac rivers, and this body of water would be deepest, and consequently would act with more force in sapping a passage for itself through the mountain at the identical spot where the gap now is than at any other, for this is the lowest spot in a very extended tract of country. A glance at the map will be sufficient to satisfy any person on this point; it will at once be seen, that all the rivers of the adjacent country bend their courses hitherwards. Whether the ridge, however, was left originally entire, or whether a break was left in it for the passage of the rivers, it is impossible at this day to ascertain; but it is very evident that the sides of the gap have been reduced to their present rugged state by some great inundation. Indeed, supposing that the Patowmac and Shenandoah ever rofe during a flood, a common circumftance in fpring and autumn, only equally high with what James River did in 1795, that is fifteen feet above their ufual level, fuch a circumftance might have occafioned a very material alteration in the appearance of the gap.

The Blue Ridge, on each fide of the Patowmac, is formed, from the foundation to the fummit, of large rocks depofited in beds of rich foft earth. This earth is very readily wafhed away, and in that cafe the rocks confequently become loofe; indeed, they are frequently loofened even by heavy fhowers of rain. A proof of this came within my own obfervation, which I fhall never forget. It had been raining exceffively hard the whole morning of that day on which I arrived at this place; the evening however was very fine, and being anxious to behold the fcene in every point of view, I croffed the river, and afcended the mountain at a fteep part on the oppofite fide, where there was no path, and many large projecting rocks. I had walked up about fifty yards, when a large ftone that I fet my foot upon, and which appeared to me perfectly firm, all at once gave way; it had been loofened by the rain, and brought down fuch a heap of others with it in its fall, with fuch a tremendous noife at the fame time,

that

that I thought the whole mountain was coming upon me, and expected every moment to be dashed to pieces. I slid down about twenty feet, and then luckily caught hold of the branch of a tree, by which I clung; but the stones still continued to roll down heap after heap; several times, likewise, after all had been still for a minute or two, they again began to fall with increased violence. In this state of suspense I was kept for a considerable time, not knowing but that some stone larger than the rest might give way, and carry down with it even the tree by which I held. Unacquainted also with the paths of the mountain, there seemed to me to be no other way of getting down, excepting over the fallen stones, a way which I contemplated with horror. Night however was coming on very fast; it was absolutely necessary to quit the situation I was in, and fortunately I got to the bottom without receiving any further injury than two or three slight contusions on my hips and elbows. The people congratulated me when I came back on my escape, and informed me, that the stones very commonly gave way in this manner after heavy falls of rain; but on the dissolution of a large body of snow, immense rocks, they said, would sometimes roll down with a crash that might be heard for miles. The consequences then of a large

rock

rock towards the bottom of the mountain being undermined by a flood, and giving way, may be very readily imagined: the rock above it, robbed of its support, would also fall; this would bring down with it numbers of others with which it was connected, and thus a disruption would be produced from the base to the very summit of the mountain.

The passage of the rivers through the ridge at this place is certainly a curious scene, and deserving of attention; but I am far from thinking with Mr. Jefferson, that it is "one of the most stupendous scenes in nature, and worth a voyage across the Atlantic;" nor has it been my lot to meet with any person that had been a spectator of the scene, after reading his description of it, but what also differed with him very materially in opinion. To find numberless scenes more stupendous, it would be needless to go farther than Wales. A river, it is true, is not to be met with in that country, equal in size to the Patowmac; but many are to be seen there rushing over their stony beds with much more turbulence and impetuosity than either the Patowmac or Shenandoah: the rocks, the precipices, and the mountains of the Blue Ridge at this place are diminutive and uninteresting also, compared with those which abound in that country. Indeed, from every part of Mr. Jefferson's description, it appears as if he had beheld the scene, not in its present state, but at the very moment when the disruption happened, and when every thing was in a state of tumult and confusion.

After crossing the Patowmac, I passed on to Frederic in Maryland, which has already been mentioned, and from thence to Baltimore. The country between Frederic and Baltimore is by no means so rich as that west of the Blue Ridge, but it is tolerably well cultivated. Iron and copper are found here in many places. No works of any consequence have as yet been established for the manufacture of copper, but there are several extensive iron works. The iron is of a remarkably tough quality; indeed, throughout the states of Maryland, Virginia, and Pennsylvania, it is generally so; and the utensils made of it, as pots, kettles, &c. though cast much thinner than usual in England, will admit of being pitched into the carts, and thrown about, without any danger of being broken. The forges and furnaces are all worked by negroes, who seem to be particularly suited to such an occupation, not only on account of their sable complexions, but because they can sustain a much greater degree of heat than white persons without any inconvenience. In the hottest days in summer they are never without fires in their huts.

The farms and plantations in Maryland confift, in general, of from one hundred to one thoufand acres. In the upper parts of the ftate, towards the mountains, the land is divided into fmall portions. Grain is what is principally cultivated, and there are few flaves. In the lower parts of the ftate, and in this part of the country between Frederic and Baltimore, the plantations are extenfive; large quantities of tobacco are raifed, and the labour is performed almoft entirely by negroes. The perfons refiding upon thefe large plantations live very fimilar to the planters in Virginia: all of them have their ftewards and overfeers, and they give themfelves but little trouble about the management of the lands. As in Virginia, the clothing for the flaves, and moft of the implements for hufbandry, are manufactured on each eftate. The quarters of the flaves are fituated in the neighbourhood of the principal dwelling houfe, which gives the refidence of every planter the appearance of a little village, juft the fame as in Virginia. The houfes are for the moft part built of wood, and painted with Spanifh brown; and in front there is generally a long porch, painted white.

From Baltimore I returned to Philadelphia, where I arrived on the fourteenth day of June, after having been abfent about three months.

During

During the whole of that period the weather had been extremely variable, scarcely ever remaining alike four days together. As early as the fourteenth of March, in Pennsylvania, Fahrenheit's thermometer stood at 65° at noon day, though not more than a week before it had been so low as 14°. At the latter end of the month, in Maryland, I scarcely ever observed it higher than 50° at noon: the evenings were always cold, and the weather was squally and wet. In the northern neck of Virginia, for two or three days together, during the second week in April, it rose from 80° to 84°, in the middle of the day; but on the wind suddenly shifting, it fell again, and remained below 70° for some days. As I passed along through the lower parts of Virginia, I frequently afterwards observed it as high as 80° during the month of April; but on no day in the month of May, previous to the fourteenth, did it again rise to the same height; indeed, so far from it, many of the days were too cold to be without fires; and on the night of the ninth instant, when I was in the neighbourhood of the South-west Mountains, so sharp a frost took place, that it destroyed all the cherries, and also most of the early wheat, and of the young shoots of Indian corn; in some particular places, for miles together, the young leaves of the forest trees even were all withered ed, and the country had exactly the appearance of November. On the tenth inftant, the day after the froft, the thermometer was as low as 46° in the middle of the day; yet four days afterwards it ftood at 81°. During the remainder of the month, and during June, until I reached Philadelphia, it fluctuated between 60° and 80°; the weather was on the whole fine, but frequently for a day or two together the air felt extremely raw and difagreeable. The changes in the ftate of the atmofphere were alfo fometimes very fudden. On the fixth day of June, when on my way to Frederic Town, after paffing the Patowmac River, the moft remarkable change of this nature took place which I ever witneffed. The morning had been oppreffively hot; the thermometer at 81°, and the wind S. S. W. About one o'clock in the afternoon, a black cloud appeared in the horizon, and a tremendous guft came on, accompanied by thunder and lightning; feveral large trees were torn up by the roots by the wind; hailftones, about three times the fize of an ordinary pea, fell for a few minutes, and afterwards a torrent of rain came pouring down, nearly as if a waterfpout had broken over head. Juft before the guft came on, I had fufpended my thermometer from a window with a northern afpect, when it ftood at 81°; but on looking at it at the

end

end of twenty-three minutes, by which time the guſt was completely over, I found it down to 59°, a change of 22°. A north-weſt wind now ſet in, the evening was moſt delightful, and the thermometer again roſe to 65°. In Pennſylvania the thermometer has been known to vary fifty degrees in the ſpace of twenty-ſix hours.

The climate of the middle and ſouthern ſtates is extremely variable; the ſeaſons of two ſucceeding years are ſeldom alike; and it ſcarcely ever happens that a month paſſes over without very great viciſſitudes in the weather taking place. Doctor Rittenhouſe remarked, that whilſt he reſided in Pennſylvania, he diſcovered nightly froſts in every month of the year excepting July, and even in that month, during which the heat is always greater than at any other time of the year, a cold day or two ſometimes intervene, when a fire is found very agreeable.

The climate of the ſtate of New York is very ſimilar to that of Pennſylvania, excepting that in the northern parts of that ſtate, bordering upon Canada, the winters are always ſevere and long. The climate of New Jerſey, Delaware, and the upper parts of Maryland, is alſo much the ſame with that of Pennſylvania; in the lower parts of Maryland the climate does not differ materially from that of Virginia to the

the eastward of the Blue Ridge, where it very rarely happens that the thermometer is as low as 6° above cipher.

In Pennsylvania, the range of the mercury in Fahrenheit's thermometer has been observed to be from 24° below cipher to 105° above it; but it is an unusual occurrence for the mercury to stand at either of these extreme points; in its approach towards them it commonly draws much nearer to the extreme of heat than to that of cold. During the winter of 1795, and the three preceding years, it did not sink lower than 10° above cipher; a summer however seldom passes over that it does not rise to 96°. It was mentioned as a singular circumstance, that in 1789 the thermometer never rose higher than 90°.

Of the oppression that is felt from the summer heats in America, no accurate idea can be formed without knowing the exact state of the hygrometer as well as the height of the thermometer. The moisture of the air varies very much in different parts of the country; it also varies in all parts with the winds; and it is surprising to find what a much greater degree of heat can be borne without inconvenience when the air is dry than when it is moist. In New England, in a remarkably dry air, the heat is not found more insupportable when the thermometer stands at 100°, than it
is

is in the lower parts of the southern states, where the air is moist, when the thermometer stands perhaps at 90°, that is, supposing the wind to be in the same quarter in both places. In speaking of Virginia I have taken notice of the great difference that is found between the climate of the mountains and the climate of the low country in that state. The case is the same in every other part of the country. From the mountains in New England, along the different ridges which run through New York, New Jersey, Pennsylvania, Maryland, and the southern states, even to the extremity of Georgia, the heat is never found very oppressive; whilst as far north as Pennsylvania and New York, the heat in the low parts of the country, between the mountains and the ocean, is frequently intolerable.

In the course of the few days that I have spent in Philadelphia during this month, the thermometer has risen repeatedly to 86° and for two or three days it stood at 93°. During these days no one stirred out of doors that was not compelled to do so; those that could make it convenient with their business always walked with umbrellas to shade them from the sun; light white hats were universally worn, and the young men appeared dressed in cotton or linen jackets and trowsers; every gleam of sunshine seemed to be considered as baneful

and

and deftructive; the window fhutters of each houfe were clofed early in the morning, fo as to admit no more light than what was abfolutely neceffary for domeftic bufinefs; many of the houfes, indeed, were kept fo dark, that on going into them from the ftreet, it was impoffible at firft entrance to perceive who was prefent. The beft houfes in the city are furnifhed with Venetian blinds, at the outfide, to the windows and hall doors, which are made to fold together like common window fhutters. Where they had thefe they conftantly kept them clofed, and the windows and doors were left open behind them to admit air. A very different fcene was prefented in the city as foon as the fun was fet; every houfe was then thrown open, and the inhabitants all crowded into the ftreets to take their evening walks, and vifit their acquaintance. It appeared every night as if fome grand fpectacle was to be exhibited, for not a ftreet or alley was there but what was in a ftate of commotion. This varied fcene ufually lafted till about ten o'clock; at eleven there is no city in the world, perhaps, fo quiet all the year round; at that hour you may walk over half the town without feeing the face of a human being, except the watchmen. Very heavy dews fometimes fall after thefe hot days, as foon as the fun is down, and the nights are then found very cold; at other times

times there are no dews, and the air remains hot all the night through. For days together in Philadelphia, the thermometer has been obferved never to be lower than 80° during any part of the twenty-four hours.

I obferve now that meat can never be kept, but in an ice houfe or a remarkable cold cellar, for one day, without being tainted. Milk generally turns four in the courfe of one or two hours after it comes from the cow. Fifh is never brought to market without being covered with lumps of ice, and notwithftanding that care, it frequently happens that it is not fit to be eat. Butter is brought to market likewife in ice, which they generally have in great plenty at every farm houfe; indeed it is almoft confidered as a neceffary of life in thefe low parts of the country. Poultry intended for dinner is never killed till about four hours before the time it is wanted, and then it is kept immerfed in water, without which precaution it would be tainted. Notwithftanding all this, I have been told, that were I to ftay in Philadelphia till the latter end of July or beginning of Auguft, I fhould find the heat much more intolerable than it has been hitherto. Moft of the other large fea port towns, fouth of Philadelphia, are equally hot and difagreeable in fummer; and Baltimore,

Baltimore, Norfolk, and some others, even more so.

The winds in every part of the country make a prodigious difference in the temperature of the air. When the north-west wind blows, the heat is always found more tolerable than with any other, although the thermometer should be at the same height. This wind is uncommonly dry, and brings with it fresh animation and vigour to every living thing. Although this wind is so very piercing in winter, yet I think the people never complain so much of cold as when the north-east wind blows; for my own part I never found the air so agreeable, let the season of the year be what it would, as with the north-west wind. The north-east wind is also cold, but it renders the air raw and damp. That from the south-east is damp but warm. Rain or snow usually falls when the wind comes from any point towards the east. The south-west wind, like the north-west, is dry; but it is attended generally with warm weather. When in a southerly point, gusts, as they are called, that is, storms attended with thunder, lightning, hail, and rain, are common.

It is a matter of no difficulty to account for these various effects of the winds in America. The north-west wind, from coming over

over such an immense tract of land, must necessarily be dry; and coming from regions eternally covered with mounds of snow and ice, it must also be cold. The north-east wind, from traversing the frozen seas, must be cold likewise; but from passing over such a large portion of the watry main afterwards, it brings damps and moistures with it. All those from the east are damp, and loaded with vapours, from the same cause. Southerly winds, from crossing the warm regions between the tropics, are attended with heat; and the southwest wind, from passing, like the north-west, over a great extent of land, is dry at the same time; none however is so dry as that from the north-west. It is said, but with what truth I cannot take upon me to say, that west of the Alleghany and Appalachian mountains, which are all in the same range, the southwest winds are cold and attended with rain. Those great extremes of heat and cold, observable on the eastern side of the mountains, are unknown to the westward of them.

LETTER XIX.

Travelling in America without a Companion not pleasant.—Meet two English Gentlemen.—Set out together for Canada.—Description of the Country between Philadelphia and New York.— Bristol. —Trenton. — Princeton.— College there.—Some Account of it.—Brunswick.—Posaik Water-fall.—Copper Mine.—Singular Discovery thereof.—New York.—Description of the City.—Character and Manners of the Inhabitants.—Leave it abruptly on Account of the Fevers.—Passage up North River from New York to Albany.—Great Beauty of the North River.—West Point.—Highlands.—Gusts of Wind common in passing them.—Albany.—Description of the City and Inhabitants.—Celebration of the 4th of July.—Anniversary of American Independence.

MY DEAR SIR,   Albany, July.

I Was on the point of leaving Philadelphia for New York, intending from thence to proceed to Canada, when chance brought me into the company of two young gentlemen from England, each of whom was separately preparing to set off on a similar excursion. A rational and agreeable companion, to whom you might communicate the result of your

obser-

observations, and with whom you might interchange sentiments on all occasions, could not but be deemed a pleasing acquisition, I should imagine, by a person on a journey through a foreign land. Were any one to be found, however, of a different opinion, I should venture to affirm, that ere he travelled far through the United States of America, where there are so few inhabitants in proportion to the extent of the country; where, in going from one town to another, it is frequently necessary to pass for many miles together through dreary woods; and where, even in the towns, a few of those sea-ports indeed excepted which are open to the Atlantic, there is such sameness in the customs, manners, and conversation of the inhabitants, and so little amongst them that interests either the head or the heart; he would not only be induced to think that a companion must add to the pleasure of a journey, but were absolutely necessary to prevent its appearing insipid, and at times highly irksome to him.

For my own part, I had fully determined in my own mind, upon returning from my tour beyond the Blue Mountains, never again to set out on a journey alone through any part of America, if I could possibly procure an agreeable companion. The gentlemen I met with had, as well as myself, travelled widely through different parts of the United States, and formed nearly the same resolution; we accordingly agreed to go forward to Canada together, and having engaged a carriage for ourselves as far as New York, we quitted the close and disagreeable city of Philadelphia on the twentieth of June.

The road, for the first twenty-five miles, runs very near the River Delaware, which appears to great advantage through openings in the woods that are scattered along its shores. From the town of Bristol in particular, which stands on an elevated part of the banks, twenty miles above Philadelphia, it is seen in a most pleasing point of view. The river, here about one mile wide, winds majestically round the point whereon the town is built, and for many miles, both upwards and downwards, it may be traced through a rich country, flowing gently along: in general it is covered with innumerable little sloops and schooners. Opposite to Bristol stands the city of Burlington, one of the largest in New Jersey, built partly upon an island and partly on the main shore. It makes a good appearance, and adds considerably to the beauty of the prospect from Bristol.

Ten miles farther on, opposite to Trenton, which stands at the head of the sloop navigation, you cross the river. The falls or rapids,

pids, that prevent boats from afcending any higher, appear in full view as you pafs, but their profpect is in no way pleafing; beyond them, the navigation may be purfued for upwards of one hundred miles in fmall boats. Trenton is the capital of New Jerfey, and contains about two hundred houfes, together with four churches. The ftreets are commodious, and the houfes neatly built. The ftate-houfe, in which congrefs met for fome time during the war, is a heavy clumfy edifice.

Twelve miles from Trenton, ftands Princeton, a neat town, containing about eighty dwellings in one long ftreet. Here is a large college, held in much repute by the neighbouring ftates. The number of ftudents amounts to upwards of feventy; from their appearance, however, and the courfe of ftudies they feem to be engaged in, like all the other American colleges I ever faw, it better deferves the title of a grammar fchool than a college. The library, which we were fhewn, is moft wretched, confifting, for the moft part, of old theological books, not even arranged with any regularity. An orrery, contrived by Mr. Rittenhoufe, whofe talents are fo much boafted of by his countrymen, ftands at one end of the apartment, but it is quite out of repair, as well as a few detached parts of a philofophical apparatus,

apparatus, enclosed in the same glass case. At the opposite end of the room are two small cupboards, which are shewn as the museum. These contain a couple of small stuffed alligators, and a few singular fishes, in a miserable state of preservation, the skins of them being tattered in innumerable places, from their being repeatedly tossed about. The building is very plain, and of stone; it is one hundred and eighty feet in front, and four stories high.

The next stage from Princeton is Brunswick, containing about two hundred houses; there is nothing very deserving of attention in it, excepting it be the very neat and commodious wooden bridge that has been thrown across the Raritan River, which is about two hundred paces over. The part over the channel is contrived to draw up, and on each side is a footway guarded by rails, and ornamented with lamps. Elizabeth Town and Newark, which you afterwards pass through in succession, are both of them cheerful lively looking places: neither of them is paved. Newark is built in a straggling manner, and has very much the appearance of a large English village: there is agreeable society in this town. These two towns are only eight miles apart, and each of them has one or two excellent churches, whose tall spires appear very beautiful

tiful as you approach at a diftance, peeping up above the woods by which they are encircled.

The ftate of New Jerfey, meafured from north to fouth, is about one hundred and fixty miles in length; it varies in breadth from forty to eighty miles. The northern part of it is croffed by the blue ridge of mountains, running through Pennfylvania; and fhooting off in different directions from this ridge, there are feveral other fmall mountains in the neighbourhood. The fouthern part of the ftate, on the contrary, which lies towards the fea, is extremely flat and fandy; it is covered for miles together with pine trees alone, ufually called pine barrens, and is very little cultivated. The middle part, which is croffed in going from Philadelphia to New York, abounds with extenfive tracts of good land; the foil varies, however, confiderably, in fome places being fandy, in others ftoney, and in others confifting of a rich brown mould. This part of the ftate, as far as Newark, is on the whole well cultivated, and fcattered about in different places are fome excellent farm houfes; a good deal of uncleared land, however, ftill remains. Beyond Newark the country is extremely flat and marfhy. Between the town and the Pofaick River there is one marfh, which alone extends upwards of twenty miles, and is about

two

two miles wide where you pafs over it. The road is here formed with large logs of wood laid clofe together, and on each fide are ditches to keep it dry. This was the firft place where we met with mufquitoes, and they annoyed us not a little in paffing. Towards the latter end of the fummer Philadelphia is much infefted with them; but they had not made their appearance when we left that city. The Pofaik River runs clofe upon the borders of this marfh, and there is an excellent wooden bridge acrofs it, fomewhat fimilar to that at New Brunfwick over the Raritan River. About fifteen miles above it there is a very remarkable fall in the river. The river, at the fall, is about forty yards wide, and flows with a gentle current till it comes within a few perches of the edge of the fall, when it fuddenly precipitates itfelf, in one entire fheet, over a ledge of rocks of nearly eighty feet in perpendicular height; below, it runs on through a chafm, formed of immenfe rocks on each fide; they are higher than the fall, and feem to have been once united together.

In this neighbourhood there is a very rich copper mine: repeated attempts have been made to work it; but whether the price of labour be too great for fuch an undertaking, or the proprietors have not proceeded with judgment, certain it is, that they have always miscarried,

miscarried, and sustained very considerable losses thereby. This mine was first discovered in 1751, by a person who, passing along about three o'clock in the morning, observed a blue flame, about the size of a man, issuing from the earth, which afterwards soon died away: he marked the place with a stake, and when the hill was opened, several large lumps of virgin copper were found. The vein of copper in the mine is said to be much richer now than when first opened.

From the Posaik to the North River the country is hilly, barren, and uninteresting, till you come very near the latter, when a noble view opens all at once of the city of New York on the opposite shore, of the harbour, and shipping. The river, which is very grand, can be traced for several miles above the city; the banks are very steep on the Jersey side, and beautifully wooded, the trees almost dipping into the water: numbers of vessels plying about in every part render the scene extremely sprightly and interesting.

New York is built on an island of its own name, formed by the North and the East Rivers, and a creek or inlet connecting both of these together. The island is fourteen miles long, and, on an average, about one mile in breadth; at its southern extremity stands the city, which extends from one river to the other.

The North, or Hudson River, is nearly two miles wide; the East, or the North-east one, as it should rather be called, is not quite so broad. The depth of water in each, close to the city, is sufficient for the largest merchant vessels. The principal seat of trade, however, is on the East River, and most of the vessels lie there, as during winter the navigation of that river is not so soon impeded by the ice. At this side of the town the houses and stores are built as closely as possible. The streets are narrow and inconvenient, and, as but too commonly is the case in seaport towns, very dirty, and, consequently, during the summer season, dreadfully unhealthy. It was in this part of the town that the yellow fever raged with such violence in 1795; and during 1796, many persons that remained very constantly there also fell victims to a fever, which, if not the yellow fever, was very like it. The streets near the North River are much more airy; but the most agreeable part of the town is in the neighbourhood of the battery, on the southern point of the island, at the confluence of the two rivers. When New York was in possession of the English, this battery consisted of two or more tiers of guns, one above the other; but it is now cut down, and affords a most charming walk, and, on a summer's evening, is crowded with people, as it is open to the

breezes

breezes from the sea, which render it particularly agreeable at that season. There is a fine view from it of the roads, Long and Staten Islands, and Jersey shore. At the time of high water the scene is always interesting on account of the number of vessels sailing in and out of port; such as go into the East River pass within a few yards of the walls of the battery.

From the battery a handsome street, about seventy feet wide, called Broadway, runs due north through the town; between it and the North River run several streets at right angles, as you pass which you catch a view of the water, and boats plying up and down; the distant shore of the river also is seen to great advantage. Had the streets on the opposite side of Broadway been also carried down to the East River, the effect would have been beautiful, for Broadway runs along a ridge of high ground between the two rivers; it would have contributed also very much to the health of the place; if, added to this, a spacious quay had been formed the entire length of the city, on either side, instead of having the borders of the rivers crowded with confused heaps of wooden store houses, built upon wharfs projecting one beyond another in every direction, New York would have been one of the most beautiful sea-ports in the world. All the sea-ports in America appear to great disadvantage from the water,
when

when you approach near to them, from the shores being crowded in this manner with irregular maſſes of wooden houſes, ſtanding as it were in the water. The federal city, where they have already begun to erect the ſame kind of wooden wharfs and ſtore-houſes without any regularity, will be juſt the ſame. It is aſtoniſhing, that in laying out that city a grand quay was not thought of in the plan; it would certainly have afforded equal, if not greater accommodation for the ſhipping, and it would have added wonderfully to the embelliſhment of the city.

Many of the private houſes in New York are very good, particularly thoſe in Broadway. Of the public buildings there are none which are very ſtriking. The churches and houſes for public worſhip amount to no leſs than twenty-two; four of them are for Preſbyterians, three for Epiſcopalians of the church of England, three for Dutch Reformiſts, two for German Lutherans and Calviniſts, two for Quakers, two for Baptiſts, two for Methodiſts, one for French Proteſtants, one for Moravians, one for Roman Catholics, and one for Jews.

According to the cenſus in 1790, the number of inhabitants in New York was found to be thirty thouſand one hundred and forty-eight free perſons, and two thouſand one hundred

dred and eighty slaves; but at present the number is supposed to amount at least to forty thousand. The inhabitants have long been distinguished above those of all the other towns in the United States, except it be the people of Charleston, for their politeness, gaiety, and hospitality; and, indeed, in these points they are most strikingly superior to the inhabitants of the other large towns. Their public amusements consist in dancing and card assemblies, and theatrical exhibitions; for the former a spacious suite of rooms has lately been erected. The theatre is of wood, and a most miserable edifice it is; but a new one is now building on a grand scale, which, it is thought, will be as much too large for the town as the other is too small.

Being anxious to proceed on our journey before the season was too far advanced, and also particularly desirous of quitting New York on account of the fevers, which, it was rumoured, were increasing very fast, we took our passage for Albany in one of the sloops trading constantly on the North River, between New York and that place, and embarked on the second day of July, about two o'clock in the afternoon. Scarcely a breath of air was stirring at the time; but the tide carried us up at the rate of about two miles and a half an hour. The sky remained all day as serene as possible, and as the water was perfectly smooth, it reflected in a most beautiful manner the images of the various objects on the shore, and of the numerous vessels dispersed along the river at different distances, and which seemed to glide along, as it were, by the power of magic, for the sails all hung down loose and motionless. The sun, setting in all his glory, added fresh beauties to this calm and peaceable scene, and permitted us for the last time to behold the distant spires of New York, illumined by his parting rays. To describe all the grand and beautiful prospects presented to the view on passing along this noble river, would be an endless task; all the various effects that can be supposed to arise from a happy combination of wood and water, of hill and dale, are here seen in the greatest perfection. In some places the river expands to the breadth of five or six miles, in others it narrows to that of a few hundred yards, and in various parts it is interspersed with islands; in some places again its course can be traced as far as the eye can reach, whilst in others it is suddenly lost to the view, as it winds between its lofty banks; here mountains covered with rocks and trees rise almost perpendicularly out of the water; there a fine champaign country presents itself, cultivated to the very margin of the river, whilst

VIEW on the HUDSON RIVER

whilst neat farm houses and distant towns embellish the charming landscapes.

After sunset, a brisk wind sprang up, which carried us on at the rate of six or seven miles an hour for a considerable part of the night; but for some hours we had to lie at anchor at a place where the navigation of the river was too difficult to proceed in the dark. Our sloop was no more than seventy tons burthen by register; but the accommodations she afforded were most excellent, and far superior to what might be expected on board so small a vessel; the cabin was equally large with that in a common merchant vessel of three hundred tons, built for crossing the ocean. This was owing to the great breadth of her beam, which was no less than twenty-two feet and a half although her length was only fifty-five feet. All the sloops engaged in this trade are built nearly on the same construction; short, broad, and very shallow, few of them draw more than five or six feet water, so that they are only calculated for sailing upon smooth water.

Early the next morning we found ourselves opposite to West Point, a place rendered remarkable in history by the desertion of General Arnold, during the American war, and the consequent death of the unfortunate Major André. The fort stands about one hundred and fifty feet above the level of the water, on the

the side of a barren hill; no human creature appearing in it except the solitary centinel, who marched backwards and forwards on the ramparts overgrown with long grass, it had a most melancholy aspect that perhaps was heightened by the gloominess of the morning, and the recollection of all the circumstances attending the unhappy fate of poor André.

Near West Point there is also another post, called Fort Putnam, which, since the peace, has been suffered to get very much out of repair; however, steps are now taking to have it put in good order. Supposing that a rupture should ever unfortunately again take place between Great Britain and the United States of America, these posts would be of the greatest consequence, as they form a link in that chain of posts which extend the whole way along the navigable waters that connect the British settlements with New York.

In this neighbourhood the highlands, as they are called, commence, and extend along the river on each side for several miles. The breadth of the river is here considerably contracted, and such sudden gusts of wind, coming from between the mountains, sometimes blow through the narrow passes, that vessels frequently have their topmasts carried away. The captain of the sloop we were in, said, that

that his mainsail was once blown into tatters in an instant, and a part of it carried on shore. When the sky is lowering, they usually take in sail going along this part of the river.

About four o'clock in the morning of the fourth of July we reached Albany, the place of our destination, one hundred and sixty miles distant from New York.

Albany is a city, and contains about eleven hundred houses; the number however is increasing fast, particularly since the removal of the state government from New York. In the old part of the town the streets are very narrow and the houses are frightful; they are all built in the old Dutch taste, with the gable end towards the street, and ornamented on the top with large iron weather cocks; but in that part which has been lately erected, the streets are commodious, and many of the houses are handsome. Great pains have been taken to have the streets well paved and lighted. Here are four places for public worship, and an hospital. Albany is in summer time a very disagreeable place; it stands in a low situation, just on the margin of the river, which runs very slowly here, and towards the evening often exhales clouds of vapours; immediately behind the town, likewise, is a large sand bank, that prevents a free circulation of air, while at the same time it

powerfully

powerfully reflects the rays of the sun, which shines in full force upon it the whole day. Notwithstanding all this, however, the climate is deemed very salubrious.

The inhabitants of this place, a few years ago, were almost entirely of Dutch extraction; but now strangers are flocking to it from all quarters, as there are few places in America more advantageously situated for commerce. The flourishing state of its trade has already been mentioned; it bids fair to rival that of New York in process of time.

The fourth of July, the day of our arrival at Albany, was the anniversary of the declaration of American independence, and on our arrival we were told that great preparations were making for its celebration *. A drum and trumpet, towards the middle of the day, gave notice of the commencement of the rejoicings, and on walking to a hill about a

---

* Our landlord, as soon as he found out who we were, immediately came to us, to request that we would excuse the confused state in which his house was, as this was the anniversary day of " American Independence," or, as some, indeed, more properly called it, of " American Repentance." We were all of us not a little surprised at this address, and from such a person; instances, however, are not wanting of people openly declaring, that they have never enjoyed so much quiet and happiness in their own homes since the revolution as they did when the states were the colonies of Great Britain. Amongst the planters in Virginia I heard language of this sort more than once.

quarter

quarter of a mile from the town, we saw sixty men drawn up, partly militia, partly volunteers, partly infantry, partly cavalry; the latter were clothed in scarlet, and mounted on horses of various descriptions. About three hundred spectators attended. A few rounds were fired from a three pounder, and some volleys of small arms. The firing was finished before one hour was expired, and then the troops returned to town, a party of militia officers in uniform marching in the rear, under the shade of umbrellas, as the day was excessively hot. Having reached town, the whole body immediately dispersed. The volunteers and militia officers afterwards dined together, and so ended the rejoicings of the day; no public ball, no general entertainment was there of any description. A day still fresh in the memory of every American, and which appears so glorious in the annals of their country, would, it might be expected, have called forth more brilliant and more general rejoicings; but the downright phlegmatic people in this neighbourhood, intent upon making money, and enjoying the solid advantages of the revolution, are but little disposed to waste their time in what they consider idle demonstrations of joy.

LETTER XX.

Departure from Albany.—Difficulty of hiring a Carriage.—Arrival at Cohoz.—Description of the curious Fall there of the Mohawk River.—Still-water.—Saratoga.—Few of the Works remaining there.—Singular Mineral Springs near Saratoga.—Fort Edward. —Miss M'Crea cruelly murdered there by Indians.—Fort Ann, wretched Road thither. —Some Observations on the American Woods. —Horses jaded.—Difficulty of getting forward.—Arrive at Skenesborough.—Dreadfully infested by Musquitoes.—Particular Description of that Insect.—Great Danger ensues sometimes from their Bite.—Best Remedy.

MY DEAR SIR, Skenesborough, July.

WE remained in Albany for a few days, and then set off for Skenesborough, upon Lake Champlain, in a carriage hired for the purpose. The hiring of this vehicle was a matter attended with some trouble, and detained us longer in the town than we wished to stay. There were only two carriages to be had in the whole place, and the owners having an understanding with each other, and thinking

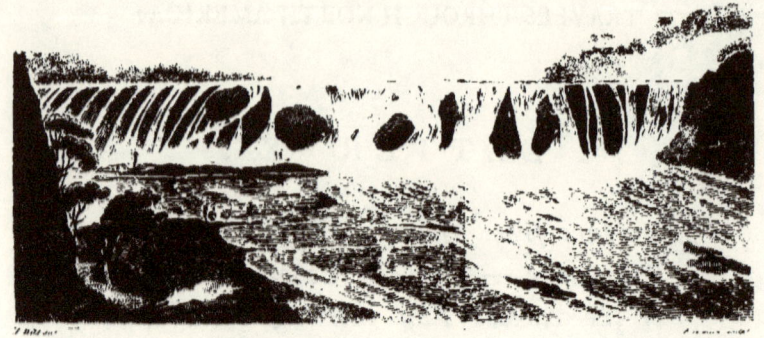

F. Weld   P. Thomson sculpt.

ing that we should be forced to give whatever price they asked, positively refused to let us have either of them for less than seventy dollars, equal to fifteen guineas. We on our part as positively refused to comply with a demand which we knew to be exorbitant, and resolved to wait patiently in Albany for some other conveyance, rather than submit to such an imposition. The fellows held out for two days, but at the end of that time one of them came to tell us we might have his carriage for half the price, and accordingly we took it.

Early the next morning we set off, and in about two hours arrived at the small village of Cohoz, close to which is the remarkable fall in the Mohawk River. This river takes its rise to the north-east of Lake Oneida, and after a course of one hundred and forty miles, disembogues into the Hudson or North River, about ten miles above Albany. The Cohoz Fall is about three miles distant from its mouth. The breadth of the river is three hundred yards; a ledge of rocks extends quite across, and from the top of them the water falls about fifty feet perpendicular; the line of the fall from one side of the river to the other is nearly straight. The appearance of this fall varies very much, according to the quantity of water; when the river is full, the water descends in an unbroken sheet from one bank to the other, whilft at other times the greater part of the rocks are left uncovered. The rocks are of a remarkable dark colour, and fo alfo is the earth in the banks, which rife to a great height on either fide. There is a very pleafing view of this cataract as you pafs over the bridge acrofs the river, about three quarters of a mile lower down.

From hence we proceeded along the banks of the Hudfon River, through the town of Stillwater, which receives its name from the uncommon ftillnefs of the river oppofite to it, and late in the evening reached Saratoga, thirty-five miles from Albany. This place contains about forty houfes, and a Dutch reformed church, but they are fo fcattered about that it has not the fmalleft appearance of a town.

In this neighbourhood, upon the borders of a marfh, are feveral very remarkable mineral fprings; one of them, in the crater of a rock, of a pyramidical form, about five feet in height, is particularly curious. This rock feems to have been formed by the petrifaction of the water: all the other fprings are likewife furrounded with petrifactions of the fame kind. The water in the principal fpring, except at the beginning of the fummer, when it regularly overflows, remains about eight inches below the rim of the crater, and bubbles up

as

as if boiling. The crater is nine inches in diameter. The various properties of the water have not been yet ascertained with any great accuracy; but it is said to be impregnated with a fossile acid and some saline substance; there is also a great portion of fixed air in it. An opportunity is here afforded for making some curious experiments.

If animals be put down into the crater, they will be immediately suffocated; but if not kept there too long they recover again upon being brought into the open air.

If a lighted candle be put down, the flame will be extinguished in an instant, and not even the smallest spark left in the wick.

If the water immediately taken from the spring be put into a bottle, closely corked, and then shaken, either the cork will be forced out with an explosion, or the bottle will be broken; but if left in an open vessel it becomes vapid in less than half an hour. The water is very pungent to the taste, and acts as a cathartic on some people, as an emetic on others.

Of the works thrown up at Saratoga by the British and American armies during the war, there are now scarcely any remains. The country round about is well cultivated, and the trenches have been mostly levelled by the plough. We here crossed the Hudson River, and proceeded along its eastern shore as far as Fort Edward, where it is lost to the view, for the road still runs on towards the north, whilst the river takes a sudden bend to the west.

Fort Edward was dismantled prior to the late American war; but the opposite armies, during that unhappy contest, were both in the neighbourhood. Many of the people, whom we found living here, had served as soldiers in the army, and told us a number of interesting particulars relative to several events which happened in this quarter. The landlord of the tavern where we stopped, for one, related all the circumstances attending Miss M'Crea's death, and pointed out on a hill, not far from the house, the very spot where she was murdered by the Indians, and the place of her interment. This beautiful young lady had been engaged to an officer in General Burgoyne's army, who, anxious for her safety, as there were several marauding parties going about in the neighbourhood where she lived, sent a party of trusty Indians to escort her to the camp. These Indians had partly executed their commission, and were approaching with their charge in sight of the British camp, when they were met by another set of Indians belonging to a different tribe, that was also attending the British army at this time. In a few minutes it became a matter of dispute between

between them which should have the honour of conducting her to the camp; from words they came to blows, and blood was on the point of being drawn, when one of their chiefs, to settle the matter without farther mischief, went up to Miss M'Crea, and killed her on the spot with a blow of his tomahawk. The object of contention being thus removed, the Indians returned quietly to the camp. The enormity of the crime, however, was too great not to attract public notice, and it turned the minds of every person against the Indians, who had not before witnessed their ferocity on occasions equally shocking to humanity. The impolicy of employing such barbarians was now strongly reprobated, and in a short time afterwards most of them were dismissed from our army.

Fort Edward stands near the river. The town of the same name, is at the distance of one or two hundred yards from it, and contains about twenty houses. Thus far we had got on tolerably well; but from hence to Fort Anne, which was also dismantled prior to the late war, the road is most wretched, particularly over a long causeway between the two forts, formed originally for the transporting of cannon, the soil here being extremely moist and heavy. The causeway consists of large trees laid side by side transversely, some of which having decayed, great intervals are left, wherein the wheels of the carriage were sometimes locked so fast that the horses alone could not possibly extricate them. To have remained in the carriage over this part of the road would really have been a severe punishment; for although boasted of as being the very best in Albany, it had no sort of springs, and was in fact little better than a common waggon; we therefore alighted, took our guns, and amused ourselves with shooting as we walked along through the woods. The woods here had a much more majestic appearance than any that we had before met with on our way from Philadelphia; this, however, was owing more to the great height than to the thickness of the trees, for I could not see one that appeared more than thirty inches in diameter; indeed, in general, the girt of the trees in the woods of America is but very small in proportion to their height, and trifling in comparison of that of the forest trees in Great Britain. The thickest tree I ever saw in the country was a sycamore, which grew upon the banks of the Shenandoah River, just at its junction with the Patowmac, in a bed of rich earth, close to the water; yet this tree was no more than about four feet four inches in diameter. On the low grounds in Kentucky, and on some of the bottoms in the western territory,

territory, it is said that trees are commonly to be met with seven and eight feet in diameter. Where this is the case, the trees must certainly grow much farther apart than they do in the woods in the middle states, towards the Atlantic, for there they spring up so very close to each other, that it is absolutely impossible for them to attain to a great diameter.

The woods here were composed chiefly of oaks *, hiccory, hemlock, and beech trees, intermixed with which, appeared great numbers of the smooth bark or Weymouth pines, as they are called, that seem almost peculiar to this part of the country. A profusion of wild raspberries were growing in the woods here, really of a very good flavour: they are commonly found in the woods to the northward of this; in Canada they abound every where.

Beyond Fort Anne, which is situated at the distance of eight miles from Fort Edward, the roads being better, we once more mounted into our vehicle; but the miserable horses, quite jaded, now made a dead stop; in vain the driver bawled, and stamped, and swore; his whip had been previously worn out some hours, owing to the frequent use he had made of it, and the animals no longer feeling

* There are upwards of twenty different kinds of oaks in America.

its

its heavy lafh, feemed as determined as the mules of the abbefs of Andouillets to go no farther. In this fituation we could not help bantering the fellow upon the excellence of his cattle, which he had boafted fo much of at fetting out, and he was ready to cry with vexation at what we faid; but having accidentally mentioned the fum we had paid for the carriage, his paffion could no longer be reftrained, and it broke forth in all its fury. It appeared that he was the owner of two of the horfes, and for the ufe of them, and for driving the carriage, was to have had one half of the hire; but the man whom we had agreed with, and paid at Albany, had given him only ten dollars as his moiety, affuring him, at the fame time, that it was exactly the half of what we had given, although in reality it fell fhort of the fum by feven dollars and a half. Thus cheated by his companion, and left in the lurch by his horfes, he vowed vengeance againft him on his return; but as proteftations of this nature would not bring us any fooner to our journey's end, and as it was neceffary that fomething fhould be immediately done, if we did not wifh to remain all night in the woods, we fuggefted the idea, in the mean time, of his conducting the foremoft horfes as poftillion, whilft one of our fervants fhould drive the pair next to the wheel. This plan

was

was not started with any degree of seriousness, for we could not have supposed that a tall meagre fellow, upwards of six feet high, and clad in a pair of thin nankeen breeches, would very readily bestride the raw boned back of a horse, covered with the profuse exudations which the intense heat of the weather, and the labour the animal had gone through, necessarily excited. As much tired, however, of our pleasantries as we were of his vehicle, and thinking of nothing, I believe, but how he could best get rid of us, he eagerly embraced the proposal, and accordingly, having furnished himself with a switch from the adjoining thicket, he mounted his harnessed Rosinante. In this style we proceeded; but more than once did our gigantic postillion turn round to bemoan the sorry choice he had made; as often did we urge the necessity of getting out of the woods; he could make no answer; so jogging slowly along, we at last reached the little town of Skenesborough, much to the amusement of every one who beheld our equipage, and much to our own satisfaction; for, owing to the various accidents we had met with, such as traces breaking, bridles slipping off the heads of the horses, and the noble horses themselves sometimes slipping down, &c. &c. we had been

no

no less than five hours in travelling the last twelve miles.

Skenesborough stands just above the junction of Wood Creek with South River, as it is called in the best maps, but which, by the people in the neighbourhood, is considered as a part of Lake Champlain. At present there are only about twelve houses in the place; but if the navigation of Wood Creek is ever opened, so as to connect Lake Champlain with the North River, a scheme which has already been seriously thought of, it will, doubtless, soon become a trading town of considerable importance, as all the various productions of the shores of the lake will then be collected there for the New York and Albany markets. Notwithstanding all the disadvantages of a land carriage of forty miles to the North River, a small portion of flour and pot-ash, the staple commodities of the state of New York, is already sent to Skenesborough from different parts of the lake, to be forwarded to Albany. A considerable trade also is carried on through this place, and over Lake Champlain, between New York and Canada. Furs and horses principally are sent from Canada, and in return they get East Indian goods and various manufactures. Lake Champlain opens a very ready communication

tion between New York and the country bordering on the St. Lawrence; it is emphatically called by the Indians, Caniad—Eri Guarunte, the mouth or door of the country.

Skenefborough is moſt dreadfully infeſted with muſquitoes; ſo many of them attacked us the firſt night of our ſleeping there, that when we aroſe in the morning our faces and hands were covered all over with large puſtules, preciſely like thoſe of a perſon in the ſmall pox. This happened too notwithſtanding that the people of the houſe, before we went to bed, had taken all the pains poſſible to clear the room of them, by fumigating it with the ſmoke of green wood, and afterwards ſecuring the windows with gauze blinds; and even on the ſecond night, although we deſtroyed many dozens of them on the walls, after a ſimilar fumigation had been made, yet we ſuffered nearly as much. Theſe inſects were of a much larger ſize than any I ever ſaw elſewhere, and their bite was uncommonly venomous. General Waſhington told me, that he never was ſo much annoyed by muſquitoes in any part of America as in Skeneſborough, for that they uſed to bite through the thickeſt boot. The ſituation of the place is indeed peculiarly favourable for them, being juſt on the margin of a piece of water, almoſt ſtagnant, and ſhaded with thick woods.

The

The mufquito is of the fame fpecies with the common gnat in England, and refembles it very clofely both in fize and fhape. Like the gnat it lays its eggs on the furface of the water, where they are hatched in the courfe of a few days, unlefs the water is agitated, in which laft cafe they are all deftroyed. From the egg is produced a grub, which changes to a chryfalis, and afterwards to a mufquito; this laft change takes place on the furface of the water, and if at the moment that the infect firft fpreads its wings the water is not perfectly ftill and the air calm, it will be inevitably deftroyed; at thofe parts of the lake, therefore, which are moft expofed, and where the water is often agitated, no fuch thing as a mufquito is ever feen; neither are they ever found along a large and rapid river, where the fhores are lofty and dry; but in the neighbourhood of marfhes, low grounds, and ftagnant waters, they always abound. Mufquitoes appear to be particularly fond of the frefh blood of Europeans, who always fuffer much more the firft year of their arrival in America than they do afterwards. The people of the country feem quite to difregard their attacks. Wherever they fix their fting, a little tumor or puftule ufually arifes, fuppofed to be occafioned by the fermentation, when mixed with the blood, of a fmall quantity

tity of liquor which the insect always injects into the wound it makes with its spicula, as may be seen through a microscope, and which it probably does to render the blood more fluid. The disagreeable itching this excites is most effectually allayed by the application of volatile alkali; or if the part newly stung be scratched and immediately bathed in cold water, that also affords considerable relief; but after the venom has been lodged for any time, scratching only increases the itching, and it may be attended with great danger. Repeated instances have occurred of people having been laid up for months, and narrowly escaping the loss of a limb, from imprudently rubbing a part which had been bitten for a long time. Great ease is also derived from opening the pustules on the second day with a lancet, and letting out the blood and watery matter.

LETTER XXI.

Embark on Lake Champlain.—Difficulty of procuring Provisions at Farms bordering upon it.— Ticonderoga.— Crown Point.— Great Beauty of the Scenery.—General Description of Lake Champlain and the adjacent Country. Captain Thomas and his Indians arrive at Crown Point.— Character of Thomas.— Reach St. John's.—Description of that Place. —Great Difference observable in the Face of the Country, Inhabitants, &c. in Canada and in the States.—Chambly Castle.—Calashes.— Bons Dieux.—Town of La Prarie.—Great Rapidity of the River Saint Lawrence.— Cross it to Montreal.—Astonishment on seeing large Ships at Montreal.—Great Depth of the River.

Montreal, July.

SHORTLY after our arrival in Skenesborough, we hired a small boat of about ten tons for the purpose of crossing Lake Champlain. It was our wish to proceed on the voyage immediately; but the owner of the boat asserting that it was impossible to go out with the wind then blowing, we were for three days detained in Skenesborough, a delicious feast for the hungry musquitoes. The wind

wind shifted again and again, still it was not fair in the opinion of our boatman. At last, being most heartily tired of our quarters, and suspecting that he did not understand his business as well as he ought to have done, we resolved not to abide by his opinion any longer, but to make an attempt at beating out; and we had great reason to be pleased with having done so, as we arrived in Canada three days before any of the other boats, that did not venture to move till the wind was quite aft.

We set off about one o'clock; but from the channel being very narrow, it was impossible to make much way by tacking. We got no farther than six miles before sun-set. We then stopped, and having landed, walked up to some farm houses, which appeared at a distance, on the Vermont shore, to procure provisions; for the boatman had told us it was quite unnecessary to take in any at Skenesborough, as there were excellent houses close to the shore the whole way, where we could get whatever we wished. At the first we went to, which was a comfortable log-house, neither bread, nor meat, nor milk, nor eggs, were to be had; the house was crowded with children of all ages, and the people, I suppose, thought they had but little enough for themselves. At a second house, we found a venerable old man at the door, reading a news-paper, who civilly offered

offered it to us for our perusal, and began to talk upon the politics of the day; we thanked him for his offer, and gave him to understand, at the same time, that a loaf would be much more acceptable. Bread there was none; we got a new Vermont cheese, however. A third house now remained in sight, and we made a third attempt at procuring something to eat. This one was nearly half a mile off, but alas! it afforded still less than the last; the people had nothing to dispose of but a little milk. With the milk and the cheese, therefore, we returned to our boat, and adding thereto some biscuits and wine, which we had luckily on board, the whole afforded us a frugal repast.

The people at the American farm houses will cheerfully lie three in a bed, rather than suffer a stranger to go away who comes to seek for a lodging. As all these houses, however, which we had visited, were crowded with inhabitants, we felt no great inclination to ask for accommodation at any of them, but determined to sleep on board our little vessel. We accordingly moored her at a convenient part of the shore, and each of us having wrapped himself up in a blanket, which we had been warned to provide on leaving New York, we laid ourselves down to sleep. The boat was decked two thirds of her length forward, and had a commodious hold; we gave the preference,

ference, however, becauſe more airy, to the cabin or after part, fitted up with benches, and covered with a wooden awning, under which a man could juſt ſit upright, provided he was not very tall. The benches, which went lengthwiſe, accommodated two of us; and the third was obliged to put up with the cabin floor; but a blanket and a bare board, out of the way of muſquitoes, were luxuries after our accommodations at Skeneſborough; our ears were not aſſailed by the noiſe even of a ſingle one the whole night, and we enjoyed ſounder repoſe than we had done for many nights preceding.

The wind remained nearly in the ſame point the next morning, but the lake being wider, we were enabled to proceed faſter. We ſtopped at one houſe to breakfaſt, and at another to dine. At neither of theſe, although they bore the name of taverns, were we able to procure much more than at the houſes where we had ſtopped the preceding evening. At the firſt we got a little milk, and about two pounds of bread, abſolutely the whole of what was in the houſe; and at the ſecond, a few eggs, and ſome cold ſalted fat pork; but not a morſel of bread was to be had. The wretched appearance alſo of this laſt habitation was very ſtriking; it conſiſted of a wooden frame, merely with a few boards nailed againſt it, it, the crevices between which were the only apertures for the admiſſion of light, except the door; and the roof was ſo leaky, that we were ſprinkled with the rain even as we ſat at the fire ſide. That people can live in ſuch a manner, who have the neceſſaries and conveniencies of life within their reach, as much as any others in the world, is really moſt aſtoniſhing! It is, however, to be accounted for, by that deſire of making money, which is the predominant feature in the character of the Americans in general, and leads the petty farmer in particular to ſuffer numberleſs inconveniencies, when he can gain by ſo doing. If he can ſell the produce of his land to advantage, he keeps as ſmall a part of it as poſſible for himſelf, and lives the whole year round upon ſalt proviſions, bad bread, and the fiſh he can catch in the rivers or lakes in the neighbourhood; if he has built a comfortable houſe for himſelf, he readily quits it, as ſoon as finiſhed, for money, and goes to live in a mere hovel in the woods till he gets time to build another. Money is his idol, and to procure it he gladly foregoes every ſelf-gratification.

From this miſerable habitation, juſt mentioned, we departed as ſoon as the rain was over, and the wind coming round in our favour, we got as far as Ticonderoga that night. The only dwelling here is the tavern, which

is

is a large houfe built of ftone. On entering it we were fhewn into a fpacious apartment, crowded with boatmen and people that had juft arrived from St. John's, in Canada. Seeing fuch a number of guefts in the houfe, we expected nothing lefs than to be kept an hour or two till fufficient fupper was prepared for the whole company, fo that all might fit down at once together, which, as I have before faid, is the cuftom in the country parts of the United States. Our furprife therefore was great at perceiving a neat table and a comfortable little fupper fpeedily laid out for us, and no attempts made at ferving the reft of the company till we had quite finifhed. This was departing from the fyftem of equality in a manner which we had never witneffed before, and we were at a lofs for fome time to account for it; but we prefently heard that the woman of the houfe had kept a tavern for the greater part of her life at Quebec, which refolved the knotty point. The wife is generally the active perfon in managing a country tavern, and the hufband attends to his farm, or has fome independent occupation. The man of this houfe was a judge, a fullen demure old gentleman, who fat by the fire *, with tattered clothes and difhevelled

---

* Though this was the 14th day of July, the weather was fo cold that we found a fire extremely agreeable.

locks, reading a book, totally regardless of every person in the room.

The old fort and barracks of Ticonderoga are on the top of a rising ground, just behind the tavern; they are quite in ruins, and it is not likely that they will ever be rebuilt, for the situation is very insecure, being commanded by a lofty hill called Mount Defiance. The British got possession of the place the last war by dragging cannon and mortars up the hill, and firing down upon the fort.

Early the next morning we left Ticonderoga, and pursued our voyage to Crown Point, where we landed to look at the old fort. Nothing is to be seen there, however, but a heap of ruins; for shortly before it was given up by the British, the powder magazine blew up, by which accident a great part of the works was destroyed; since the evacuation of it also, the people in the neighbourhood have been continually digging in different parts, in hopes of procuring lead and iron shot; a considerable quantity was in one instance got out of the stores that had been buried by the explosion. The vaults, which were bomb proof, have been demolished for the sake of the bricks for building chimneys. At the south side alone the ditches remain perfect; they are wide and deep, and cut through immense rocks of limestone; and from being overgrown towards the top with different kinds of shrubs, have a grand

and

and picturesque appearance. The view from this spot of the fort, and the old buildings in it overgrown with ivy, of the lake, and of the distant mountains beyond it, is indeed altogether very fine. The fort, and seven hundred acres of good cleared land adjoining to it, are the property of the state of New York, and are leased out at the rate of one hundred and fifty dollars, equal to £. 33. 10 s. sterling per annum, which is appropriated for the use of a college. The farmer who rented it told us, he principally made use of the land for grazing cattle; these, in the winter season, when the lake was frozen, he drove over the ice to Albany, and there disposed of.

Crown Point is the most advantageous spot on the shores of Lake Champlain for a military post, not being commanded by any rising grounds in the neighbourhood, as Ticonderoga is, and as the lake is so narrow here, owing to another point running out on the opposite side, that it would be absolutely impossible for a vessel to pass, without being exposed to the fire of the fort. The Indians call this place Tek-ya-dough-nigarigee, that is, the two points immediately opposite to each other: the one opposite to Crown Point is called Chimney Point; upon it are a few houses, one of which is a tavern. While we staid there we were very agreeably surprised, for the first time, with the sight of a large birch canoe upon the lake, navigated by two or three Indians in the dresses of their nation. They made for the shore and soon landed; and shortly after another party, amounting to six or seven, arrived, that had come by land.

On board our little vessel we had a poor Canadian, whom we took in at Skenesborough. Tempted by the accounts he had heard of the United States, he quitted his own home in Canada, where he lived under one of the seigniors, and had gone as far as Albany, in the neighbourhood of which place he had worked for some time with a farmer; but finding, that although he got higher wages, he had to pay much more for his provisions than in Canada, and that he was also most egregiously cheated by the people, and particularly by his employer, from whom he could not get even the money he had earned; finding likewise that he was unable to procure any redress, from being ignorant of the English language, the poor fellow determined to return to Canada, and on his way thither we met him, without a shilling in his pocket.

Having asked this little fellow, as we sailed along, some questions about the Indians, he immediately gave us a long account of a Captain Thomas, a chief of the Cachenonaga nation, in the neighbourhood of whose village he said

said he lived. Thomas, he told us, was a very rich man, and had a most excellent house, in which he said he lived as well as a seignior, and he was sure we should be well received if we went to see him; he told us also that he had built a church, and was a christian; that he was very charitable, and that if he were acquainted with his present distress he would certainly make him a present of four or five dollars. " Oh je vous assure, messieurs, que " c'est un bon sauvage." It was impossible not to smile at the little Canadian, who, half naked himself, and nearly as dark as a mulatto, concluded his panegyric upon Thomas, by assuring us, " he was a good savage;" at the same time we felt a strong desire to behold this chief, of whom we had heard so much. It was not long before we were gratified, for the party of Indians that arrived whilst we were at Chimney Point were from the Cachenonaga village, and at their head was Captain Thomas.

Thomas appeared to be about forty-five years of age; he was nearly six feet high, and very bulky in proportion: this is a sort of make uncommon among the Indians, who are generally slender. He was dressed like a white man, in boots; his hair untied, but cut short; the people who attended him were all in the Indian habit. Not one of his followers could speak a word of English or French; Thomas, however,

however, could himself speak both languages. English he spoke with some little hesitation, and not correctly; but French seemed as familiar to him as his native tongue. His principal attention seemed to be directed towards trade, which he had pursued with great success, so much so, indeed, that, as we afterwards heard, he could get credit in any store in Montreal for five hundred pounds. He had along with him at Chimney Point thirty horses and a quantity of furs in the canoe, which he was taking for sale to Albany. His people, he told us, had but very few wants; he took care to have these always supplied; in return they brought him furs, taken in hunting; they attended his horses, and voluntarily accompanied him when he went on a trading expedition: his profits therefore must be immense. During the course of conversation he told us, that if we came to see him he would make us very happy; that there were some very handsome squaws * in his village, and that each of us should have a wife: we promised to visit him if it was in our power, and parted very good friends. Thomas, as we afterwards found, is not a man respected among the Indians in general, who think much more of a chief that is a good warrior and hunter, and that retains the

* Female Indians.

habits

habits of his nation, than of one that becomes a trader, and aſſimilates his manners to thoſe of the whites.

Lake Champlain is about one hundred and twenty miles in length, and is of various breadths; for the firſt thirty miles, that is, from South River to Crown Point, it is in no place more than two miles wide; beyond this, for the diſtance of twelve miles, it is five or ſix miles acroſs, but then again it narrows, and again at the end of a few miles expands. That part called the Broad Lake, becauſe broader than any other, commences about twenty-five miles north of Crown Point, and is eighteen miles acroſs in the wideſt part. Here the lake is interſperſed with a great number of iſlands, the largeſt of which, formerly called Grande Iſle, now South Hero, is fifteen miles in length, and, on an average, about four in breadth. The ſoil of this iſland is fertile, and it is ſaid that five hundred people are ſettled upon it. The Broad Lake is nearly fifty miles in length, and gradually narrows till it terminates in a large river called Chambly, Richlieu, or Sorelle, which runs into the St. Lawrence.

The ſoundings of Lake Champlain, except at the narrow parts at either end, are in general very deep; in many places ſixty and ſeventy, and in ſome even one hundred fathoms. In proportion to its breadth and depth, the water

is

is more or less clear; in the broad part it is as pure and transparent as possible. On the west side, as far as Cumberland Bay, the lake is bounded for the most part by steep mountains close to the edge of the water; at Cumberland Bay the ridge of mountains runs off to the north west, and the shore farther on is low and swampy. The East or Vermont shore is not much elevated, except in a few particular places; at the distance of twelve miles, however, from the lake is a considerable mountain. The shores on both sides are very rocky; where there are mountains these rocks jut out very boldly; but at the east side, where the land is low, they appear but a little above the water. The islands also, for the most part, are surrounded with rocks, in some parts, shelving down into the lake, so that it is dangerous to approach within one or two miles of them at particular sides. From some parts of the eastern shore the rocks also run out in the same manner for a considerable distance. Sailing along the shore when a breeze is blowing, a hollow murmuring noise is always heard from the waters splashing into the crannies of these rocks. There are many streams which fall into the lake: the mouths of all those on the western side are obstructed by falls, so that none of them are navigable. Of those on the eastern or Vermont side, a few only are navigable for small boats, and that for a short distance.

The

The scenery along various parts of the lake is extremely grand and picturesque, particularly beyond Crown Point; the shores are there beautifully ornamented with hanging woods and rocks, and the mountains on the western side rise up in ranges one behind the other in the most magnificent manner. It was on one of the finest evenings possible that we passed along this part of the lake, and the sun setting in all his glory behind the mountains, spread the richest tints over every part of the prospect; the moon also appearing nearly in the full, shortly after the day had closed, afforded us an opportunity of beholding the surrounding scenery in fresh though less brilliant colours. Our little bark was now gliding smoothly along, whilst every one of us remained wrapt up in silent contemplation of the solemn scene, when suddenly she struck upon one of the shelving rocks: nothing but hurry and confusion was now visible on board, every one lending his assistance; however, at last, with some difficulty, we got her off; but in a minute she struck a second time, and after we had again extricated her, even a third and a fourth time; at last she stuck so fast that for a short time we despaired of being able to move her. At the end of a quarter of an hour, however, we again fortunately got her into deep water. We had before suspected that our boatman did not know

know a great deal about the navigation of the lake, and on queftioning him now, it came out, that he had been a cobler all his life, till within the laſt nine months, when he thought proper to change his bufinefs, and turn failor. All the knowledge he had of the fhores of the lake, was what he had picked up during that time, as he failed ftraight backward and forward between St. John's and Skenefborough. On the prefent occafion he had miftaken one bay for another, and had the waves been as high as they fometimes are, the boat would inevitably have been dafhed to pieces.

The humble roof of another judge, a plain Scotch labourer, afforded us fhelter for this night. It was near eleven o'clock, however, when we got there, and the family having retired to reft we had to remain rapping and calling at the door for half an hour at leaft; before we could get admittance. The people at laft being roufed, opened their doors, cheerfully got us fome fupper, and prepared their beft beds for us. In the morning, having paid our reckoning to the judge, he returned to his plough, and we to our boat to profecute our voyage.

We fet off this day with a remarkable fine breeze, and being defirous of terminating our voyage as foon as poffible, of which we began now to be fomewhat tired, we ftopped but once

once in the courſe of the day, and determined to ſail on all night. A ſhort time after ſun ſet we paſſed the boundary between the Britiſh dominions and the United States. Here we were brought to by an armed brig of twenty guns, under Engliſh colours, ſtationed for the purpoſe of examining all boats paſſing up and down the lake: the anſwers which we gave to the ſeveral queſtions aſked being ſatisfactory, we were accordingly ſuffered to proceed. Since the ſurrender of the poſts, purſuant to the late treaty with the United States, this brig has been removed, and laid up at St. John's. When night came on, we wrapped ourſelves up in our blankets, as we had done on the firſt night of our voyage, and laid down upon the cabin floor, where we might poſſibly have ſlept until we got to St. John's, had we not been awakened at midnight by the loud hollas of the ſentinel at the Britiſh fort on Iſle aux Noix. On examining into the matter, it appeared that the boat had been driven on ſhore, while our ſleepy pilot enjoyed his nap at the helm; and the centinel, unable to imagine what we were about, ſeeing the boat run up cloſe under the fort, and ſuſpicious of ſome attack, I ſuppoſe, had turned out the whole guard; by whom, after being examined and re-examined, we were finally diſmiſſed. We now took the command of the boat upon
our-

ourselves, for the boatman, although he was more anxious to get to St. John's than any one of us, and though he had himself in some-measure induced us to go on, was so sleepy that he could not keep his eyes open.. Relieving each other at the helm, we reached St. John's by day-break; one hundred and fifty miles distant from Skenesborough.

Immediately on our landing we were conducted to the guard house, where we had to deliver to the serjeant on duty, to be by him forwarded to the commanding officer, an account of our names, occupation, and place of abode, the strictest orders having been issued by the governor not to suffer any Frenchmen or other foreigners, or any people who could not give an exact account of their business in Canada, to enter into the country.

St. John's is a garrison town; it contains about fifty miserable wooden dwellings, and barracks, in which a whole regiment is generally quartered. The fortifications are entirely out of order, so much so that it would be cheaper to erect fresh works than to attempt to repair them. There is a king's dock yard here, well stored with timber, at least, when we saw it; but in the course of the summer, after the armed brig which I mentioned was laid up, all the timber was sold off. The old hulks of several vessels of force were lying
opposite

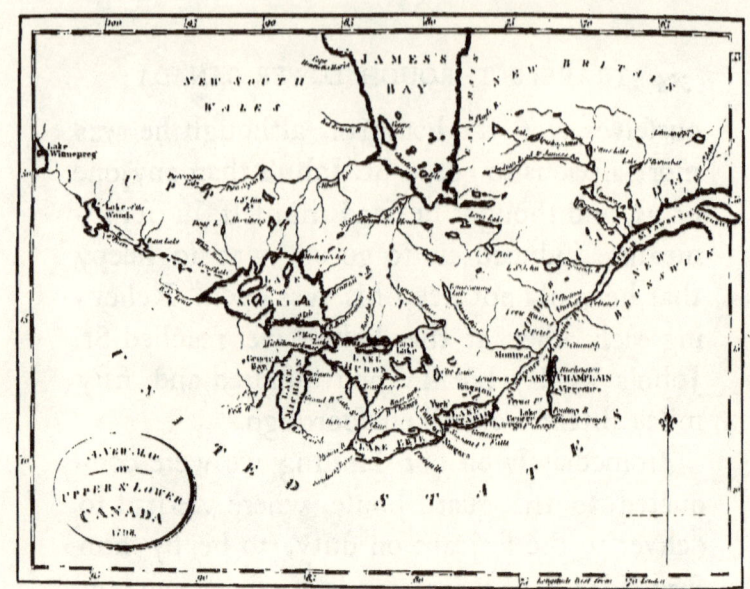

oppofite the yard. In proportion to the increafe of trade between New York and Lower Canada this town muft improve, as it is the Britifh port of entry on Lake Champlain.

The country about St. John's is flat, and very bare of trees, a dreadful fire in the year 1788 having done great mifchief, and deftroyed all the woods for feveral miles: in fome parts of the neighbourhood the people fuffer extremely during winter from the want of fuel.

At St. John's we hired a light waggon, fimilar to thofe made ufe of in the United States, and fet off about noon for La Prarie, on the banks of the river St. Lawrence. By the direct road, this is only eighteen miles diftant; but the moft agreeable way of going thither is by Chambly, which is a few miles farther, on account of feeing the old caftle built there by the French. The caftle ftands clofe to the rapids in Chambly or Sorelle River, and at a little diftance has a grand appearance; the adjacent country alfo being very beautiful, the whole together forms a moft interefting fcene. The caftle is in tolerably good repair, and a garrifon is conftantly kept in it.

As you travel along this road to La Prarie, after having juft arrived from the United States over Lake Champlain, a variety of objects forcibly remind you of your having got into a new country. The Britifh flag, the foldiers

Vol. I.   X   on

on duty, the French inhabitants running about in their red nightcaps, the children coming to the doors to falute you as you pafs, a thing unknown in any part of the United States; the compact and neat exterior appearance of the houfes, the calafhes, the bons dieux, the large Roman Catholic churches and chapels, the convents, the priefts in their robes, the nuns, the friars; all ferve to convince you that you are no longer in any part of the United States: the language alfo differs, French being here univerfally fpoken.

The calafh is a carriage very generally ufed in Lower Canada; there is fcarcely a farmer indeed in the country who does not poffefs one: it is a fort of one horfe chaife, capable of holding two people befides the driver, who fits on a kind of box placed over the foot board exprefsly for his accommodation. The body of the calafh is hung upon broad ftraps of leather, round iron rollers that are placed behind, by means of which they are fhortened or lengthened. On each fide of the carriage is a little door about two feet high, whereby you enter it, and which is ufeful when fhut, in preventing any thing from flipping out. The harnefs for the horfe is always made in the old French tafte, extremely heavy; it is ftudded with brafs nails, and to particular parts

of

J. B. Drayton, sculp.

of it are attached small bells, of no use that I could ever discover but to annoy the passenger.

The bons dieux are large wooden crucifixes, sometimes upwards of twenty feet in height, placed on the highway; some of them are highly ornamented and painted: as the people pass they pull off their hats, or in some other way make obeisance to them.

La Prarie de la Madelene contains about one hundred houses: after stopping an hour or two there we embarked in a bateau for Montreal.

Montreal is situated on an island of the same name, on the opposite side of the River St. Lawrence to that on which la Prarie stands, but somewhat lower down. The two towns are nine miles apart, and the river is about two miles and a quarter wide. The current here is prodigiously strong, and in particular places as you cross, the boats are hurried down the stream, in the midst of large rocks, with such impetuosity that it seems as if nothing could save them from being dashed to pieces; indeed this would certainly be the case if the men were not uncommonly expert; but the Canadians are the most dexterous people perhaps in the world at the management of bateaux in rapid rivers. After such a prospect of the River St. Lawrence, it was not without astonishment that on approaching

X 2   the

the town of Montreal we beheld ships of upwards of four hundred tons burthen lying close to the shore. The difficulties which vessels have to encounter in getting to Montreal are immense; I have myself seen them with all their sails set, and with a smart and favourable breeze, stationary for an hour together in the stream, unable to stem it, between the island of St. Helene and the main land, just below the town: to stem the current at this place it is almost necessary that the vessel should be aided by a storm. The ascent is equally difficult in several other parts of the river. Owing to this it is, that the passage from Quebec to Montreal is generally more tedious than that across the Atlantic; those ships, therefore, which trade between Europe and Montreal, never attempt to make more than one voyage during the year. Notwithstanding the rapidity of the stream, the channel of the river is very deep, and in particular just opposite to the town. The largest merchant vessels can there lie so close to the banks, which are in their natural state, that you may nearly touch them with your hand as you stand on the shore.

LETTER XXII.

Description of the Town of Montreal.—Of the public Buildings.—Churches.—Funeral Ceremonies.—Convents.—Barracks.—Fortifications.—Inhabitants mostly French.—Their Character and Manners.—Charming Prospects in the Neighbourhood of the Town.—Amusements during Summer.—Parties of Pleasure up the Mountain.—Of the Fur Trade.—The Manner in which it is carried on.—Great Enterprise of the North West Company of Merchants.—Sketch of Mr. M'Kenzie's Expeditions over Land to the Pacific Ocean.—Differences between the North West and Hudson's Bay Companies.

Montreal, July.

THE town of Montreal was laid out pursuant to the orders of one of the kings of France, which were, that a town should be built as high up on the St. Lawrence as it were possible for vessels to go by sea. In fixing upon the spot where it stands, his commands were complied with in the strictest sense. The town at present contains about twelve hundred houses, whereof five hundred only are within the walls; the rest are in the suburbs, which commence from the north, east, and west gates. The houses in the suburbs are mostly built of wood, but the others are all of stone; none of them are elegant, but there are many very comfortable habitations. In the lower part of the town, towards the river, where most of the shops stand, they have a very gloomy appearance, and look like so many prisons, being all furnished at the outside with sheet iron shutters to the doors and windows, which are regularly closed towards evening, in order to guard against fire. The town has suffered by fire very materially at different times, and the inhabitants have such a dread of it, that all who can afford it cover the roofs of their houses with tin-plates instead of shingles. By law they are obliged to have one or more ladders, in proportion to the size of the house, always ready on the roofs.

The streets are all very narrow; three of them run parallel to the river, and these are intersected by others at right angles, but not at regular distances. On the side of the town farthest from the river, and nearly between the northern and southern extremities, there is a small square, called La Place d'Armes, which seems originally to have been left open to the walls on one side, and to have been intended for the military to exercise in; the troops, however, never make use of it now,

now, but parade on a long walk, behind the walls, nearer to the barracks. On the opposite side of the town, towards the water, is another small square, where the market is held.

There are six churches in Montreal; one for English Episcopalians, one for Presbyterians, and four for Roman Catholics. The cathedral church belonging to the latter, which occupies one side of La Place d'Armes, is a very spacious building, and contains five altars, all very richly decorated. The doors of this cathedral are left open the greater part of the day, and there are, generally, numbers of old people in it at their prayers, even when no regular service is going on. On a fine Sunday in the summer season such multitudes flock to it, that even the steps at the outside are covered with people, who, unable to get in, remain there kneeling with their hats off during the whole time of divine service. Nearly all the christenings, marriages, and burials of the Roman Catholic inhabitants of Montreal are performed in this church, on which occasions, as well as before and during the masses, they always ring the bells, to the great annoyance of every person that is not a lover of discords; for instead of pulling the bells, which are five in number, and really well toned, with regularity, they jingle them all at once, without any sort of cadence whatever.

Our lodgings happened to be in La Place d'Armes; and during three weeks that we remained there, I verily believe the bells were never suffered to remain still for two hours together, at any one time, except in the night.

The funerals, as in other Roman Catholic countries, are conducted with great ceremony; the corpse is always attended to the church by a number of priests chanting prayers, and by little boys in white robes and black caps carrying wax lights. A morning scarcely ever passed over that one or more of these processions did not pass under our windows whilst we were at breakfast; for on the opposite side of the square to that on which the cathedral stood, was a sort of chapel, to which the bodies of all those persons, whose friends could not afford to pay for an expensive funeral, were brought, I suppose, in the night, for we could never see any carried in there, and from thence conveyed in the morning to the cathedral. If the priests are paid for it they go to the house of the deceased, though it be ever so far distant, and escort the corpse to the church. Until within a few years past it was customary to bury all the bodies in the vaults underneath the cathedral; but now it is prohibited, left some putrid disorder should break out in the town in consequence of such numbers

numbers being deposited there. The burying grounds are all without the walls at present.

There are in Montreal four convents, one of which is of the order of St. Francis; the number of the friars, however, is reduced now to two or three, and as by the laws of the province men can no longer enter into any religious order, it will of course in a few years dwindle entirely away. On the female orders there is no restriction, and they are still well filled. The Hotel Dieu, founded as early as 1644, for the relief of the sick poor, and which is the oldest of the convents, contains thirty " religieuses"—nuns; La Congregation de Notre Dame, instituted for the instruction of young girls, contains fifty-seven sœurs, another sort of nuns; and L'Hospital Generale, for the accommodation of the infirm poor, contains eighteen sœurs.

The barracks are agreeably situated near the river, at the lower end of the town; they are surrounded by a lofty wall, and calculated to contain about three hundred men.

The walls round the town are mouldering away very fast, and in some places are totally in ruins; the gates, however, remain quite perfect. The walls were built principally as a defence against the Indians, by whom the country was thickly inhabited when Montreal was founded, and they were found necessary,

to

to repel the open attacks of these people as late as the year 1736. When the large fairs used to be held in Montreal, to which the Indians from all parts resorted with their furs, they were also found extremely useful, as the inhabitants were thereby enabled to shut out the Indians at night, who, had they been suffered to remain in the town, addicted as they are to drinking, might have been tempted to commit great outrages, and would have kept the inhabitants in a continual state of alarm. In their best state the walls could not have protected the town against cannon, not even against a six pounder; nor, indeed, would the strongest walls be of any use in defending it against artillery, as it is completely commanded by the eminences in the island of St. Helene*, in the River St. Lawrence. Montreal has always been an easy conquest to regular troops.

By far the greater number of the inhabitants of Montreal are of French extraction; all the eminent merchants, however, and principal people in the town, are either English, Scotch, Irish, or their descendants, all of whom pass for English with the French inhabitants. The French retain, in a great

---

* This island was the last place which the French surrendered to the British.

meafure,

measure, the manners and customs of their ancestors, as well as the language; they have an unconquerable aversion to learn English, and it is very rare to meet with any person amongst them that can speak it in any manner; but the English inhabitants are, for the most part, well acquainted with the French language.

The people of Montreal, in general, are remarkably hospitable and attentive to strangers; they are sociable also amongst themselves, and fond in the extreme of convivial amusements. In winter, they keep up such a constant and friendly intercourse with each other, that it seems then as if the town were inhabited but by one large family. During summer they live somewhat more retired; but throughout that season a club, formed of all the principal inhabitants, both male and female, meet every week or fortnight, for the purpose of dining at some agreeable spot in the neighbourhood of the town.

The island of Montreal is about twenty-eight miles in length and ten in breadth; it is the largest of several islands which are situated in the St. Lawrence, at the mouth of the Utawa River. Its soil is luxuriant, and in some parts much cultivated and thickly inhabited. It is agreeably diversified with hill and dale, and towards its center, in the neighbourhood

bourhood of Montreal, there are two or three confiderable mountains. The largeft of thefe ftands at the diftance of about one mile from the town, which is named from it. The bafe of this mountain is furrounded with neat country houfes and gardens, and partial improvements have been made about one third of the way up; the remainder is entirely covered with lofty trees. On that fide towards the river is a large old monaftery, with extenfive inclofures walled in, round which the ground has been cleared for fome diftance. This open part is covered with a rich verdure, and the woods encircling it, inftead of being overrun with brufhwood, are quite clear at bottom, fo that you may here roam about at pleafure for miles together, fhaded, by the lofty trees, from the rays of the fun.

The view from hence is grand beyond defcription. A prodigious expanfe of country is laid open to the eye, with the noble river St. Lawrence winding through it, which may be traced from the remoteft part of the horizon. The river comes from the right, and flows fmoothly on after paffing down the tremendous rapids above the town, where it is hurried over huge rocks with a noife that is heard even up the mountain. On the left below you appears the town of Montreal, with its churches, monafteries, glittering
spires,

spires, and the shipping under its old walls; several little islands in the river near the town, partly improved, partly overgrown with wood, add greatly to the beauty of the scene. La Prarie with its large church on the distant side of the river, is seen to the greatest advantage, and beyond it is a range of lofty mountains which terminates the prospect. Such an endless variety and such a grandeur is there in the view from this part of the mountain, that even those who are most habituated to the view always find it a fresh subject of admiration whenever they contemplate it; and on this part of the mountain it is that the club which I mentioned generally assembles. Two stewards are appointed for the day, who always chuse some new spot where there is a spring or rill of water, and an agreeable shade: each family brings cold provisions, wine, &c.; the whole is put together, and the company, often amounting to one hundred persons, sits down to dinner.

The fur trade is what is chiefly carried on at Montreal, and it is there that the greater part of the furs are shipped, which are sent from Canada to England.

This very lucrative trade is carried on, partly by what is called the North West Company, and partly by private individuals on their own account. The company does not possess any

particular

particular privileges by law, but from its great capital merely it is enabled to trade to certain remote parts of the continent, to the exclusion of those who do not hold any shares in it. It was formed originally by the merchants of Montreal themselves, who wisely considered that the trade could be carried on to those distant parts of the continent, inhabited solely by Indians, with more security and greater profit, if they joined together in a body, than if they continued to trade separately. The stock of the company was divided into forty shares, and as the number of merchants in the town at that time was not very great, this arrangement afforded an opportunity to every one of them to join in the company if he thought proper. At present these shares have all fallen into the hands of a few persons.

The company principally carries on its trade by means of the Utawas or Grand River, that falls into the St. Lawrence about thirty miles above Montreal, and which forms, by its confluence with that river, " Le Lac de Deux Montagnes et le Lac St. Louis,"—the lake of the Two Mountains and the Lake of St. Louis, wherein are several large islands. To convey the furs down this river, they make use of canoes, formed of the bark of the birch tree, some of which are upon such a large scale that they are capable of containing two tons, but they seldom put so much in them, especially on this river, it being in many places shallow, rapid, and full of rocks, and contains no less than thirty-two portages.

The canoes are navigated by the French Canadians, who are particularly fond of the employment, preferring it in general to that of cultivating the ground. A fleet of them sets off from Montreal about the month of May, laden with provisions, consisting chiefly of biscuit and salt pork, sufficient to last the crews till their return, and also with the articles given in barter to the Indians. At some of the shallow places in the river, it is sufficient if the men merely get out of the canoes, and push them on into the deep water; but at others, where there are dangerous rapids and sharp rocks, is it necessary for the men to unlade the canoes, and carry both them and the cargoes on their shoulders, till they come again to a safe part of the river. At night they drag the canoes upon shore, light a fire, cook their provisions for the following day, and sleep upon the ground wrapped up in their blankets. If it happens to rain very hard, they sometimes shelter themselves with boughs of trees, but in general they remain under the canopy of heaven, without any covering but their blankets: they copy exactly the Indian mode of life on these occasions, and many of

them

them even wear the Indian dresses, which they find more convenient than their own

Having ascended the Utawas River for about two hundred and eighty miles, which it takes them about eighteen days to perform, they then cross by a portage into Lake Nispissing, and from this lake by another portage they get upon French River, that falls into Lake Huron on the north-east side; then coasting along this last lake they pass through the Straits of St. Mary, where there is another portage into Lake Superior; and coasting afterwards along the shores of Lake Superior, they come to the Grand Portage on the north-west side of it; from hence by a chain of small lakes and rivers they proceed on to the Rainy Lake, to the Lake of the Woods, and for hundreds of miles beyond it, through Lake Winnipeg, &c.

The canoes, however, which go so far up the country, never return the same year; those intended to bring back cargoes immediately, stop at the Grand Portage, where the furs are collected ready for them by the agents of the company. The furs are made up in packs of a certain weight, and a particular number is put into each canoe. By knowing thus the exact weight of every pack, there can be no embezzlement; and at the portages there is no time wasted in allotting to each
man

man his load, every one being obliged to carry so many packs.

At the Grand Portage, and along that immense chain of lakes and rivers, which extend beyond Lake Superior, the company has regular posts, where the agents reside; and with such astonishing enterprize and industry have the affairs of this company been carried on, that trading posts are now established within five hundred miles of the Pacific Ocean. One gentleman, indeed, a partner in the house at Montreal, which now holds the greatest part of the shares of the company, has even penetrated to the Pacific Ocean itself. The journal kept by this gentleman upon the expedition is, it is said, replete with information of the most interesting nature. That it has not been laid before the public long ago, together with an accurate map of his track, is to be imputed solely to an unfortunate misunderstanding which took place between him and a noble lord high in the confidence of government.

In the first attempt which this adventurous gentleman, a Mr. M'Kenzie, made to penetrate to the ocean, he set out early in the spring from the remotest of the posts belonging to the company. He took with him a single canoe, and a party of chosen men; and after passing over prodigious tracts of land, never before traverfed by any white perfon, at laft came to a large river. Here the canoe, which was carried by the men on their fhoulders, was launched, and having all embarked, they proceeded down the ftream. From the courfe this river took for a very great diftance, Mr. M'Kenzie was led to imagine that it was one of thofe rivers he was in queft of; namely, one which emptied itfelf into the Pacific Ocean; but at the end of feveral weeks, during which they had worked their way downward with great eagernefs, he was convinced, from the gradual inclination of the river towards another quarter, that he muft have been miftaken; and that it was one of thofe immenfe rivers, fo numerous on the continent of North America, that ran into Baffin's Bay, or the Arctic Ocean.

The party was now in a very critical fituation; the feafon was far advanced, and the length of way which they had to return was prodigious. If they attempted to go back, and were overtaken by winter, they muft in all probability perifh for want of provifions in an uninhabited country; if, on the contrary, they made up their minds to fpend the winter where they were, they had no time to lofe in building huts, and going out to hunt and fifh, that they might have fufficient ftores to fupport them through that dreary feafon. Mr. M'Kenzie

M'Kenzie represented the matter, in the most open terms, to his men, and left it to themselves to determine the part they would take. The men were for going back at all hazards; and the result was, that they reached their friends in safety. The difficulties they had to contend with, and the exertions they made in returning, were almost surpassing belief.

The second expedition entered upon by Mr. M'Kenzie, and which succeeded to his wishes, was undertaken about three years ago. He set out in the same manner, but well provided with several different things, which he found the want of in the first expedition. He was extremely well furnished this time with astronomical instruments, and in particular with a good time-piece, that he procured from London. He took a course somewhat different from the first, and passed through many nations of Indians who had never before seen the face of a white man, amongst some of whom he was for a time in imminent danger; but he found means at last to conciliate their good will. From some of these Indians he learned, that there was a ridge of mountains at a little distance, beyond which the rivers all ran in a western direction. Having engaged some of them therefore for guides, he proceeded according to their directions until he came to the mountains, and after ascending them

them with prodigious labour, found, to his great fatisfaction, that the account the Indians had given was true, and that the rivers on the oppofite fide did indeed all run to the weft. He followed the courfe of one of them, and finally came to the Pacific Ocean, not far from Nootka Sound.

Here he was given to underftand by the natives, and their account was confirmed by the fight of fome little articles they had amongft them, that an Englifh veffel had quitted the coaft only fix weeks before. This was a great mortification to Mr. M'Kenzie; for had there been a fhip on the coaft, he would moft gladly have embarked in it rather than encounter the fame difficulties, and be expofed to the fame perils, which he had experienced in getting there; however there was no alternative; he fet out after a fhort time on his journey back again, and having found his canoe quite fafe under fome bufhes, near the head of the river, where he had hid it, together with fome provifions, left on going down to the coaft the natives might have proved unfriendly, and have cut off his retreat by feizing upon it, he finally arrived at one of the trading pofts in fecurity. When I was at Montreal Mr. M'Kenzie was not there, and I never had an opportunity of feeing him afterwards. What I have here related refpecting his two expeditions

ditions is the substance, to the best of my recollection, of what I heard from his partners.

Many other individuals belonging to the North West Company, before Mr. M'Kenzie set out, penetrated far into the country in different directions, and much beyond what any person had done before them, in order to establish posts. In some of these excursions they fell in with the agents of the Hudson Bay Company, who were also extending their posts from another quarter: this unexpected meeting between the two companies, at one time gave rise to some very unpleasant altercations, and the Hudson Bay Company threatened the other with an immediate prosecution for an infringement of its charter.

By its charter, it seems, the Hudson Bay Company was allowed the exclusive privilege of trading to the Bay, and along all the rivers and waters connected with it. This charter, however, was granted at a time when the northern parts of the continent were much less known than they are now, for to have the exclusive trade along all the waters connected with Hudson Bay was, literally speaking, to have the exclusive trade of the greater part of the continent of North America. Hudson Bay by a variety of rivers and lakes, is closely connected with Lake Superior, and from that chain of lakes, of which Lake Superior is one, there

there is a water communication throughout all Canada, and a very great part of the United States; however, when the agents of the North-weſt Company were fixing trading poſts upon ſome rivers which ran immediately into Hudſon's Bay, it undoubtedly appeared to be an infringement of the charter, and ſo indeed it muſt ſtrictly have been, had not the Hudſon's Bay Company itſelf infringed its own charter in the firſt inſtance, or at leaſt neglected to comply with all the ſtipulations contained therein. A clauſe ſeems to have been in the charter, which, at the ſame time that it granted to the company the excluſive privilege of trading to Hudſon's Bay, and along all the waters connected with it, bound it to erect a new poſt twelve miles farther to the weſtward every year, otherwiſe the charter was to become void. This had not been done; the North-weſt Company therefore reſted perfectly eaſy about the menaces of a proſecution, ſatisfied that the other company did not in fact legally poſſeſs thoſe privileges to which it laid claim.

The Hudſon's Bay Company, though it threatened, never indeed attempted to put its threats into execution, well knowing the weakneſs of its cauſe, but continued nevertheleſs to watch the motions of its rival with a moſt jealous eye; and as in extending their reſpective

tive trades, the posts of the two companies were approximating nearer and nearer to each other every year, there was great reason to imagine that their differences, instead of abating, would become still greater than they were, and finally, perhaps, lead to consequences of the most serious nature. A circumstance, however, unexpectedly took place, at a time when the greatest enmity subsisted between the parties, which happily reconciled them to each other, and terminated all their disputes.

A very powerful nation of Indians, called the Assiniboins, who inhabit an extended tract of country to the south-west of Lake Winnipeg, conceiving that the Hudson's Bay Company had encroached unreasonably upon their territories, and had otherwise maltreated a part of their tribe, formed the resolution of instantly destroying a post established by that company in their neighbourhood. A large body of them soon collected together, and breathing the fiercest spirit of revenge, marched unperceived and unsuspected by the party against whom their expedition was planned, till within a short distance of their post. Here they halted according to custom, waiting only for a favourable moment to pounce upon their prey. Some of the agents of the North-west Company, however, who were scattered about this part of the country, fortunately got intelligence of their design.

design. They knew the weakness of the place about to be attacked, and forgetting the rivalship subsisting between them, and thinking only how to save their countrymen, they immediately dispatched a messenger to give the party notice of the assault that was meditated; they at the same time sent another messenger to one of their own posts, desiring that instant succour might be sent to that belonging to the Hudson Bay Company, which the Indians were about to plunder. The detachment arrived before the attack commenced, and the Indians were repulsed; but had it not been for the timely assistance their rivals had afforded, the Hudson Bay people were fully persuaded that they must have fallen victims to the fury of the Indians.

This signal piece of service was not undervalued or forgotten by those who had been saved; and as the North-west Company was so much stronger, and on so much better terms with the Indians in this part of the country than its rivals, it now evidently appeared to be the interest of the latter to have the posts of the North-west Company established as near its own as possible. This is accordingly done for their mutual safety, and the two companies are now on the most friendly terms, and continue to carry on their trade close to each other.

About two thousand men are employed by
the

the North-west Company in their posts in the upper country. Those who are stationed at the remote trading posts lead a very savage life, but little better indeed than that of Indians: some of them remain far up in the country for four or five years together. The head clerk or principal agent generally marries an Indian girl, the daughter of some eminent chief, by which he gains in a peculiar manner the affections of the whole tribe, a matter of great importance. These marriages, as may be supposed, are not considered as very binding by the husband; but that is nothing in the opinion of an Indian chief, who readily brings his sister or daughter to you; at the same time he can only be appeased by blood if a person attempts to take any improper liberties with his wife. Amongst no people are the wives more chaste, or more devoted to their husbands.

Besides the furs and pelts conveyed down to Montreal from the north-western parts of the continent, by means of the Utawas River, there are large quantities also brought there across the lakes, and down the River St. Lawrence. These are collected at the various towns and posts along the Lakes Huron, Erie, and Ontario, where the trade is open to all parties, the several posts being protected by regular troops, at the expence of the government.

ment. Added likewise to what are thus collected by the agents of the company, and of private merchants, there are considerable quantities brought down to Montreal for sale by traders, on their own account. Some of these traders come from parts as remote as the Illinois Country, bordering on the Mississippi. They ascend the Mississippi as far as Onisconsing River, and from that by a portage of three miles get upon Fox River, which falls into Lake Michigan. In the fall of the year, as I have before mentioned, these two rivers overflow, and it is then sometimes practicable to pass in a light canoe from one river to the other, without any portage whatsoever. From Lake Michigan they get upon Lake Huron, afterwards upon Lake Erie, and so on to the St. Lawrence. Before the month of September is over, the furs are all brought down to Montreal; as they arrive they are immediately shipped, and the vessels dispatched in October, beyond which month it would be dangerous for them to remain in the river on account of the setting in of winter.

Furs are also shipped in considerable quantities at Quebec, and at the town of Trois Rivieres. These furs are brought down the rivers that fall into the St. Lawrence, on the north side, by Indians.

LETTER XXIII.

Voyage to Quebec down the St. Lawrence.—A Bateau preferable to a Keel Boat.—Town of Sorelle.—Ship-building there.—Description of Lake St. Pierre.—Baliscon.—Charming Scenery along the Banks of St. Lawrence.—In what respects it differs from the Scenery along any other River in America.—Canadian Houses.—Sketch of the Character and manners of the lower Classes of Canadians.—Their Superstition.—Anecdote.—St. Augustin Calvaire.—Arrive at Quebec.

Quebec, August.

WE remained in Montreal until the first day of August, when we set off in a bateau for Quebec, about one hundred and sixty miles lower down the St. Lawrence. A bateau is a particular kind of boat, very generally used upon the large rivers and lakes in Canada. The bottom of it is perfectly flat, and each end is built very sharp, and exactly alike. The sides are about four feet high, and for the convenience of the rowers, four or five benches are laid across, sometimes more, according to the length of the bateau. It is a very heavy awkward sort of vessel, either for rowing or sailing, but

but it is preferred to a boat with a keel for two very obvious reasons; first, because it draws less water, at the same time that it carries a larger burthen; and secondly, because it is much safer on lakes or wide rivers, where storms are frequent: a proof of this came under our observation the day of our leaving Montreal. We had reached a wide part of the river, and were sailing along with a favourable wind, when suddenly the horizon grew very dark, and a dreadful storm arose, accompanied with loud peals of thunder and torrents of rain. Before the sail could be taken in, the ropes which held it were snapped in pieces, and the waves began to dash over the sides of the bateau, though the water had been quite smooth five minutes before. It was impossible now to counteract the force of the wind with oars, and the bateau was consequently driven on shore, but the bottom of it being quite flat, it was carried smoothly upon the beach without sustaining any injury, and the men leaping out drew it up on dry land, where we remained out of all danger till the storm was over. A keel boat, however, of the same size, could not have approached nearer to the shore than thirty feet, and there it would have stuck fast in the sand, and probably have been filled with water. From being fitted up as it was, our bateau proved to be a very pleasant conveyance: it was one of

a large

a large size, and over the widest part of it an oilcloth awning was thrown, supported by hoops similar to the roof of a waggon: thus a most excellent cabin was formed, large enough to contain half a dozen chairs and a table, and which, at the same time that it afforded shelter from the inclemency of the weather, was airy, and sufficiently open to let us see all the beauties of the prospect on each shore to the greatest advantage.

It was about eleven o'clock in the morning when we left Montreal, and at five in the afternoon we reached the town of Sorelle, fifteen leagues distant. The current is very strong the whole way between the two places. Sorelle stands at the mouth of the river of the same name, which runs from Lake Champlain into the St. Lawrence. It was laid out about the year 1787, and on an extensive plan, with very wide streets and a large square, but at present it contains only one hundred houses, are all very indifferent, and standing widely asunder. This is the only town on the St. Lawrence, between Montreal and Quebec, wherein English is the predominant language. The inhabitants consist principally of loyalists from the United States, who took refuge in Canada. The chief business carried on here is that of ship-building; there are several vessels annually launched from fifty to two hundred tons burthen;

then; thefe are floated down to Quebec, and there rigged. Ship-building is not carried on to fo much advantage in Canada as might be imagined, all the bolts and other articles of iron, the blocks, and the cordage, being imported; fo that what is gained by having excellent timber on the fpot is loft in bringing over thefe different articles, which are fo bulky, from Europe. The river of Sorelle is deep at the mouth, and affords good fhelter for fhips from the ice, at the breaking up of winter: it is not navigable far beyond the town, even in boats, on account of the rapids.

The next morning we left Sorelle, beyond which place the St. Lawrence expands to a great breadth. Here it abounds with fmall iflands, fituated fo clofely to each other, that it is impoffible to think without aftonifhment of large veffels, like thofe that go to Montreal, paffing between them: the channel through them is very intricate. This wide part of the river is called Lac St. Pierre; the greateft breadth of it is about four leagues and a half, and its length from the iflands at the head of the lake downwards about eight leagues. From hence to Quebec the river is in no place more than two miles acrofs, and in fome parts it narrows to the breadth of three quarters of a mile. The tide ebbs and flows in the river within a few leagues of Lac St. Pierre; the great

great expansion of the water at the lake, and the strong current which sets out from it, prevents its action higher up.

From Montreal as far as the town of Trois Rivieres, which stands about four leagues below Lac St. Pierre, the shores on each side of the St. Lawrence are very flat; the land then begins to rise, and on the south-east side it continues lofty the whole way down to Quebec. On the opposite side, however, below Trois Rivieres, the banks vary considerably; in some places they are high, in others very low, until you approach within a few leagues of Quebec, when they assume a bold and grand appearance on each side. The scenery along various parts of the river is very fine: it is impossible, indeed, but that there must be a variety of pleasing views along a noble river like the St. Lawrence, winding for hundreds of miles through a rich country, diversified with rising grounds, woodlands, and cultivated plains. What particularly attracts the attention, however, in going down this river, is, the beautiful disposition of the towns and villages on its banks. Nearly all the settlements in Lower Canada are situated close upon the borders of the rivers, and from this circumstance the scenery along the St. Lawrence and others differs materially from that along the rivers in the United States. The banks

banks of the Hudson river, which are more cultivated than those of any of the other large rivers there, are wild and desolate in comparison with those of the St. Lawrence. For several leagues below Montreal the houses stand so closely together, that it appears as if it were but one village, which extended the whole way. All the houses have a remarkably neat appearance at a distance; and in each village, though it be ever so small, there is a church. The churches are kept in the neatest repair, and most of them have spires, covered, according to the custom of the country, with tin, that, from being put on in a particular manner, never becomes rusty *. It is pleasing beyond description to behold one of these villages opening to the view, as you sail round a point of land covered with trees, the houses in it overhanging the river, and the spires of the churches sparkling through the groves with which they are encircled, before the rays of the setting sun.

There is scarcely any part of the river, where you pass along, for more than a league, without seeing a village and church.

The second night of our voyage we landed

---

* The square plates of tin are nailed on diagonally, and the corners are carefully folded over the heads of the nails, so as to prevent any moisture from getting to them.

at

at the village of Batiscon. It stands on the north-west side of the river, about eighty miles below Montreal. Here the shore is very flat and marshy, and for a considerable distance from it the water is so shallow when the tide is out, that a bateau even, cannot at that time come within one hundred yards of the dry ground. Lower down the river the shore is in some places extremely rocky.

The first habitation we came to at Batiscon was a farm house, where we readily got accommodation for the night. The people were extremely civil, and did all in their power to serve us. A small table was quickly set out, covered with a neat white table cloth, and bread, milk, eggs, and butter, the best fare which the house afforded, were brought to us. These things may always be had in abundance at every farm house; but it is not often that you can procure meat of any sort; in going through Canada, therefore, it is customary for travellers to carry a provision basket with them. The houses in Lower Canada are in general well furnished with beds, all in the French style, very large, and raised four or five feet high, with a paillasse, a mattrass, and a feather bed.

The houses for the most part are built of logs; but they are much more compact and better built than those in the United States;

the logs are made to fit more closely together, and instead of being left rough and uneven on the outside, are planed and white washed. At the inside also the walls are generally lined with deal boards, whereas in the United States the common log-houses are left as rough within as they are without. One circumstance, however, renders the Canadian houses very disagreeable, and that is the inattention of the inhabitants to air them occasionally by opening the windows, in consequence of which they have a close heavy smell within doors. As we travelled by land from Quebec to Montreal, we scarcely observed ten houses the whole way with the windows open, notwithstanding that the weather was very warm. If you ask the people why they don't let a little fresh air into their houses, their constant answer is, as it is to all questions of a similar tendency, " Ce n'est " pas la maniere des habitans"—It is not the custom of the people of the country.

Some of the lower classes of the French Canadians have all the gaiety and vivacity of the people of France; they dance, they sing, and seem determined not to give way to care; others, to appearance, have a great deal of that sullenness and bluntness in their manners characteristic of the people of the United States; vanity, however, is the ascendant feature

ture in the character of all of them, and by working upon that you may make them do what you please. Few of the men can read or write; the little learning there is amongst the inhabitants is confined to the women: a Canadian never makes a bargain, or takes any step of importance, without consulting his wife, whose opinion is generally abided by. Both men and women are sunk in ignorance and superstition, and blindly devoted to their priests. The following anecdote may serve to shew how much they are so.

On the evening before we reached Quebec, we stopped at the village of St. Augustin Calvaire, and after having strolled about for some time, returned to the farm-house where we had taken up our quarters for the night. The people had cooked some fish, that had been just caught, while we had been walking about, and every thing being ready on our return, we sat down to supper by the light of a lamp, which was suspended from the ceiling. The glimmering light, however, that it afforded, scarcely enabled us to see what was on the table; we complained of it to the man of the house, and the lamp was in consequence trimmed; it was replenished with oil; taken down and set on the table; still the light was very bad. " Sacre Dieu!" exclaimed he, " but you shall not eat your fish
" in

"in the dark;" so saying, he stepped aside to a small cupboard, took out a candle, and having lighted it, placed it beside us. All was now going on well, when the wife, who had been absent for a few minutes, suddenly returning, poured forth a volley of the most terrible execrations against her poor husband for having presumed to have acted as he had done. Unable to answer a single word, the fellow stood aghast, ignorant of what he had done to offend her; we were quite at a loss also to know what could have given rise to such a sudden storm; the wife, however, snatching up the candle, and hastily extinguishing it, addressed us in a plaintive tone of voice, and explained the whole affair. It was the holy candle—"La chandelle benite," which her giddy husband had set on the table; it had been consecrated at a neighbouring church, and supposing there should be a tempest at any time, with thunder and lightning ever so terrible, yet if the candle were but kept burning while it lasted, the house, the barn, and every thing else belonging to it, were to be secured from all danger. If any of the family happened to be sick, the candle was to be lighted, and they were instantly to recover. It had been given to her that morning by the priest of the village, with an assurance that it possessed the miraculous power of preserving

preserving the family from harm, and she was confident that what he told her was true.—To have contradicted the poor woman would have been useless; for the sake of our ears, however, we endeavoured to pacify her, and that being accomplished, we sat down to supper, and e'en made the most of our fish in the dark.

The village of St. Augustin Calvaire is about five leagues from Quebec, at which last place we arrived early on the next morning, the fourth of our voyage. When the wind is fair, and the tide favourable also, it does not take more than two days to go from Montreal to Quebec.

LETTER XXIV.

Situation of the City of Quebec.—Divided into Upper and Lower Town.—Description of each.—Great Strength of the Upper Town.—Some Observations on the Capture of Quebec by the English Army under General Wolfe.—Observations on Montgomery's and Arnold's Attack during the American War.—Census of Inhabitants of Quebec.—The Chateau, the Residence of the Governor.—Monastery of the Recollets.—College of the Jesuits.—One Jesuit remaining of great Age.—His

—*His great Wealth.—His Character.—Nunneries.—Engineer's Drawing Room.—State House.—Armoury.—Barracks.—Market-place.—Dogs used in Carts.—Grandeur of the Prospects from Parts of the Upper Town.—Charming Scenery of the Environs.—Description of Montmorenci Water Fall.—Of La Chaudiere Water Fall.*

Quebec, August.

THE city of Quebec is situated on a very lofty point of land, on the north-west side of the River St. Lawrence. Nearly facing it, on the opposite shore, there is another point, and between the two the river is contracted to the breadth of three quarters of a mile, but after passing through this strait it expands to the breadth of five or six miles, taking a great sweep behind that point whereon Quebec stands. The city derives its name from the word Quebec or Quebeio, which signifies in the Algonquin tongue, a sudden contraction of a river. The wide part of the river, immediately before the town, is called The Bason; and it is sufficiently deep and spacious to float upwards of one hundred sail of the line.

Quebec is divided into two parts; the upper town, situated on a rock of limestone, on the top of the point; and the lower town, built

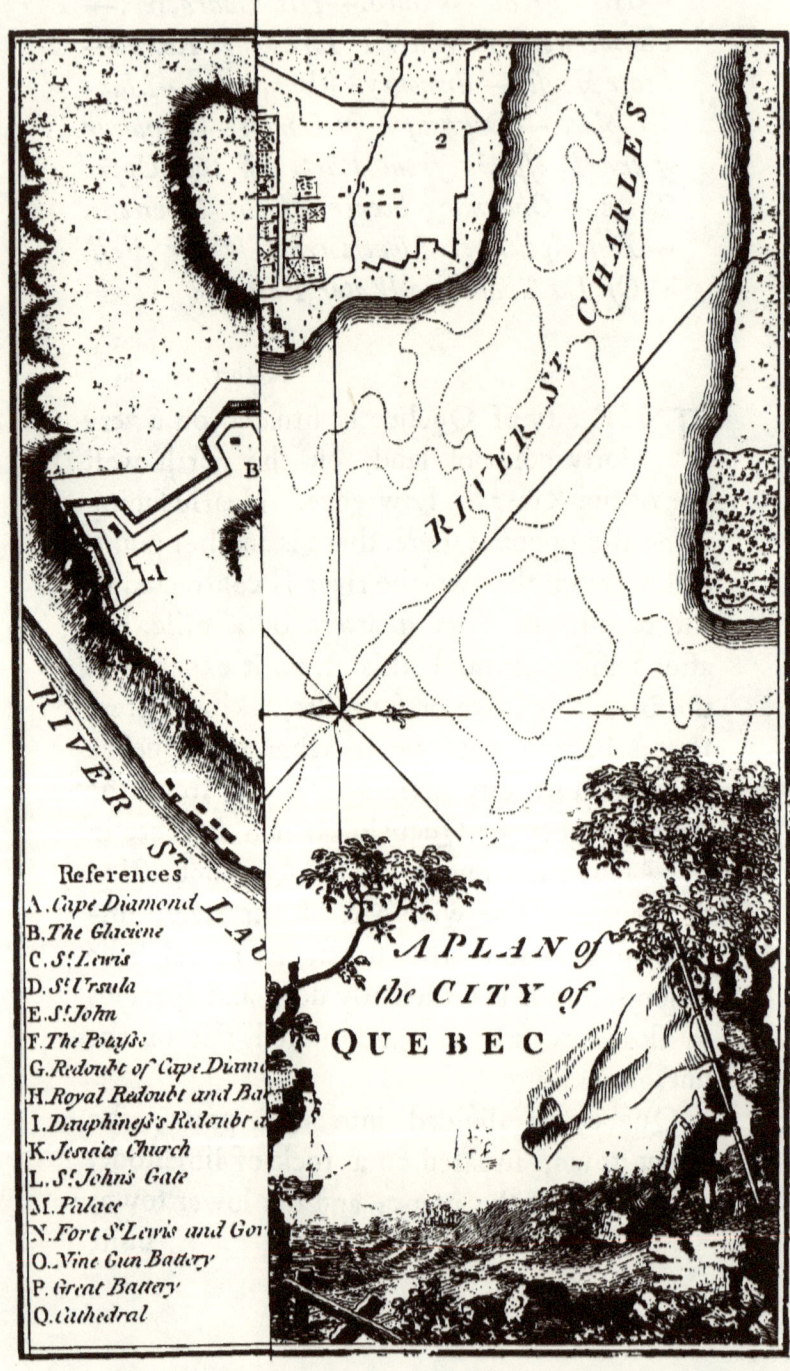

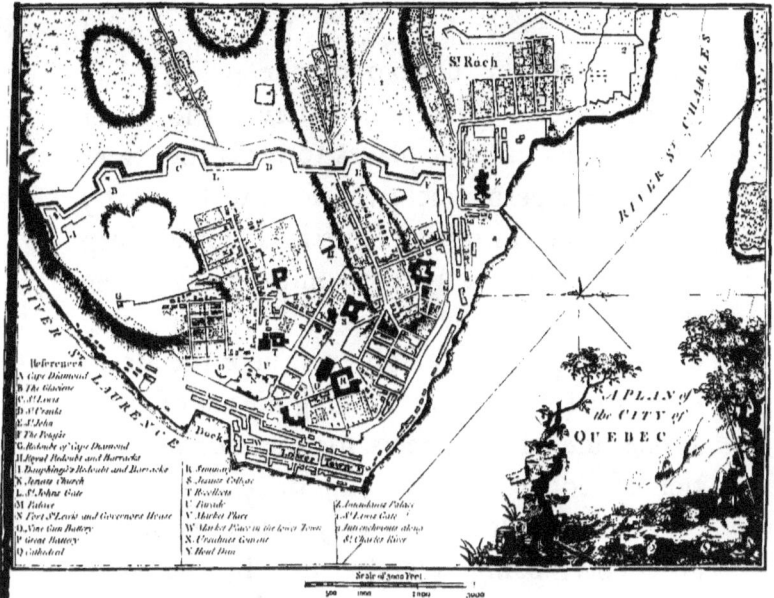

built round the bottom of the point, close to the water. The rock whereon the upper town stands, in some places towards the water rises nearly perpendicularly, so as to be totally inaccessible; in other places it is not so steep but that there is a communication between the two towns, by means of streets winding up the side of it, though even here the ascent is so great, that there are long flights of stairs at one side of the streets for the accommodation of foot passengers.

The lower town lies very much exposed to an enemy, being defended merely by a small battery towards the bason, which at the time of high tides is nearly on a level with the water, and by barriers towards the river, in which guns may be planted when there is any danger of an attack.

The upper town, however, is a place of immense strength. Towards the water it is so strongly guarded by nature, that it is found unnecessary to have more than very slight walls; and in some particular places, where the rock is inaccessible, are no walls at all. There are several redoubts and batteries however here. The principal battery, which points towards the bason, consists of twenty-two twenty-four pounders, two French thirty-six pounders, and two large iron mortars; this battery is flanked by another of six guns,

guns, that commands the passes from the lower town.

On the land side, the town owes its strength solely to the hand of art, and here the fortifications are stupendous. Considerable additions and improvements have been made to them since the place has been in the possession of Great Britain; but even at the time when it belonged to France, the works were so strong, that had it not been for the conduct of M. de Montcalm, the French general, it is almost doubtful whether the genius of the immortal Wolfe himself would not have been baffled in attempting to reduce it.

Had M. de Montcalm, when the first intelligence of the British army's having ascended the Heights of Abraham was carried to him, instead of disbelieving the account, and laughing at it as a thing impossible, marched immediately to the attack, without giving General Wolfe time to form his men; or had he, when the account was confirmed of the enemy's procedure, and of their having formed on the plain, waited for a large division of his troops, whose station was below the town, and who might have joined him in two hours, instead of marching out to give General Wolfe battle with the troops he had with him at the time, the fate of the day might have turned out very differently; or had he,

* instead

instead of hazarding a battle at all, retired within the walls of the city and defended it, the place was so strong that there is reason to think it might have held out until the approach of winter, when the British ships must have quitted the river, and General Wolfe would consequently have been under the necessity of raising the siege.

General Wolfe thought it a vain attempt to make an assault on the side of the town which lies towards the water, where the rock is so steep, and so easily defended; his object was to get behind it, and to carry on the attack on the land side, where there is an extensive plain adjoining the town, and not a great deal lower than the highest part of the point. In order to do so, he first of all attempted to land his troops some miles below the town, near the Falls of Montmorenci. Here the banks of the river are by no means so difficult of ascent as above the town; but they were defended by a large division of the French forces, which had thrown up several strong redoubts, and, in attempting to land, Wolfe was repulsed with loss.

Above Quebec, the banks of the river are extremely high, and so steep at the same time, that by the French they were deemed inaccessible. Foiled, however, in his first attempt to get on shore, General Wolfe formed the bold

bold design of ascending to the top of these banks, commonly called the Heights of Abraham. To prepare the way for it, possession was taken of Point Levi, the point situated opposite to that on which Quebec stands, and from thence a heavy bombardment was commenced on the town, in order to deceive the enemy. In the mean time boats were prepared; the troops embarked; they passed the town with muffled oars, in the night, unobserved, and landed at a cove, about two miles above. The soldiers clambered up the heights with great difficulty, and the guns were hauled up by means of ropes and pullies fixed round the trees, with which the banks are covered from top to bottom. At the top the plain commences, and extends close under the walls of the city: here it was that the memorable battle was fought, in which General Wolfe unhappily perished, at the very moment when all his noble exertions were about to be crowned with that success which they so eminently deserved. The spot where the illustrious hero breathed his last is marked with a large stone, on which a true meridional line is drawn.

Notwithstanding that the great Wolfe found it such a very difficult task to get possession of Quebec, and that it has been rendered so much stronger since his time, yet

the

the people of the United States confidently imagine, at this day, that if there were a rupture with Great Britain, they need only send an army thither, and the place muſt fall into their hands immediately. Arnold, after his return from the expedition againſt the place, under Montgomery, in the year 1775, uſed frequently to declare, that if he had not been wounded he ſhould certainly have carried it. But however that expedition may be admired for its great boldneſs, it was, in reality, far from being ſo nearly attended with ſucceſs as the vanity of Arnold has led his countrymen to imagine.

All thoughts of taking the city by a regular ſiege were abandoned by the Americans, when they came before it; it was only by attempting to ſtorm it at an unexpected hour that they ſaw any probability of wreſting it from the Britiſh. The night of the thirty-firſt of December was accordingly fixed upon, and the city was attacked at the ſame moment in three places. But although the garriſon were completely ſurpriſed, and the greater part of the rampart guns had been diſmounted, and laid up for the winter, during which ſeaſon it was thought impoſſible for an army to make an attack ſo vigorous that cannon would be wanting to repel it, yet the Americans were at once baffled in their attempt. Arnold,

Arnold, in endeavouring to force St. John's Gate, which leads out on the back part of the town, not far from the plains of Abraham, was wounded, and repulsed with great loss. Montgomery surprised the guard of the first barrier, at one end of the lower town, and passed it; but at the second he was shot, and his men were driven back. The third division of the Americans entered the lower town in another quarter, which, as I have before said, lies very much exposed, by passing over the ice: they remained there for a day or two, and during that time they set fire to some buildings, amongst which was one of the religious houses; but they were finally dislodged without much difficulty. The two divisions under Montgomery and Arnold were repulsed with a mere handful of men: the different detachments, sent down from the upper town against the former, did not altogether amount, it is said, to two hundred men. Arnold's attack was the maddest possible; for St. John's Gate, and the walls adjoining, are stupendous, and a person need but see them to be convinced that any attempt to storm them must be fruitless without the aid of heavy artillery, which the Americans had not.

Independent of what it owes to its fortifications, and situation on the top of a rock, Quebec

Quebec is indebted for much of its strength to the severity and great length of the winter, as in that season it is wholly impracticable for a besieging army either to carry on any works or blockade the town.

It requires about five thousand soldiers to man the works at Quebec completely. A large garrison is always kept in it, and abundance of stores of every description. The troops are lodged partly in barracks, and partly in block houses near Cape Diamond, which is the most elevated part of the point, and is reckoned to be upwards of one thousand feet above the level of the river. The Cape is strongly fortified, and may be considered as the citadel of Quebec; it commands the town in every direction, and also the plains at the outside of the walls. The evening and morning guns, and all salutes and signals, are fired from hence. Notwithstanding the great height of the rock above the river, water may readily be had even at the very top of it, by sinking wells of a moderate depth, and in some particular places, at the sides of the rock, it gushes out in large streams. The water is of a very good quality.

No census has been lately taken of the number of houses and inhabitants in Quebec; but it is supposed that, including the upper and lower towns and suburbs, there are at least

two

two thousand dwellings; at the rate of six therefore to each house, the number of inhabitants would amount to twelve thousand. About two thirds of the inhabitants are of French extraction. The society in Quebec is agreeable, and very extensive for a place of the size, owing to its being the capital of the lower province, and therefore the residence of the governor, different civil officers, principal lawyers, &c. &c. The large garrison constantly kept in it makes the place appear very gay and lively.

The lower town of Quebec is mostly inhabited by the traders who are concerned with the shipping, and it is a very disagreeable place. The streets are narrow and dirty, and owing to the great height of the houses in most of them, the air is much confined; in the streets next to the water also, there is oftentimes an intolerable stench from the shore when the tide is out. The upper town, on the contrary, is extremely agreeable: from its elevated situation the air is as pure as possible, and the inhabitants are never oppressed with heat in summer; it is far, however, from being well laid out, the streets being narrow and very irregular. The houses are for the most part built of stone, and except a few, erected of late years, small, ugly, and inconvenient.

The

The chateau, wherein the governor refides, is a plain building of common ftone, fituated in an open place, the houfes round which, form three fides of an oblong fquare. It confifts of two parts. The old and the new are feparated from each other by a fpacious court. The former ftands juft on the verge of an inacceffible part of the rock; behind it, on the outfide, there is a long gallery, from whence, if a pebble were let drop, it would fall at leaft fixty feet perpendicularly. This old part is chiefly taken up with the public offices, and all the apartments in it are fmall and ill contrived; but in the new part, which ftands in front of the other, facing the fquare, they are fpacious, and tolerably well finifhed, but none of them can be called elegant. This part is inhabited by the governor's family. The chateau is built without any regularity of defign, neither the old nor the new part having even an uniform front. It is not a place of ftrength, as commonly reprefented. In the garden adjoining to it is merely a parapet wall along the edge of the rock, with embrafures, in which a few fmall guns are planted, commanding a part of the lower town. Every evening during fummer, when the weather is fine, one of the regiments of the garrifon parades in the open place before the chateau, and the band plays for an hour or two, at which time the place becomes the refort.

sort of numbers of the most genteel people of the town, and has a very gay appearance.

Opposite to the chateau there is a monastery belonging to the Recollets or Francifcan friars; a very few only of the order are now left. Contiguous to this building is the college belonging to the Jesuits, whose numbers have diminished even still faster than that of the Recollets; one old man alone of the brotherhood is left, and in him are centered the immense poffessions of that once powerful body in Canada, bringing in a yearly revenue of £. 10,000 sterling. This old man, whose lot it has been to outlive all the rest of the order, is by birth a Swifs: in his youth he was no more than a porter to the college, but having some merit he was taken notice of, promoted to a higher situation, and in the end created a lay brother. Though a very old man he is extremely healthy; he possesses an amiable disposition, and is much beloved on account of the excellent use he makes of his large fortune, which is chiefly employed in charitable purposes. On his death the property falls to the crown.

The nunneries are three in number, and as there is no restriction upon the female religious orders, they are all well filled. The largest of them, called L'Hospital General, stands in the suburbs, outside of the walls; another, of the order of St. Ursule, is not far distant from the chateau.

The

The engineer's drawing room, in which are kept a variety of models, together with plans of the fortifications of Quebec and other fortresses in Canada, is an old building, near the principal battery. Adjoining thereto stands the house where the legislative council and assembly of representatives meet, which is also an old building, that has been plainly fitted up to accommodate the legislature.

The armoury is situated near the artillery barrack, in another part of the town. About ten thousand stand of arms are kept in it, arranged in a similar manner with the arms in the Tower of London, but, if possible, with greater neatness and more fancy.

The artillery barracks are capable of containing about five hundred men, but the principal barracks are calculated to contain a much larger number; they stand in the market place, not far distant from the square in which the chateau is situated, but more in the heart of the town.

The market of Quebec is extremely well supplied with provisions every kind, which may be purchased at a much more moderate price than in any town I visited in the United States. It is a matter of curiosity to a stranger to see the number of dogs yoked in little carts, that are brought into this market by the people who attend it. The Canadian dogs are found extremely

tremely useful in drawing burthens, and there is scarcely a family in Quebec or Montreal, that does not keep one or more of them for that purpose. They are somewhat similar to the Newfoundland breed, but broader across the loins, and have shorter and thicker legs; in general they are handsome, and wonderfully docile and sagacious; their strength is prodigious; I have seen a single dog, in more than one instance, draw a man for a considerable distance that could not weigh less than ten stone. People, during the winter season, frequently perform long journeys on the snow with half a dozen or more of these animals yoked in a cariole or sledge.

I must not conclude this letter without making mention of the scenery that is exhibited to the view, from various parts of the upper town of Quebec, which, for its grandeur, its beauty, and its diversity, surpasses all that I have hitherto seen in America, or indeed in any other part of the globe. In the variegated expanse that is laid open before you, stupendous rocks, immense rivers, trackless forests and cultivated plains, mountains, lakes, towns, and villages, in turn strike the attention, and the senses are almost bewildered in contemplating the vastness of the scene. Nature is here seen on the grandest scale; and it is scarcely possible for the imagination to paint to itself any thing more
sublime

sublime than are the several prospects presented to the sight of the delighted spectator. From Cape Diamond, situated one thousand feet above the level of the river, and the loftiest part of the rock on which the city is built, the prospect is considered by many as superior to that from any other spot. A greater extent of country opens upon you, and the eye is here enabled to take in more at once, than at any other place; but to me it appears, that the view from the cape is by no means so fine as that, for instance, from the battery; for in surveying the different objects below you from such a stupendous height, their magnitude is in a great measure lost, and it seems as if you were looking at a draft of the country more than at the country itself. It is the upper battery that I allude to, facing the bason, and is about three hundred feet above the level of the water. Here, if you stand but a few yards from the edge of the precipice, you may look down at once upon the river, the vessels upon which, as they sail up to the wharfs before the lower town, appear as if they were coming under your very feet. The river itself, which is between five and six miles wide, and visible as far as the distant end of the island of Orleans, where it loses itself amidst the mountains that bound it on each side, is one of the most beautiful objects in nature, and on a fine still summer's

A a 2   evening

evening it often wears the appearance of a vaſt mirror, where the varied rich tints of the ſky, as well as the images of the different objects on the banks, are ſeen reflected with inconceivable luſtre. The ſouthern bank of the river, indented fancifully with bays and promontories, remains nearly in a ſtate of nature, cloathed with lofty trees; but the oppoſite ſhore is thickly covered with houſes, extending as along other parts of the river already mentioned, in one uninterrupted village, ſeemingly, as far as the eye can reach. On this ſide the proſpect is terminated by an extenſive range of mountains, the flat lands ſituated between and the villages on the banks not being viſible to a ſpectator at Quebec, it ſeems as if the mountains roſe directly out of the water, and the houſes were built on their ſteep and rugged ſides.

Beautiful as the environs of the city appear when ſeen at a diſtance, they do not appear leſs ſo on a more cloſe inſpection; and in paſſing through them the eye is entertained with a moſt pleaſing variety of fine landſcapes, whilſt the mind is equally gratified with the appearance of content and happineſs that reigns in the countenances of the inhabitants. Indeed, if a country as fruitful as it is picturesque, a genial and healthy climate, and a tolerable ſhare of civil and religious liberty, can make

people

people happy, none ought to appear more so than the Canadians, during this delightful season of the year.

Before I dismiss this subject entirely, I must give you a brief account of two scenes in the vicinity of Quebec, more particularly deserving of attention than any others. The one is the Fall of the River Montmorenci; the other, that of the Chaudiere. The former stream runs into the St. Lawrence, about seven miles below Quebec; the latter joins the same river nearly at an equal distance above the city.

The Montmorenci River runs in a very irregular course, through a wild and thickly wooded country, over a bed of broken rocks, till it comes to the brink of a precipice, down which it descends in one uninterrupted and nearly perpendicular fall of two hundred and forty feet. The stream of water in this river, except at the time of floods, is but scanty, but being broken into foam by rushing with such rapidity as it does over the rocks at the top of the precipice, it is thereby much dilated, and in its fall appears to be a sheet of water of no inconsiderable magnitude. The breadth of the river at top, from bank to bank, is about fifty feet only. In its fall, the water has the exact appearance of snow, as when thrown in heaps from the roof of a house, and it seemingly descends

scends with a very flow motion. The spray at the bottom is confiderable, and when the fun happens to shine bright in the middle of the day, the prifmatic colours are exhibited in it in all their variety and luftre. At the bottom of the precipice the water is confined in a fort of bafon, as it were, by a mafs of rock, extending nearly acrofs the fall, and out of this it flows with a gentle current to the St. Lawrence, which is about three hundred yards diftant. The banks of the Montmorenci, below the precipice, are nearly perpendicular on one fide, and on both inacceffible, fo that if a perfon be defirous of getting to the bottom of the fall, he muft defcend down the banks of the St. Lawrence, and walk along the margin of that river till he comes to the chafm through which the Montmorenci flows. To a perfon failing along the St. Lawrence, paft the mouth of the chafm, the fall appears in great beauty.

General Haldimand, formerly governor of Canada, was fo much delighted with this cataract, that he built a dwelling houfe clofe to it, from the parlour windows of which it is feen in a very advantageous point of view. In front of the houfe is a neat lawn, that runs down the whole way to the St. Lawrence, and in various parts of it little fummer-houfes have been erected, each of which commands a view of the fall. There is alfo a fummer-houfe,
fituated

situated nearly at the top of the fall, hanging directly over the precipice, so that if a bullet were dropped from the window, it would descend in a perpendicular line at least two hundred feet. This house is supported by large beams of timber, fixed into the sides of the chasm, and in order to get to it you have to pass over several flights of steps, and one or two wooden galleries, which are supported in the same manner. The view from hence is tremendously grand. It is said, that the beams whereon this little edifice is erected are in a state of decay, and many persons are fearful of entering into it, lest they should give way; but being ignorant of the danger, if indeed there was any, our whole party ventured into it at once, and staid there a considerable time, notwithstanding its tremulous motion at every step we trod. That the beams cannot last for ever is certain; it would be a wise measure, therefore, to have them removed or repaired in proper time, for as long as they remain standing, persons will be found that will venture into the unsteady fabrick they support, and should they give way at a moment when any persons are in it, the catastrophe must inevitably be fatal.

The fall in the River Chaudiere is not half the height of that of the Montmorenci, but then it is no less than two hundred and fifty feet

feet in breadth. The scenery round this cataract is much superior in every respect to that in the neighbourhood of the Montmorenci. Contiguous to the latter there are few trees of any great magnitude, and nothing is near it to relieve the eye; you have the fall, and nought but the fall, to contemplate. The banks of La Chaudiere, on the contrary, are covered with trees of the largest growth, and amidst the piles of broken rocks, which lie scattered about the place, you have some of the wildest and most romantic views imaginable. As for the fall itself, its grandeur varies with the season. When the river is full, a body of water comes rushing over the rocks of the precipice that astonishes the beholder; but in dry weather, and indeed during the greater part of the summer, we may say, the quantity of water is but trifling. At this season there are few but what would prefer the falls of the Montmorenci River, and I am tempted to imagine that, upon the whole, the generality of people would give it the preference at all times.

LETTER XXV.

Of the Constitution, Government, Laws, and Religion of the Provinces of Upper and Lower Canada.—Estimate of the Expenses of the Civil List, of the Military Establishment, and the Presents to the Indians.—Salaries of certain Officers of the Crown.—Imports and Exports. —Taxes.

Quebec.

FROM the time that Canada was ceded to Great Britain until the year 1774, the internal affairs of the province were regulated by the ordinance of the governor alone. In pursuance of the Quebec Bill, which was then passed, a legislative council was appointed by his Majesty in the country; the number of members was limited to twenty-three. This council had full power to make all such ordinances and regulations as were thought expedient for the welfare of the province; but it was prohibited from levying any taxes, except for the purpose of making roads, repairing public buildings, or the like. Every ordinance was to be laid before the governor, for his Majesty's approbation, within six months from the time it was passed, and no ordinance, imposing a greater punishment on any person or persons

persons than a fine, or imprisonment for three months, was valid without his Majesty's assent, signified to the council by the governor.

Thus were the affairs of the province regulated until the year 1791, when an act was passed in the British parliament, repealing so much of the Quebec Bill as related to the appointment of a council, and to the powers that had been granted to it; and which established the present form of government.

The country, at the same time, was divided into two distinct provinces; the province of Lower Canada, and the province of Upper Canada. The former is the eastern part of the old province of Canada; the latter, the western part, situated on the northern sides of the great lakes and rivers through which the boundary line runs that separates the British territories from those of the United States. The two provinces are divided from each other by a line, which runs north, 24° west, commencing at Point au Baudet, in that part of the river St. Lawrence called Lake Francis, and continuing on from thence to the Utawas or Grand River. The city of Quebec is the capital of the lower province, as the town of Niagara is of the upper one.

The executive power in each province is vested in the governor, who has for his advice an executive council appointed by his Majesty.

jesty. The legislative power of each province is vested in the governor, a legislative council, and an assembly of the representatives of the people. Their acts, however, are subject to the controul of his Majesty, and in some particular cases to the controul of the British parliament.

Bills are passed in the council and in the assembly in a form somewhat similar to that in which bills are carried through the British houses of parliament; they are then laid before the governor, who gives or withholds his assent, or reserves them for his Majesty's pleasure.

Such bills as he assents to are put in force immediately; but he is bound to transmit a true copy of them to the King, who in council may declare his disallowance of them within two years from the time of their being received, in which case they become void.

Such as are reserved for his Majesty's assent are not to be put in force until that is received.

Moreover, every act of the assembly and council, which goes to repeal or vary the laws or regulations that were in existence at the time the present constitution was established in the country respecting tithes; the appropriation of land for the support of a protestant clergy; the constituting and endowing of parsonages or rectories; the right of presentation
to

to the fame, and the manner in which the incumbents shall hold them; the enjoyment and exercise of any form or mode of worship; the imposing of any burdens and disqualifications on account of the same; the rights of the clergy to recover their accustomed dues; the imposing or granting of any farther dues or emoluments to any ecclesiastics; the establishment and discipline of the church of England; the King's prerogative, touching the granting of waste lands of the crown within the province; every such act, before it receives the royal assent, must be laid before both houses of parliament in Great Britain, and the King must not give his assent thereto until thirty days after the same has been laid before parliament; and in case either house of parliament presents an address to the King to withhold his assent to any such act or acts, it cannot be given.

By an act passed in the eighteenth year of his present Majesty's reign, the British parliament has also the power of making any regulations which may be found expedient, respecting the commerce and navigation of the province, and also of imposing import and export duties; but all such duties are to be applied solely to the use of the province, and in such a manner only as the laws made in the council and assembly direct.

The

The legislative council of Lower Canada consists of fifteen members; that of Upper Canada of seven. The number of the members in each province must never be less than this; but it may be increased whenever his Majesty thinks fit.

The counsellors are appointed for life, by an instrument under the great seal of the province, signed by the governor, who is invested with powers for that purpose by the King. No person can be a counsellor who is not twenty-one years of age, nor any one who is not a natural born subject, or who has not been naturalized according to act of parliament.

Whenever his Majesty thinks proper, he may confer on any persons hereditary titles of honour, with a right annexed to them of being summoned to sit in this council, which right the heir may claim at the age of twenty-one; the right, however, cannot be acknowledged if the heir has been absent from the province without leave of his Majesty, signified to the council by the governor, for four years together, between the time of his succeeding to the right and the time of his demanding it. The right is forfeited also, if the heir takes an oath of allegiance to any foreign power before he demands it, unless his Majesty, by an an inftrument under the great feal of the province, fhould decree to the contrary.

If a counfellor, after having taken his feat, abfent himfelf from the province for two years fucceffively, without leave from his Majefty, fignified to the council by the governor, his feat is alfo thereby vacated.

All hereditary rights, however, of fitting in council, fo forfeited, are only to be fufpended during the life of the defaulters, and on their death they defcend with the titles to the next heirs *.

In cafes of treafon, both the title and right of fitting in the council are extinguifhed.

All queftions concerning the right of being fummoned to the council are to be determined by the council; but an appeal may be had from their decifion to his Majefty in his parliament of Great Britain.

The governor has the power of appointing and removing the fpeaker of the council.

The affembly of Lower Canada confifts of fifty members, and that of Upper Canada of fixteen; neither affembly is ever to confift of a lefs number.

The members for diftricts, circles, or coun-

---

* No hereditary titles, with this right annexed, have yet been conferred on any perfons in Canada by his Britannic Majefty.

THE ASSEMBLY.

ties, are chosen by a majority of the votes of such persons as are possessed of lands or tenements in freehold, in fief, in boture, or by certificate derived under the authority of the governor and council of Quebec, of the yearly value of forty shillings, clear of all rents, charges, &c. The members for towns or townships are chosen by a majority of the votes of such persons as possess houses and lands for their own use, of the yearly value of five pounds sterling, or as have resided in the town or township for one year, and paid a rent for a house during the time, at the rate of ten pounds yearly.

No person is eligible to serve as a member of the assembly, who is a member of the legislative council, or a minister, priest, ecclesiastic, or religious personage of the church of England, Rome, or of any other church.

No person is qualified to vote or serve, who is not twenty-one years of age; nor any peron, not a natural born subject, or who has not been naturalized, either by law or conquest; nor any one who has been attainted of treason in any court in his Majesty's dominions, or who has been disqualified by an act of assembly and council.

Every voter, if called upon, must take an oath, either in French or English, that he is of age; that he is qualified to vote according to law; and that he has not voted before at that election.

The governor has the power of appointing the place of seſſion, and of calling together, of proroguing, and of diſſolving the aſſembly.

The aſſembly is not to laſt longer than four years, but it may be diſſolved ſooner. The governor is bound to call it at leaſt once in each year.

The oath of a member, on taking his ſeat, is compriſed in a few words: he promiſes to bear true allegiance to the King, as lawful ſovereign of Great Britain, and the province of Canada dependant upon it; to defend him againſt all traitorous conſpiracies and attempts againſt his perſon; and to make known to him all ſuch conſpiracies and attempts, which he may at any time be acquainted with; all which he promiſes without mental evaſion, reſervation, or equivocation, at the ſame time renouncing all pardons and diſpenſations from any perſon or power whatſoever.

The governors of the two provinces are totally independent of each other in their civil capacity: in military affairs, the governor of the lower province takes precedence, as he is uſually created captain general of his Majeſty's forces in North America.

The preſent ſyſtem of judicature in each province was eſtabliſhed by the Quebec bill of of 1774. By this bill it was enacted, that all persons in the country should be entitled to hold their lands or possessions in the same manner as before the conquest, according to the laws and usages then existing in Canada; and that all controversies relative to property or civil rights should also be determined by the same laws and usages. These old laws and usages, however, were not to extend to the lands which might thereafter be granted by his Britannic Majesty in free and common socage: here English laws were to be in full force; so that the * English inhabitants, who have settled for the most part on new lands, are not subject to the controul of these old French laws, that were existing in Canada when the country was conquered, except a dispute concerning property or civil rights should arise between any of them and the French inhabitants, in which case the matter is to be determined by the French laws. Every friend to civil liberty would wish to see these laws abolished, for they weigh very unequally in favour of the rich and of the poor; but as long as the French inhabitants remain so wedded as they are at present to old cus-

---

* I must observe here once for all that by English inhabitants I mean all those whose native language is English, in contradistinction to the Canadians of French extraction, who universally speak the French language, and no other.

toms, and so very ignorant, there is little hope of seeing any alteration of this nature take place. At the same time that the French laws were suffered by the Quebec bill to exist, in order to conciliate the affections of the French inhabitants, who were attached to them, the criminal law of England was established throughout every part of the country; " and " this was one of the happiest circumstances," as the Abbé Raynal observes, " that Canada " could experience; as deliberate, rational, " public trials took place of the impenetrable " mysterious transactions of a cruel inquisi- " tion; and as a tribunal, that had theretofore " been dreadful and sanguinary, was filled " with humane judges, more disposed to ac- " knowledge innocence than to suppose cri- " minality."

The governor, the lieutenant governor, or the person administering the government, the members of the executive council, the chief justices of the province, and the judges of the court of king's bench, or any five of them, form a court of appeal, the judges however excepted of that district from whence the appeal is made. From the decision of this court an appeal may be had in certain cases to the King in council.

Every religion is tolerated, in the fullest extent of the word, in both provinces; and

no

no disqualifications are imposed on any persons on account of their religious opinions. The Roman Catholic religion is that of a great majority of the inhabitants; and by the Quebec bill of 1774, the ecclesiastics of that persuasion are empowered by law to recover all the dues which, previous to that period, they were accustomed to receive, as well as tithes, that is, from the Roman Catholic inhabitants; but they cannot exact any dues or tithes from Protestants, or off lands held by Protestants, although formerly such lands might have been subjected to dues and tithes for the support of the Roman Catholic church. The dues and tithes from off these lands are still, however, to be paid; but they are to be paid to persons appointed by the governor, and the amount of them is to be reserved, in the hands of his Majesty's receiver general, for the support of the Protestant clergy actually residing in the province.

By the act of the year 1791, also, it was ordained, that the governor should allot out of all lands belonging to the crown, which should be granted after that period, one-seventh for the benefit of a Protestant clergy, to be solely applicable to their use; and all such allotments must be particularly specified in every grant of waste lands, otherwise the grant is void.

With the advice of the executive council, the governor is authorized to conſtitute or erect parſonages or rectories, and to endow them out of theſe appropriations, and to preſent incumbents to them, ordained according to the rites of the church of England; which incumbents are to perform the ſame duties, and to hold their parſonages or rectories in the ſame manner as incumbents of the church of England do in that country.

The clergy of the church of England, in both provinces, conſiſts at preſent of twelve perſons only, including the biſhop of Quebec; that of the church of Rome, however, conſiſts of no leſs than one hundred and twenty-ſix; viz. a biſhop, who takes his title from Quebec, his "coadjuteur élu," who is biſhop of Canathe, three vicars general, and one hundred and ſixteen curates and miſſionaries, all of whom are reſident in the lower province, except five curates and miſſionaries.

The number of the diſſenting clergy, in both provinces, is conſiderably ſmaller than that of the clergy of the church of England.

The expences of the civil liſt in Lower Canada are eſtimated at £.20,000 ſterling per annum, one half of which is defrayed by Great Britain, and the remainder by the province, out of the duties paid on the importation of certain articles. The expence of the

PRESENTS AND SALARIES. 373

civil list in Upper Canada is considerably less; perhaps not so much as a fourth of that of the lower province.

The military establishment in both provinces, together with the repairs of fortifications, &c. are computed to cost Great Britain annually £.100,000 sterling.

The presents distributed amongst the Indians, and the salaries paid to the different officers in the Indian department, are estimated at £.100,000 sterling more, annually.

Amongst the officers in the Indian department are, superintendants general, deputy superintendants, inspectors general, deputy inspectors general, secretaries, assistant secretaries, storekeepers, clerks, agents, interpreters, issuers of provisions, surgeons, gunsmiths, &c. &c. &c. most of whom, in the lower province, have now sinecure places, as there are but few Indians in the country; but in the upper province they have active service to perform. Of the policy of issuing presents to such a large amount amongst the Indians, more will be said in the afterpart of this work.

The following is a statement of some of the salaries paid to the officers of government in Lower Canada.

	£.
Governor general	2,000
Lieutenant governor	1,500

	£
Executive counsellors, each	100
Attorney general	300
Solicitor general	200
Secretary and regifter to the province	400
Clerk of the court of appeals, with fire wood and ftationary	120
Secretary to the governor	200
French fecretary to the governor, and tranflator to the council	200
Chief juftice of Quebec, who is chief juftice of the province	1,200
Chief juftice of Montreal	900
Chief juftice of Three Rivers	300
Receiver general	400
Surveyor general of lands	300
Deputy, and allowance for an office	150
Surveyor of woods	200
Grand voyer of Quebec	100
Grand voyer of Montreal	100
Grand voyer of Three Rivers	60
Superintendant of provincial poft houfes	100
Clerk of the terraro of the king's domain	90
Clerk of the crown	100
Infpector of police at Quebec	100
Infpector of police at Montreal	100
Four miffionaries to Indians, each	50
One miffionary to Indians	45

School-

		£.
Schoolmaster at Quebec	- -	100
Schoolmaster at Montreal	- -	50
Schoolmaster at Carlisle, Bay de Chaleurs	- - - - -	25
Overseers, to prevent fires at Quebec, and to sweep the chimneys of the poor	- - - - -	60
Salary of the bishop of Quebec, who is bishop of both provinces	-	2,000

The pensions, between January 1794 and January 1795, amounted to £.1,782 - 6 s. 7 d.

A STATEMENT of the Articles subject to Duty on Importation into Canada, and of the Duties payable thereon.

	s.	d.
Brandy and other spirits, the manufacture of Great Britain, per gallon	-	. 3
Rum and other spirits, imported from the colonies in the West Indies, per gallon	-	. 6
Brandy and spirits of foreign manufacture, imported from Great Britain, per gallon	-	1 0
Additional duty on the same, per gallon		. 3
Rum or spirits manufactured in the United States, per gallon	-	1 0

	d.
Molasses and Syrups imported in British shipping, per gallon	3
Additional duty, per gallon	3
Molasses or Syrups legally imported in other than British shipping, per gallon	6
Additional duty, per gallon	3
Madeira wine, per gallon	6
Other wine	3

N. B. Wine can be imported directly from Madeira, or from any of the African islands, into Canada; but no European wine or brandy can be imported, except through England.

	d.
Loaf or lump sugar, per lb.	1
Muscovado or clayed sugar	½
Coffee, per lb.	2
Leaf tobacco, per lb.	2
Playing cards, per pack	2
Salt, the minot	4

N. B. The minot is a measure commonly used in Canada, which is to the Winchester bushel, as 100 is to 108,765.

The imports into Canada consist of all the various articles which a young country, that does not manufacture much for its own use, can be supposed to stand in need of; such as earthen

earthen ware, hardware, and houfehold furniture, except of the coarfer kinds; woollen and linen cloths, haberdafhery, hofiery, &c.; paper, ftationary, leather and manufactures of leather, groceries, wines, fpirits, Weft Indian produce, &c. &c.; cordage of every defcription, and even the coarfer manufactures of iron, are alfo imported.

The foil of the country is well adapted to the growth of hemp, and great pains have been taken to introduce the culture of it. Handbills, explaining the manner in which it can be raifed to the beft advantage, have been affiduoufly circulated amongft the farmers, and pofted up at all the public houfes. It is a difficult matter, however, to put the French Canadians out of their old ways, fo that very little hemp has been raifed in confequence of the pains that have been thus taken; and it is not probable that much will be raifed for a confiderable time to come.

Iron ore has been difcovered in various parts of the country; but works for the fmelting and manufacturing of it have been erected at one place only, in the neighbourhood of Trois Rivieres. Thefe works were erected by the king of France fome time before the conqueft: they are now the property of the Britifh government, and are rented out to the perfons who hold them

at

at prefent. When the leafe expires, which will be the cafe about the year 1800, it is thought that no one will be found to carry on the works, as the bank of ore, from whence they are fupplied, is nearly exhaufted. The works confift of a forge and a foundry: iron ftoves are the principal articles manufactured in the latter; but they are not fo much efteemed as thofe from England.

Domeftic manufactures are carried on in moft parts of Canada, confifting of linen and of coarfe woollen cloths; but by far the greater part of thefe articles ufed in the country is imported from Great Britain.

The exports from Canada confift of furs and pelts in immenfe quantities; of wheat, flour, flax-feed, potafh, timber, ftaves, and lumber of all forts; dried fifh, oil, ginfeng, and various medicinal drugs.

The trade between Canada and Great Britain employs, it is faid, about feven thoufand tons of fhipping annually.

LETTER XXVI.

Of the Soil and Productions of Lower Canada. —Observations on the Manufacture of Sugar from the Maple-tree.—Of the Climate of Lower Canada.—Amusements of People of all Descriptions during Winter.—Carioles. —Manner of guarding against the Cold.— Great Hardiness of the Horses.—State of the River St. Lawrence on the Dissolution of Winter.—Rapid Progress of Vegetation during Spring.—Agreeableness of the Summer and Autumn Seasons.

Quebec.

THE eastern part of Lower Canada, between Quebec and the Gulph of St. Lawrence, is mountainous; between Quebec and the mouth of the Utawas River also a few scattered mountains are to be met with; but higher up the River St. Lawrence the face of the country is flat.

The soil, except where small tracts of stony and sandy land intervene, consists principally of a loose dark coloured earth, and of the depth of ten or twelve inches, below which there is a bed of cold clay. This earth towards the surface is extremely fertile, of which there

there cannot be a greater proof than that it continues to yield plentiful crops, notwithstanding its being worked year after year by the French Canadians, without ever being manured. It is only within a few years back, indeed, that any of the Canadians have begun to manure their lands, and many ſtill continue, from father to ſon, to work the ſame fields without intermiſſion, and without ever putting any manure upon them, yet the land is not exhauſted, as it would be in the United States. The manure principally made uſe of by thoſe who are the beſt farmers is marl, found in prodigious quantities in many places along the ſhores of the River St. Lawrence.

The ſoil of Lower Canada is particularly ſuited to the growth of ſmall grain. Tobacco alſo thrives well in it; it is only raiſed, however, in ſmall quantities for private uſe, more than one half of what is uſed in the country being imported. The Canadian tobacco is of a much milder quality than that grown in Maryland and Virginia: the ſnuff made from it is held in great eſtimation.

Culinary vegetables of every deſcription come to the greateſt perfection in Canada, as well as moſt of the European fruits: the currants, gooſeberries, and raſpberries are in particular very fine; the latter are indigenous, and are found in profuſion in the woods; the vine

vine is also indigenous, but the grapes which it produces in its uncultivated state are very poor, sour, and but little larger than fine currants.

The variety of trees found in the forests of Canada is prodigious, and it is supposed that there many kinds are still unknown: beech trees, oaks, elms, ashes, pines, sycamores, chesnuts, walnuts, of each of which several different species are commonly met with; the sugar maple tree is also found in almost every part of the country, a tree never seen but upon good ground. There are two kinds of this very valuable tree in Canada; the one called the swamp maple, from its being generally found upon low lands; the other, the mountain or curled maple, from growing upon high dry ground, and from the grain of the wood being very beautifully variegated with little stripes and curls. The former yields a much greater quantity of sap, in proportion to its size, than the other, but this sap does not afford so much sugar as that of the curled maple. A pound of sugar is frequently procured from two or three gallons of the sap of the curled maple, whereas no more than the same quantity can be had from six or seven gallons of that of the swamp.

The most approved method of getting the sap is by piercing a hole with an auger in the side of the tree, of one inch or an inch and a half in diameter, and two or three inches in depth, obliquely upwards; but the moſt common mode of coming at it is by cutting a large gaſh in the tree with an axe. In each caſe a ſmall ſpout is fixed at the bottom of the wound, and a veſſel is placed underneath to receive the liquor as it falls.

A maple tree of the diameter of twenty inches will commonly yield ſufficient ſap for making five pounds of ſugar each year, and inſtances have been known of trees yielding nearly this quantity annually for a ſeries of thirty years. Trees that have been gaſhed and mangled with an axe will not laſt by any means ſo long as thoſe which have been carefully pierced with an auger; the axe, however, is generally uſed, becauſe the ſap diſtils much faſter from the wound made by it than from that made by an auger, and it is always an object with the farmer, to have the ſap brought home, and boiled down as ſpeedily as poſſible, in order that the making of ſugar may not interfere with his other agricultural purſuits. The ſeaſon for tapping the trees is when the ſap begins to riſe, at the commencement of ſpring, which is juſt the time that the farmer is moſt buſied in making preparations for ſowing his grain.

It is a very remarkable fact, that theſe trees, after

after having been tapped for six or seven succeſſive years, always yield more ſap than they do on being firſt wounded; this ſap, however, is not ſo rich as that which the trees diſtil for the firſt time; but from its coming in an increaſed portion, as much ſugar is generally procured from a ſingle tree on the fifth or ſixth year of its being tapped as on the firſt.

The maple is the only ſort of raw ſugar made uſe of in the country parts of Canada; it is very generally uſed alſo by the inhabitants of the towns, whither it is brought for ſale by the country people who attend the markets, juſt the ſame as any other kind of country produce. The moſt common form in which it is ſeen is in loaves or thick round cakes, preciſely as it comes out of the veſſel where it is boiled down from the ſap. Theſe cakes are of a very dark colour in general, and very hard; as they are wanted they are ſcraped down with a knife, and when thus reduced into powder, the ſugar appears of a much lighter caſt, and not unlike Weſt Indian muſcovada or grained ſugar. If the maple ſugar be carefully boiled with lime, whites of eggs, blood, or any of the other articles uſually employed for clarifying ſugar, and properly granulated, by the draining off of the melaſſes, it is by no means inferior, either in point of ſtrength, flavour, or appearance to the eye, to any

any West Indian sugar whatsoever: simply boiled down into cakes with milk or whites of eggs it is very agreeable to the taste.

The ingenious Dr. Nooth, of Quebec, who is at the head of the general hospital in Canada, has made a variety of experiments upon the manufacture of maple sugar; he has granulated, and also refined it, so as to render it equal to the best lump sugar that is made in England. To convince the Canadians also, who are as incredulous on some points as they are credulous on others, that it was really maple sugar which they saw thus refined, he has contrived to leave large lumps, exhibiting the sugar in its different stages towards refinement, the lower part of the lumps being left hard, similar to the common cakes, the middle part granulated, and the upper part refined.

Dr. Nooth has calculated, that the sale of the melasses alone would be fully adequate to the expence of refining the maple sugar, if a manufactory for that purpose were established. Some attempts have been made to establish one of the kind at Quebec, but they have never succeeded, as the persons by whom they were made were adventurers that had not sufficient capitals for such an undertaking. It ought not, however, to be concluded from this, that a manufactory of the sort would not succeed if conducted by judicious persons that had ample funds

funds for the bufinefs; on the contrary, it is highly probable that it would anfwer.

There is great reafon alfo to fuppofe, that a manufactory for making the fugar from the beginning, as well as for refining it, might be eftablifhed with advantage.

Several acres together are often met with in Canada, entirely covered with maple trees alone; but the trees are moft ufually found growing mixed with others, in the proportion of from thirty to fifty maple trees to every acre. Thoufands and thoufands of acres might be procured, within a very fhort diftance of the River St. Lawrence, for lefs than one fhilling an acre, on each of which thirty maple trees would be found; but fuppofing that only twenty-five trees were found on each acre, then on a track of five thoufand acres, fuppofing each tree to produce five pounds of fugar, 5,580 cwt. 2 qrs. 12 lbs. of fugar might be made annually.

The maple tree attains a growth fufficient for yielding five pounds of fugar annually in the fpace of twenty years; as the oaks and other kinds of trees, therefore, were cut away for different purpofes, maples might be planted in their room, which would be ready to be tapped by the time that the old maple trees failed. Moreover, if thefe trees were planted out in rows regularly, the trouble of collecting the sap from them would be much less than if they stood widely scattered, as they do in their natural state, and of course the expence of making the sugar would be considerably lessened. Added to this, if young maples were constantly set out in place of the other trees, as they were cut down, the estate, at the end of twenty years, would yield ten times as much sugar as it did originally.

It has been asserted, that the difficulty of maintaining horses and men in the woods at the season of the year proper for making the sugar would be so great, as to render every plan for the manufactory of the sugar on an extensive scale abortive. This might be very true, perhaps, in the United States, where the subject has been principally discussed, and where it is that this objection has been made; but it would not hold good in Canada. Many tracks, containing five thousand acres each, of sugar maple land, might be procured in various parts of the country, no part of any of which would be more than six English miles distant from a populous village. The whole labour of boiling in each year would be over in the space of six weeks; the trouble therefore of carrying food during that period, for the men and horses that were wanting for the manufactory, from a village into the woods, would be trifling, and a few huts might be

built

built for their accommodation in the woods at a small expence.

The great labour requisite for conveying the sap from the trees, that grow so far apart, to the boiling house, has been adduced as another objection to the establishment of an extensive sugar manufactory in the woods.

The sap, as I have before observed, is collected by private families, by setting a vessel, into which it drops, under each tree, and from thence carried by hand to the place where it is to be boiled. If a regular manufactory, however, were established, the sap might be conveyed to the boiling house with far less labour; small wooden troughs might be placed under the wounds in each trees, by which means the sap might easily be conveyed to the distance of twenty yards, if it were thought necessary, into reservoirs. Three or four of these reservoirs might be placed on an acre, and avenues opened through the woods, so as to admit carts with proper vessels to pass from one to the other, in order to convey the sap to the boiling houses. Mere sheds would answer for boiling houses, and these might be erected at various different places on the estate, in order to save the trouble of carrying the sap a great way.

The expence of cutting down a few trees, so as to clear an avenue for a cart, would not be be much; neither would that of making the spouts, and common tubs for refervoirs, be great in a country abounding with wood; the quantity of labour faved by fuch means would, however, be very confiderable.

When then, it is confidered, that private families, who have to carry the fap by hand from each tree to their own houfes, and often at a confiderable diftance from the woods, in order to boil it, can, with all this labour, afford to fell fugar, equally good with that which comes from the Weft Indies, at a much lower price than what the latter is fold at; when it is confidered alfo, that by going to the fmall expence, on the firft year, of making a few wooden fpouts and tubs, a very great portion of labour would be faved, and of courfe the profits on the fale of the fugar would be far greater; there is good foundation for thinking, that if a manufactory were eftablifhed on fuch a plan as I have hinted at, it would anfwer extremely well, and that maple fugar would in a fhort time become a principal article of foreign commerce in Canada.

The fap of the maple tree is not only ufeful in yielding fugar; moft excellent vinegar may likewife be made from it. In company with feveral gentlemen I tafted vinegar made from it by Dr. Nooth, allowed by every one prefent to be much fuperior to the beft French white

white wine vinegar; for at the same time that it possessed equal acidity, it had a more delicious flavour.

Good table beer may likewise be made from the sap, which many would mistake for malt liquor.

If distilled, the sap affords a very fine spirit.

The air of Lower Canada is extremely pure, and the climate is deemed uncommonly salubrious, except only in the western parts of the province, high up the River St. Lawrence, where, as is the case in almost every part of the United States south of New England, between the ocean and the mountains, the inhabitants suffer to a great degree from intermittent fevers. From Montreal downwards, the climate resembles very much that of the states of New England; the people live to a good old age, and intermittents are quite unknown. This great difference in the healthiness of the two parts of the province must be attributed to the different aspects of the country; to the east, Lower Canada, like New England, is mountainous, but to the west it is an extended flat.

The extremes of heat and cold in Canada are amazing; in the months of July and August the thermometer, according to Fahrenheit, is often known to rise to 96°, yet a winter scarcely passes over but even the mercury itself freezes

freezes. Thofe very fudden tranfitions, however, from heat to cold, fo common in the United States, and fo very injurious to the conftitution, are unknown in Canada; the feafons alfo are much more regular.

The fnow generally begins to fall in November; but fometimes it comes down as early as the latter end of October. This is the moft difagreeable part of the whole year; the air is then cold and raw, and the fky dark and gloomy; two days feldom pafs over together without a fall either of fnow or fleet. By the end of the firft or fecond week, however, in December, the clouds are generally diffolved, the froft fets in, the fky affumes a bright and azure hue, and for weeks together it continues the fame, without being obfcured by a fingle cloud.

The greateft degree of cold which they experience in Canada, is in the month of January, when for a few days it is fometimes fo intenfe, that it is impoffible for a human being to remain out of doors for any confiderable time, without evident danger of being froft bitten. Thefe very cold days, however, do not come altogether, but intervene generally at fome little diftance from each other; and between them, in the depth of winter, the air is fometimes fo warm that people in exercife, in the middle

middle of the day, feel difpofed to lay afide the thick fur cloaks ufually worn out of doors.

Thofe who have ever paffed a winter in Canada, have by no means that dread of its feverity, which fome would have who have never experienced a greater degree of cold than what is commonly felt in Great Britain; and as for the Canadians themfelves, they prefer the winter to every other feafon; indeed I never met with a Canadian, rich or poor, male or female, but what was of that opinion; nor ought this to excite our furprife, when it is confidered that they pafs the winter fo very differently from what we do. If a Canadian were doomed to fpend but fix weeks only in the country parts of England, when the ground was covered with fnow, I dare venture to fay that he would be as heartily tired of the famenefs which then pervaded the face of nature, and as defirous of beholding a green field once more, as any one of us.

Winter in Canada is the feafon of general amufement. The clear frofty weather no fooner commences, than all thoughts about bufinefs are laid afide, and every one devotes himfelf to pleafure. The inhabitants meet in convivial parties at each other's houfes, and pafs the day with mufic, dancing, card-playing, and every focial entertainment that can beguile the time. At Montreal, in particular,

fuch

such a constant and friendly intercourse is kept up amongst the inhabitants, that, as I have often heard it mentioned, it appears then as if the town were inhabited but by one large family.

By means of their carioles or sledges, the Canadians transport themselves over the snow, from place to place, in the most agreeable manner, and with a degree of swiftness that appears almost incredible; for with the same horse it is possible to go eighty miles in a day, so light is the draft of one of these carriages, and so favourable is the snow to the feet of the horse. The Canadian cariole or sledge is calculated to hold two persons and a driver; it is usually drawn by one horse; if two horses are made use of, they are put one before the other, as the track in the roads will not admit of their going abreast. The shape of the carriage is varied according to fancy, and it is a matter of emulation amongst the gentlemen, who shall have the handsomest one. There are two distinct kinds, however, of carioles, the open and the covered. The former is commonly somewhat like the body of a capriole, put upon two iron runners or slides, similar in shape to the irons of a pair of skates; the latter consists of the body of a chariot put on runners in the same manner, and covered entirely over with furs, which are found by experience

perience to keep out the cold much better than any other covering whatsoever. Covered carioles are not much liked, except for the purpose of going to a party in the evening; for the great pleasure of carioling consists in seeing and being seen, and the ladies always go out in most superb dresses of furs. The carioles glide over the snow with great smoothness, and so little noise do they make in sliding along, that it is necessary to have a number of bells attached to the harness, or a person continually sounding a horn to guard against accidents. The rapidity of the motion, with the sound of these bells and horns, appears to be very conducive to cheerfulness, for you seldom see a dull face in a cariole. The Canadians always take advantage of the winter season to visit their friends who live at a distance, as travelling is then so very expeditious; and this is another circumstance which contributes, probably not a little, to render the winter so extremely agreeable in their eyes.

Though the cold is so very intense in Canada, yet the inhabitants never suffer from it, constant experience having taught them how to guard against it effectually.

In the first place, by means of stoves they keep their habitations as warm and comfortable as can be desired. In large houses they generally have four or five stoves placed in the hall,

hall, and in the apartments on the ground floor, from whence flues pafs in different directions through the upper rooms. Befides thefe ftoves, they likewife frequently have open fires in the lower apartments; it is more, however, on account of the cheerful appearance they give to the room, than for the fake of the warmth they communicate, as by the ftoves the rooms can be heated to any degree. Left any cold blafts fhould penetrate from without, they have alfo double doors, and if the houfe ftands expofed, even double windows, about fix inches apart. The windows are made to open lengthwife in the middle, on hinges, like folding doors, and where they meet they lock together in a deep groove; windows of this defcription, when clofed, are found to keep out the cold air much better than the common fafhes, and in warm weather they are more agreeable than any other fort, as they admit more air when opened. Nor do the inhabitants fuffer from cold when they go abroad; for they never ftir out without firft wrapping themfelves up in furs from head to foot. Their caps entirely cover the ears, the back of the neck, and the greateft part of the face, leaving nothing expofed except the eyes and nofe; and their large and thick cloaks effectually fecure the body; befides which they wear fur gloves, muffs, and fhoes.

It

It is surprising to see how well the Canadian horses support the cold; after standing for hours together in the open air at a time when spirits will freeze, they set off as alertly as if it were summer. The French Canadians make no scruple to leave their horses standing at the door of a house, without any covering, in the coldest weather, while they are themselves taking their pleasure. None of the other domestic animals are as indifferent to the cold as the horses. During winter all the domestic animals, not excepting the poultry, are lodged together in one large stable, that they may keep each other warm; but in order to avoid the expence of feeding many through the winter, as soon as the frost sets in they generally kill cattle and poultry sufficient to last them till the return of spring. The carcases are buried in the ground, and covered with a heap of snow, and as they are wanted they are dug up; vegetables are laid up in the same manner, and they continue very good throughout the whole winter. The markets in the towns are always supplied best at this season, and provisions are then also the cheapest; for the farmers having nothing else to engage them, and having a quantity of meat on hand, that is never injured from being sent to market, flock to the towns in their carioles in great numbers, and always well supplied.

The

The winter generally continues till the latter end of April, and sometimes even till May, when a thaw comes on very suddenly. The snow soon disappears; but it is a long time before the immense bodies of ice in the rivers are dissolved. The scene which presents itself on the St. Lawrence at this season is most tremendous. The ice first begins to crack from side to side, with a report as loud as that of a cannon. Afterwards, as the waters become swollen by the melting of the snow, it is broken into pieces, and hurried down the stream with prodigious impetuosity; but its course is often interrupted by the islands and shallow places in the river; one large piece is perhaps first stopped, other pieces come drifting upon that, and at length prodigious heaps are accumulated, in some places rising several yards above the level of the water. Sometimes these mounds of ice are driven from the islands or rocks, upon which they have accumulated, by the wind, and are floated down to the sea in one entire body: if in going down they happen to strike against any of the rocks along the shore, the crash is horrible: at other times they remain in the same spot where they were first formed, and continue to obstruct the navigation of the river for weeks after every appearance of frost is banished on shore; so very widely also do they

they frequently extend in particular parts of the river, and so solid are they at the same time, that in crossing from shore to shore, the people, instead of being at the trouble of going round them, make directly for the ice, disembark upon it, drag their bateaux or canoes across, and launch them again on the opposite side. As long as the ice remains in the St. Lawrence, no ships attempt to pass up or down; for one of these large bodies of ice is equally dangerous with a rock.

The rapid progress of vegetation in Canada, as soon as the winter is over, is most astonishing. Spring has scarcely appeared, when you find it is summer. In a few days the fields are clothed with the richest verdure, and the trees obtain their foliage. The various productions of the garden come in after each other in quick succession, and the grain sown in May affords a rich harvest by the latter end of July. This part of the year, in which spring and summer are so happily blended together, is delightful beyond description; nature then puts on her gayest attire; at the same time the heat is never found oppressive; it is seldom that the mercury in Fahrenheit's thermometer then rises above 84°: in July and August the weather becomes warmer, and a few days often intervene when the heat is overcoming; during these months the

the mercury sometimes rises to 96°. There is a great difference, however, in the weather at this season in different years: during the whole of the time that I was in the country, I never observed the thermometer higher than 88°; for the greater part of the months of July and August it was not higher than 80°, and for many days together it did not rise beyond 65°, between Quebec and Montreal.

The fall of the year is a most agreeable season in Canada, as well as the summer.

It is observed, that there is in general a difference of about three weeks in the length of the winter at Montreal and at Quebec, and of course in the other seasons. When green peas, strawberries, &c. were entirely gone at Montreal, we met with them in full season at Quebec.

LETTER XXVII.

Inhabitants of Lower Canada.—Of the Tenures by which Lands are held.—Not favourable to the Improvement of the Country.—Some Observations thereon.—Advantages of settling in Canada and the United States compared.—Why Emigrations to the latter Country are more general.—Description of a Journey to Stoneham Township near Quebec—Description of the River St. Charles—Of Lake St. Charles—Of Stoneham Township.

Quebec.

ABOUT five-sixths of the inhabitants of Lower Canada are of French extraction, the bulk of whom are peasants, living upon the lands of the seigniors. Amongst the English inhabitants devoted to agriculture, but few, however, are to be found occupying land under seigniors, notwithstanding that several of the seigniories have fallen into the hands of Englishmen; the great majority of them hold the lands which they cultivate by virtue of certificates from the governor, and these people for the most part reside in the western parts of the province, bordering upon the upper parts of the river St. Lawrence.

The

The feigniors, both French and English, live in a plain simple style; for although the feigniories in general are extensive, but few of them afford a very large income to the proprietors.

The revenues of a feigniory arise from certain fines called lods and vents, which are paid by the vassals on the alienation of property, as when a farm, or any part of it, is divided by a vassal, during his lifetime, amongst his sons, or when any other than the immediate issue of a vassal succeeds to his estate, &c. &c. The revenues arise also from certain fines paid on the granting of fresh lands to the vassals, and from the profits of the mills of the feignior, to which the vassals are bound to send all their corn to be ground.

This last obligation is sometimes extremely irksome to the vassal, when, for instance, on a large feigniory there is not more than one mill; for although it should be ten miles distant from his habitation, and he could get his corn ground on better terms close to his own door, yet he cannot send it to any other mill than that belonging to the feignior, under a heavy penalty.

The extent of feigniorial rights in Canada, particularly in what relates to the levying of the lods and vents, seems to be by no means clearly ascertained, so that where the feignior
happens

happens to be a man of a rapacious difpofition, the vaffal is fometimes compelled to pay fines, which, in ftrict juftice perhaps, ought not to be demanded. In the firft provincial affembly that was called, this bufinefs was brought forward, and the equity and policy was ftrongly urged by fome of the Englifh members that poffeffed confiderable abilities, of having proper bounds fixed to the power of the feigniors, and of having all the fines and fervices due from their vaffals accurately afcertained, and made generally known: but the French members, a great number of whom were themfelves feigniors, being ftrongly attached to old habits, and thinking that it was conducive to their intereft that their authority fhould ftill continue undefined, oppofed the meafure with great warmth; and nothing was done.

Nearly all thofe parts of Canada which were inhabited when the country was under French government, as well as the unoccupied lands granted to individuals during the fame period, are comprized under different feigniories, and thefe, with all the ufages and cuftoms thereto formerly pertaining, were confirmed to the proprietaries by the Quebec bill, which began to be in force in May 1775; thefe lands, therefore, are held by unqueftionable titles. All the wafte lands, however, of the crown, that have been allotted fince the conqueft, have

have been granted simply by certificates of occupation, or licences, from the governor, giving permission to persons who applied for these lands to settle upon them, no patents, conveying a clear possession of them, have ever been made out; it is merely by courtesy that they are held; and if a governor thought proper to reclaim them on the part of the crown, he has only to say the word, and the titles of the occupiers sink into air. Thus it is, that although several persons have expended large sums of money in procuring, and afterwards improving townships *, none of them are yet enabled to sell a single acre as an indemnification for these expences; at least no title can be given with what is offered for sale, and it is not therefore to be supposed, that purchasers of such property will easily be found. It is true, indeed, that the different proprietaries of these townships have been assured, on the part of government, that patents shall be granted to every one of them, and they are fully persuaded that these will be made out some time or other; but they have in vain waited for them for three years, and they are anxiously waiting for them still †.

Different

---

* Tracts of waste land, usually ten miles square.

† I received a letter, dated early in the year 1796, from a gentleman in Canada, who has taken up one of these townships,

Different motives have been assigned for this conduct on the part of the British government. In the first place it has been alledged, that the titles are withheld, in order to prevent speculation and land-jobbing from rising to the same height in Canada as they have done in the United States.

It is a notorious fact, that in the United States land-jobbing has led to a series of the most nefarious practices, whereby numbers have already suffered, and by which still greater numbers must suffer hereafter. By the machinations of a few interested individuals, who have contrived by various methods to get immense tracts * of waste land into their possession, fictitious demands have been created in the market for land, the price of it has consequently been enhanced much beyond its in-

ships, which contains the following paragraph: "At present the "matter remains in an unsettled state, although every step has "been taken on my part to accelerate the completion of the "business. Mr. D——'s patent, which was sent home as a "model, is not yet returned. I received a letter lately from "Mr. Secretary R——, in which he informs me, that Mr. "G —— is again returned to the surveyor's office, and he "assures me, that in conjunction with him, he will do every "thing in his power to expedite my obtaining a patent. The "governor, he says, means that the land business should go for-"ward."

* There have been many instances in the United States of a single individual's holding upwards of three millions of acres at one time, and some few individuals have been known to hold even twice that quantity at once.

trinsic worth, and these persons have then taken the opportunity of selling what they had on hand at an enormous profit. The wealth that has been accumulated by particular persons in the United States, in this manner, is prodigious; and numberless others, witnesses to their prosperity, have been tempted to make purchases of land, in hopes of realizing fortunes in a similar way, by selling-out small portions at an advanced price. Thus it is that the nominal value of waste land has been raised so suddenly in the United States; for large tracts, which ten years before were selling for a few pence per acre, have sold in numberless instances, lately, for dollars per acre, an augmentation in price which the increase of population alone would by no means have occasioned. Estates, like articles of merchandize, have passed, before they have ever been improved, through the hands of dozens of people, who never perhaps were within five hundred miles of them, and the consumer or farmer, in consequence of the profits laid on by these people, to whom they have severally belonged, has had frequently to pay a most exorbitant price for the little spot which he has purchased *.

Speculation

* In the beginning of the year 1796, this traffic was at its highest pitch, and at this time General Washington, so eminently distinguished for his prudence and foresight, perceiving

Speculation and land-jobbing carried to such a pitch cannot but be deemed great evils in the community; and to prevent them from extending into Canada appears to be an object well worthy the attention of government; but it seems unnecessary to have recourse for that purpose to the very exceptionable measure of withholding a good title to all lands granted by the crown, a measure disabling the landholder from taking the proper steps to improve his estate, which gives rise to distrust and suspicion, and materially impedes the growing prosperity of the country.

It appears to me, that land-jobbing could never arrive at such a height in Canada as to be productive of similar evils to those already sprung up from it in the United States, or similar to those further ones with which the country is threatened, if no more land were granted by the crown, to any one individual, than a township of ten thousand acres; or

ceiving that land had risen beyond its actual value, and persuaded that it could not rise higher for some years to come, advertised for sale every acre of which he was possessed, except the farms of Mount Vernon. The event shewed how accurate his judgment was. In the close of the year, one of the great land-jobbers, disappointed in his calculations, was obliged to abscond; the land trade was shaken to its very foundation; bankruptcies spread like wildfire from one great city to another, and men that had begun to build palaces found themselves likely to have no better habitation for a time than the common gaol.

should it be thought that grants of such an extent even opened too wide a field for speculation, certain restrictions might be laid upon the grantee; he might be bound to improve his township by a clause in the patent, invalidating the sale of more than a fourth or fifth of it unless to actual settlers, until a certain number of people should be resident thereon*. Such a clause would effectually prevent the evil; for it is the granting of very extensive tracts of waste lands to individuals, without binding them in any way to improve them, which gives rise to speculation and land-jobbing.

By others it is imagined, that the withholding of clear titles to the lands is a measure adopted merely for the purpose of preventing a diminution of the inhabitants from taking place by emigration.

Not only townships have been granted by certificates of occupation, but also numberless small portions of land, from one hundred acres upwards, particularly in Upper Canada, to royalists and others, who have at different pe-

---

* The plan of binding every person that should take up a township to improve it, by providing a certain number of settlers, has not wholly escaped the notice of government; for in the licences of occupation, by which each township is allotted, it is stipulated, that every person shall provide forty settlers for his township; but as no given time is mentioned for the procuring of these settlers, the stipulation becomes nugatory.

riods

riods emigrated from the United States. These people have all of them improved their several allotments. By withholding any better title, therefore, than that of a certificate, they are completely tied down to their farms, unless, indeed, they think proper to abandon them, together with the fruits of many years labour, without receiving any compensation whatsoever for so doing.

It is not probable, however, that these people, if they had a clear title to their lands, would return back to the United States; the royalists, who were driven out of the country by the ill treatment of the other inhabitants, certainly would not; nor would the others, who have voluntarilly quitted the country, return, whilst self-interest, which led them originally to come into Canada, operated in favour of their remaining there. It was the prospect of getting land on advantageous terms which induced them to emigrate; land is still a cheaper article in Canada than in the United States; and as there is much more waste land in the former, than in the latter country, in proportion to the number of the inhabitants, it will probably continue so for a length of time to come. In the United States, at present, it is impossible to get land without paying for it; and in parts of the country where the soil is rich, and where some settlements are already made,

made, a tract of land, sufficient for a moderate farm, is scarcely to be procured under hundreds of dollars. In Canada, however, a man has only to make application to government, and on his taking the oath of allegiance, he immediately gets one hundred acres of excellent uncleared land, in the neighbourhood of other settlements, gratis; and if able to improve it directly, he can get even a larger quantity. But it is a fact worthy of notice, which banishes every suspicion relative to a diminution of the inhabitants taking place by emigrations into the States, that great numbers of people from the States actually emigrate into Canada annually, whilst none of the Canadians, who have it in their power to dispose of their property, emigrate into the United States, except, indeed, a very few of those who have resided in the towns.

According to the opinion of others again, it is not for either of the purposes already mentioned, that clear titles are withheld to the lands granted by the crown, but for that of binding down to their good behaviour the people of each province, more particularly the Americans that have emigrated from the States lately, who are regarded by many with an eye of suspicion, notwithstanding they have taken the oaths of allegiance to the crown. It is very unfair, however, to imagine that these

people

people would be ready to revolt a second time from Great Britain, if they were made still more independent than they are now, merely becaufe they did fo on a former occafion, when their liberties and rights as men and as fubjects of the Britifh empire were fo fhamefully difregarded; on the contrary, were clear titles granted with the lands beftowed by the crown on them, and the other fubjects of the province, inftead of giving rife to difaffection, there is every reafon to think it would make them ftill more loyal, and more attached to the Britifh government, as no invidious diftinctions could then be drawn between the condition of the landholders in the States and thofe in Canada. The material rights and liberties of the people would then be full as extenfive in the one country as in the other; and as no pofitive advantage could be gained by a revolt, it is not likely that Americans, of all people in the world the moft devoted to felf-intereft, would expofe their perfons and properties in fuch an attempt.

If, however, the Americans from the States are people that would abufe fuch favours from the crown, why were they admitted into the province at all? The government might eafily have kept them out, by refufing to them any grants of lands; but at any rate, were it thought expedient to admit them, and were fuch meafures sures necessary to keep them in due subjection, it seems hard that the same measures should be adopted in regard to the inhabitants of the province, who stood firm to the British government, even at the time when the people in every other part of the continent revolted.

For whatever reason this system of not granting unexceptionable titles with the land, which the crown voluntarily bestows on its faithful subjects, has been adopted, one thing appears evident, namely, that it has very considerably retarded the improvement of both the provinces; and indeed, as long as it is continued, they must both remain very backward countries, compared with any of the adjoining states Were an opposite system, however, pursued, and the lands granted merely with such restrictions as were found absolutely necessary, in order to prevent jobbing, the happy effects of a measure of that nature would soon become visible; the face of the country would be quickly meliorated, and it is probable that there would not be any part of North America, where they would, after a short period, be able to boast that improvement had taken place more rapidly.

It is very certain, that were the lands granted in this manner, many more people would annually emigrate into Canada from the United States than at present; for there are numbers who

who come yearly into the country to " explore it," that return back folely becaufe they cannot get lands with an indifputable title ; I have repeatedly met with thefe people myfelf in Upper Canada, and have heard them exprefs the utmoft difappointment at not being able to get lands on fuch terms even for money; I have heard others in the States alfo fpeak to the fame purport after they had been in Canada; it is highly probable, moreover, that many of the people, who leave Great Britain and Ireland for America, would then be induced to fettle in Canada inftead of the United States, and the Britifh empire would not, in that cafe, lofe, as it does now, thoufands of valuable citizens every year.

What are the general inducements, may here be afked, to people to quit Great Britain for the United States? They have been fummed up by Mr. Cooper *, in his letters publifhed in 1794, on the fubject of emigrating to America; and we cannot have recourfe, *on the whole*, to better authority.

" In my mind," he fays, " the firft and prin-
" cipal inducement to a perfon to quit Eng-
" land for America is, *the total abfence of anx-*

---

* Mr. Cooper, late of Manchefter, who emigrated to America with all his family, and whofe authority has been very generally quoted by the Americans who have fince written on the fubject of emigration.

" *iety*

" iety respecting the future success of a family.
" There is little fault to find with the govern-
" ment of America, that is, of the United
" States, either in principle or practice. There
" are few taxes to pay, and those are of ac-
" knowledged necessity, and moderate in
" amount. There are no animosities about re-
" ligion, and it is a subject about which few
" questions are asked; there are few respecting
" political men or political measures; the pre-
" sent irritation of men's minds in Great Bri-
" tain, and the discordant state of society on
" political accounts, is not known there.
" The government is the government of the
" people, and for the people. There are no
" tythes nor game laws; and excise laws upon
" spirits only, and similar to the British only in
" name. There are no great men of rank, nor
" many of great riches; nor have the rich the
" power of oppressing the less rich, for poverty
" is almost unknown; nor are the streets
" crowded with beggars. You see no where
" the disgusting and melancholy contrast, so
" common in Europe, of vice and filth, and
" rags and wretchedness, in the immediate
" neighbourhood of the most wanton extrava-
" gance, and the most useless and luxurious pa-
" rade; nor are the common people so de-
" praved as in Great Britain. Quarrels are
" uncommon, and boxing matches unknown
" in

" in the streets. There are no military to
" keep the people in awe. Robberies are very
" rare. All these are real advantages; but
" great as they are, they do not weigh with
" me so much as the single consideration first
" mentioned."

Any person that has travelled generally through the United States must acknowledge, that Mr. Cooper has here spoken with great partiality; for as to the morality and good order that prevails amongst the people, he has applied to all of them what only holds true with respect to those who live in the most improved parts of the country.

He is extremely inaccurate also, in representing the people of the States as free from all animosities about political measures; on the contrary, there is no country on the face of the globe, perhaps, where party spirit runs higher, where political subjects are more frequently the topic of conversation amongst all classes, and where such subjects are more frequently the cause of rancorous disputations and lasting differences amongst the people. I have repeatedly been in towns where one half of the inhabitants would scarcely deign to speak to the other half, on account of the difference of their political opinions; and it is scarcely possible, in any part of the country, to remain for a few hours in a mixed company of men, without

out witnessing some acrimonious dispute from the same cause.

Let us, however, compare the inducements which he holds out to people in England to leave that country for America, that is, for the United States, with the inducements there would be to settle in Canada, under the premised supposition, that the land was there granted in an unexceptionable manner.

From the land being plentiful in Canada, and consequently at a very low price, but likely to increase in value, whilst in the States, on the contrary, it has risen to an exorbitant value, beyond which it is not likely to rise for some time to come, there can be no doubt but that a man of moderate property could provide for his family with much more ease in Canada than in the United States, as far as land were his object.

In Canada, also, there is a much greater opening for young men acquainted with any business or profession that can be carried on in America, than there is in the United States. The expence of settling in Canada would be far less also than in any one of the States; for in the former country the necessaries and conveniencies of life are remarkably cheap, whilst, on the contrary, in the other they are far dearer than in England; a man therefore would certainly have no greater anxiety about the future

success

success of a family in Canada than in the United States, and the absence of this anxiety, according to Mr. Cooper, *is the great inducement to settle in the States, which weighs with him more than all other considerations put together.*

The taxes of Lower Canada have already been enumerated; they are of acknowledged necessity, and much lower in amount and number than those paid in the States.

There are no animosities in Canada about religion, and people of all persuasions are on a perfect equality with each other, except, indeed, it be the protestant dissenters, who may happen to live on lands that were subject to tithes under the French government; they have to pay tithes to the English episcopalian clergy; but there is not a dissenter living on tithe lands, perhaps, in the whole province. The lands granted since the conquest are not liable to tithes. The English episcopalian clergy are provided for by the crown out of the waste lands; and all dissenters have simply to pay their own clergy.

There are no game laws in Canada, nor any excise laws whatsoever.

As for the observation made by Mr. Cooper in respect to the military, it is almost too futile to deserve notice. If a soldier, however, be an object of terror, the timid man will not find himself

himself at ease in the United States any more than in England, as he will meet with soldiers in New York, on Governor's Island, at Mifflin Fort near Philadelphia, at the forts on the North River, at Niagara, at Detroit, and at Oswego, &c. on the lakes, and all through the western country, at the different posts which were established by General Wayne.

In every other respect, what Mr. Cooper has said of the United States holds good with regard to Canada; nay more, it must certainly in addition be allowed by every unprejudiced person that has been in both countries, that morality and good order are much more conspicuous amongst the Canadians of every description, than the people of the States; drunkenness is undoubtedly much less common amongst them, as is gambling, and also quarrels.

But independent of these inducements to settle in Canada, there is still another circumstance which ought to weigh greatly with every British emigrant, according to the opinion even of Mr. Cooper himself. After advising his friends " to go where land is cheap " and fertile, and where it is in a progress of " improvement," he recommends them " to " go somewhere, if possible, *in the neighbourhood* " *of a few English,* whose society, even in " America, is interesting to an English set-
" tler,

"tler, who cannot entirely relinquish the *memoria temporis acti*;" that is, as he particularly mentions in another passage, "he will find their manners and conversation far more agreeable than those of the Americans," and from being chiefly in their company, he will not be so often tormented with the painful reflection, that he has not only left, but absolutely renounced his native country, and the men whom he once held dear above all others, and united himself, in their stead, with people whose vain boasts and ignorant assertions, however harsh and grating they may sound to his ears, he must listen to without murmuring.

Now in Canada, particularly in Lower Canada, in the neighbourhood of Quebec and Montreal, an English settler would find himself surrounded by his countrymen; and although his moderate circumstances should have induced him to leave England, yet he would not be troubled with the disagreeable reflection that he had totally renounced his native land, and sworn allegiance to a foreign power; he would be able to consider with heartfelt satisfaction, that he was living under the protection of the country wherein he had drawn his first breath; that he was contributing to her prosperity, and the welfare of many of his countrymen, while he was ameliorating his own fortune.

VOL. I.   E e   From

From a due confideration of every one of the before menrioned circumftances, it appears evident to me, that there is no part of America fo fuitable to an Englifh or Irifh fettler as the vicinity of Montreal or Quebec in Canada, and within twenty miles of each of thefe places there is ample room for thoufands of additional inhabitants.

I muft not omit here to give fome account of a new fettlement in the neighbourhood of Quebec, which I and my fellow travellers vifited in company with fome neighbouring gentlemen, as it may in fome degree tend to confirm the truth of what I have faid refpecting the impolicy of withholding indifputable titles to the lands lately granted by the crown, and as it may ferve at the fame time to fhew how many eligible fpots for new fettlements are to be found in the neighbourhood of this city.

We fet off from Quebec in calafhes, and following, with a little deviation only, the courfe of the River St. Charles, arrived on the margin of the lake of the fame name, about twelve miles diftant from Quebec.

The River St. Charles flows from the lake into the bafon, near Quebec; at its mouth it is about thirty yards wide, but not navigable for boats, except for a few miles up, owing to the numerous rocks and falls. In the fpring of of the year, when it is much swollen by floods, rafts have been conducted down the whole way from the lake, but this has not been accomplished without great difficulty, some danger, and a considerable loss of time in passing the different portages. The distance from the lake to Quebec being so short, land carriage must always be preferred to a water conveyance along this river, except it be for timber.

The course of the St. Charles is very irregular; in some places it appears almost stagnant, whilst in others it shoots with wonderful impetuosity over deep beds of rocks. The views upon it are very romantic, particularly in the neighbourhood of Lorette, a village of the Huron Indians, where the river, after falling in a beautiful cascade over a ledge of rocks, winds through a deep dell, shaded on each side with tall trees.

The face of the country between Quebec and the lake is extremely pleasing, and in the neighbourhood of the city, where the settlements are numerous, well cultivated; but as you retire from it the settlements become fewer and fewer, and the country of course appears wilder. From the top of a hill, about half a mile from the lake, which commands a fine view of that and the adjacent country, not more than five or six houses are to be seen

seen, and beyond these there is no settlement beside that on Stoneham township, the one under immediate notice.

On arriving at the lake, we found two canoes in waiting for us, and embarked on board.

Lake St. Charles is about four miles and a half in length, and its breadth on an average about three quarters of a mile. It consists of two bodies of water nearly of the same size; they communicate together by a narrow pass, through which a smart current sets towards Quebec. The scenery along the lower part of the lake is uninteresting, but along the upper part of it the views are highly picturesque, particularly upon a first entrance through the pass. The lake is here interspersed with large rocks; and close to the water on one side, as far as the eye can reach, rocks and trees appear blended together in the most beautiful manner. The shores are bold, and richly ornamented with hanging woods; and the head of the lake being concealed from the view by several little promontories, you are led to imagine that the body of water is far more extensive than in reality. Towards the upper end the view is terminated by a range of blue hills, which appear at a distance, peeping over the tops of the tall trees. When a few settlements come to be made

made here, open to the lake, for the land bordering upon it is quite in its natural state, this must indeed be a heavenly little spot.

The depth of the water in the lake is about eight feet, in some places more, in others less. The water is clear, and as several small streams fall into it to supply what runs off by the River St. Charles, it is kept constantly in a state of circulation; but it is not well tasted, owing as is conceived to the bottom being in some parts overgrown with weeds. Prodigious numbers of bull frogs, however, are found about the shores, which shews that springs of good water abound near it, for these creatures are never met with but where the water is of a good quality.

At the upper part of the lake we landed, and having proceeded for about half a mile over some low ground bare of trees, from being annually flooded on the dissolution of the snow, we struck into the woods. Here a road newly cut soon attracted our attention, and following the course of it for a mile or two, we at last espied, through a sudden opening between the trees, the charming little settlement.

The dwelling house, a neat boarded little mansion painted white, together with the offices, were situated on a small eminence; to the right, at the bottom of the slope, stood the barn,

barn, the largest in all Canada, with a farm yard exactly in the English style; behind the barn was laid out a neat garden, at the bottom of which, over a bed of gravel, ran a purling stream of the purest water, deep enough, except in a very dry season, to float a large canoe. A small lawn laid down in grass appeared in front of the house, ornamented with clumps of pines, and in its neighbourhood were about sixty acres of cleared land. The common method of clearing land in America is to grub up all the brushwood and small trees merely, and to cut down the large trees about two feet above the ground: the remaining stumps rot in from six to ten years, according to the quality of the timber; in the mean time the farmer ploughs between them the best way he can, and where they are very numerous he is sometimes obliged to use even the spade or the hoe to turn up the soil. The lands, however, at this settlement had been cleared in a different manner, for the trees and roots had all been grubbed up at once. This mode of proceeding is extremely expensive, so that few of those destined to make new settlements could afford to adopt it; and, moreover, it has not been accurately proved that it is the most profitable one; but the appearance of lands so cleared is greatly superior to those cleared in the common method.

In

In another respect also the lands at this settlement had been cleared in a superior manner to what is commonly to be met with in America; for large clumps of trees were left adjoining to the house, and each field was encircled with wood, whereby the crops were secured from the bad effects of storms. The appearance of cultivated fields thus situated, as it were, in the midst of a forest, was inconceivably beautiful.

The economy of this little farm equalled its beauty. The fields, neatly fenced in and furnished with handsome gates, were cultivated according to the Norfolk system of husbandry, and had been brought to yield the most plentiful crops of every different sort of grain; the farm yard was filled with as fine cattle as could be seen in any country; and the dairy afforded excellent butter, and abundance of good cheese.

Besides the dwelling-house before mentioned, there were several log houses on different parts of this farm, inhabited by the people who were engaged in clearing the land. All these appeared delighted with the situation; nor were such of them as had come a short time before from England at all displeased with the climate; they informed me, that they had enjoyed perfect health from the moment of their landing, and found no inconvenience from

from the intense cold of the winter season, which appears such an insuperable objection to many against settling in Canada.

This settlement, together with the township it is situated upon, are the property of a clergyman formerly resident at Quebec. The township is ten miles square, commencing where the most remote of the old seigniories end, that is, within eighteen miles of the city of Quebec; but though within this short distance of a large city, it was almost totally unknown until about five or six years ago, when the present proprietor, with a party of Indians and a few friends, set out himself to examine the quality of the lands. They proved to be rich; the timber was luxuriant; the face of the country agreeably diversified with hill and dale, interspersed with beautiful lakes, and intersected by rivers and mill streams in every direction. Situated also within six miles of old settlements, through which there were established roads, being convenient to a market at the capital of Canada, and within the reach of society at least as agreeable, if not more so, than is to be found in all America, nothing seemed wanting to render it an eligible spot for a new settlement; accordingly the proprietor made application to government; the land was surveyed, the township marked out, and it was
allotted

allotted to him merely, however, by a certificate of occupation.

Several other gentlemen, charmed with the excellent quality and beautiful difpofition of the lands in this part of the country, have taken up adjoining townfhips; but at none of them have any fettlements been made, nor is it probable that any will be, until the proprietaries get better titles: indeed, it has excited the furprife of a numerous fet of people in the province, to fee even the little fettlement I have fpoken of eftablifhed on land held under fuch a tenure.

That unexceptionable titles may be fpeedily made out to thefe lands is fincerely to be hoped; for may we not, whenever that meafure fhall take place, expect to fee thefe beautiful provinces, that have fo long remained almoft unknown, rifing into general notice? May we not then expect to behold them increafing rapidly in population, and making hafty ftrides towards the attainment of that degree of profperity and confequence, which their foil, climate, and many other natural advantages have fo eminently qualified them for enjoying? And furely the empire at large would be greatly benefitted by fuch a change in the ftate of Canada; for as the country increafed in population, it would increafe in riches,

riches, and there would then be a proportionably greater demand for English manufactures; a still greater trade would also be carried on then between Canada and the West Indies than at present, to the great advantage of both countries *; a circumstance that would give employment to a greater number of British ships: as Canada also increased in wealth, it would be enabled to defray the expences of its own government, which at present falls so heavily upon the people of Great Britain: neither is there reason to imagine that Canada, if allowed to attain such a state of prosperity, would be ready to disunite herself from Great Britain, supposing that Great Britain should remain as powerful as at present, and that Canada continued to be governed with mildness and wisdom; for she need but turn towards the United States to be convinced that the great mass of her people were in the possession of as much happiness

---

* All those articles of American produce in demand in the West Indies may be had on much better terms in Canada than in the United States; and if the Canadian merchants had sufficient capitals to enable them to trade thither largely, there can hardly be a doubt but that the people of the British West Indian Isles would draw their supplies from Canada rather than from any other part of America. The few cargoes at present sent from Quebec always command a preference in the West Indian markets over those sent from any part of the United States.

and liberty as those of the neighbouring country; and that whatever she might lose by exposing herself to the horrors of a sanguinary war, she could gain no essential or immediate advantages whatsoever, by asserting her own independence.

END OF THE FIRST VOLUME.

www.ingramcontent.com/pod-product-compliance
Lightning Source LLC
Chambersburg PA
CBHW022108300426
44117CB00007B/631